DECCAN TRAVERSES

DECCAN

The Making

TRAVERSES

of Bangalore's Terrain

ANURADHA MATHUR / DILIP DA CUNHA

Rupa & Co

To

Luis and Claudina da Cunha who made Bangalore their home

Research Assisted by Graham Foundation for Advanced Studies in the Fine Arts and University of Pennsylvania Research Foundation

Published 2006 by
Rupa & Co
7/16, Ansari Road, Daryaganj,
New Delhi 110 002

Sales Centres
Allahabad, Bangalore, Chandigarh, Chennai, Hyderabad, Jaipur, Kathmandu, Kolkata, Mumbai, Pune

ISBN 81-291-0852-6

Design
Ram Sinam, Bangalore

Typeface
Berthold Imago

Printing
Ajanta Offset & Packaging Ltd.,
New Delhi

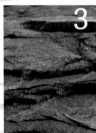

PREFACE

Deccan Traverses is about the landscape of Bangalore; but it is also about the power of landscape to determine the nature of a place and the eye through which it is seen. This aspect of landscape — an initiator of settlement — is rarely appreciated. Landscape is generally taken to be the last act of settlement, associated more with luxury than necessity. It tends to call attention to gardens, avenues, trees, lakes, parks, playgrounds and other elements of the outdoors that are low priority when funds are scarce, particularly in countries like India where poverty is a major concern. Yet landscape plays a fundamental role. Not only is it infrastructural — in that it deals with the underlying conditions of building, the nature of the built environment, and the servicing of the city — it also reaches further down to that primordial act of singling 'things' out from amorphous matter, articulating a land that is intrinsically in flux. As such, landscape creates not only the ground for habitation, but also the subjects of knowledge and the practices of everyday life; it provides the vocabulary of the land.

Nowhere is this fundamental enterprise more evident than in acts of colonisation. By this act, land is not just taken. It is taken as a *terra incognita* and given a new language which over time becomes the ordinary and everyday vocabulary of inhabitants. In Bangalore, perhaps more spectacularly than elsewhere, one sees not just the giving of this language, but its making. Here, in a place that came under the eye of British surveyors, artists and naturalists in the late 1700s and early 1800s, one sees the audacity, imagination, skill and power that it took to devise a language of the land, a language that today pervades everyday life.

Bangalore today, however, is far from considering landscape in this fundamental role. Preoccupied by problems that stem from the accelerating rate of development in recent years, coupled perhaps with a pride in Bangalore's rise and promise in the global marketplace, there is little time or interest in excavating the extraordinary roots of the vocabulary that shapes Bangalore. Besides, Bangalore's fame as the 'Garden City of India' tends to keep landscape on the surface. The word focuses attention on the trees, lakes, gardens and parks that have become objects of visual and historical significance.

We were confronted with both these preoccupations – problems and image – when we set out to do, not a book, but a landscape strategy for Bangalore. Such a strategy, we found, was expected to be about trees, open spaces, parks, avenues, lakes, what some referred to as the 'natural environment'. With development threatening climate, cleanliness, and beauty, a strategy to save the natural environment appeared necessary to many citizens. When we picked up a postcard by a local group that showed a pristine lake nestled in a temperate pine forest calling on people to 'save Bangalore's lakes', we realised that this taken-for-granted notion of the surface needed serious investigation. The more we probed the more we saw that there is little that is 'natural' in Bangalore. Almost everything is by design. The lakes are agricultural tanks constructed with bunds or embankments, trees are introductions from across the world, plants are hybrids, etc. More importantly, however, we realised that the eye, like other elements of the land, is also cultivated. Geographic maps and photographic images – the abstracted view of land from the sky and the view on the ground – are read with comfort in a land where they were introduced but two centuries ago. It is, however, difficult to open these modes of representation to question as much as it is to question the value of trees in Bangalore. To most, such questioning is a distraction, an interference with progress toward a 'better' grasp of the 'real world'. When we hear, however, calls for Bangalore to be as green and clean as Singapore, as well planned as London or as participatory as small town America, we are made aware of a generic nature not of place as much as the 'cultivated eye'. This is not landscape on the surface; this is landscape deeply embedded in education, administration, technology and everyday conversation.

It would be easy to move from the constructed nature of Bangalore's landscape to a critique of colonialism and a revival of pre-colonial landscapes. There are voices in support of this in Bangalore as well – the call for the indigenous alternative, for native wisdom. But the (British) administrator's vocabulary of the land is so deeply embedded and the modes of representation are so taken-for-granted that the indigenous tends to be presented in colonial terms, often in the guise of a local dialect. Besides, there are indications that the land where Bangalore is situated has gone through not one but many colonisations, the British being the most recent and, despite independence, still dominant in today's vocabulary. In this layered land, what is indigenous is then a matter of choice rather than truth.

Ultimately what we faced in Bangalore was neither a colonial nor an indigenous landscape but the extraordinary depth of ordinary elements – trees, gardens, and parks but also flowers, stone, rock, clay, water, tanks, quarries, maps, texts, images, and so on. We pursued these elements geographically, historically, materially, and conceptually, and the more we did the more ephemeral their constitutional boundaries appeared to be. The Bangalore that emerged in the process was neither a demarcated entity nor the sprawling metropolis, both of which speak the language of the generic city. It was rather a place of amazing beginnings and open trajectories of materials and events.

This investigation into everyday elements did not derail the idea of a landscape strategy as much as clarified the first step – a public exhibition on the making of Bangalore. It was designed to communicate three ideas: first, Bangalore's landscape is constructed as much in the eye as in the land; second, the problems – particularly infrastructural problems – that preoccupy the city do not stem necessarily from a lack of foresight, poor management or lack of funds, but perhaps more from the persistence of a vocabulary of landscape that is inadequate to the complexities of the land; and third, it is possible to seed new initiatives that cultivate fresh vocabularies and trajectories for future intervention.

The book parallels the exhibition and, with it, aims to reach beyond the agendas of development, problem-solving, and surface treatment, to encounter an extraordinary terrain at the intersection of innovative enterprises.

It is difficult to identify a starting point for this project. One of us having spent most of his life in Bangalore and regularly visiting it when away, the place tends to be within our household even while living on the other side of the earth. On one visit, however, Bangalore as a city on the Deccan Plateau was thrust into view. We were invited by the architectural community in Bangalore to present our work on the Lower Mississippi, a project that has since been published as *Mississippi Floods: Designing a Shifting Landscape* (Yale University Press, 2001). In that project we sought an alternative to the Mississippi, which from at least the advent of Europeans in America, has been objectified as a river, a representation that confines it to the space between two lines in maps. The lines are enforced today by numerous control structures which have grown in strength with each flood. We posed the Mississippi as an open, layered and dynamic landscape that demands negotiation more than control. In the conversations that followed our presentation, Bangalore became a topic and we were drawn to the idea of bringing 'home' a sensibility. City planners appeared to be working hard to control Bangalore as a city in the same vein that the United States Army Corps of Engineers was trying to control the Mississippi as a river. Like the massive structures that try to keep the Mississippi within lines, the plans that try to keep Bangalore to an order seem driven more by failure of containment than by a vision of the future. We saw the possibility of advocating landscape as a way of devising a new language of the land, a basis for inventing new tools of governance and design; it could provide a fundamental alternative to the city plan. We are grateful to the Discussions in Architecture Forum for giving us that platform in 1999 that triggered, what has been for us, a most exhilarating journey across lands, texts, images, and ideas.

Our next visit was made possible with a seed grant from the Research Foundation of the University of Pennsylvania. Edgar de Mello, whose efforts through the Architectural Gallery & Bookstore kept the architectural community open to the expansive horizons that make architecture such a boundless subject of inquiry, offered us a forum at which to present our investigations in its early stages. At the time of that presentation we were grappling with not just the physical space of Bangalore which seemed to extend all around, but also its material elements. Architecture students, Swetha Gowri and Rajalakshmi, helped us follow leads as we began tracking these extensions and materials. During this time and on our many future visits, Francis and Vatsala da Cunha opened their home to us and never hesitated to give us their car for the many short and long trips that we did, often at short notice.

Our investigation took us to places on other continents as well, where Bangalore resides in texts, images and maps: the British Library in London, Harvard University Libraries, Yale Center for British Art in New Haven, the Annenberg Rare Books Collection at the University of Pennsylvania, and the New York Public Library. We would like to specially thank John Pollack at the University of Pennsylvania for helping us find and document archival material at various stages of this project.

When the idea of an exhibition became a clear first step of this project, the Design School at Harvard University and the South Asia Studies department at the University of Pennsylvania were venues for 'work-in-progress'. We are thankful here to the support of George Hargreaves at Harvard and James Corner and Michael Meister at Penn, both of whom have encouraged and provoked our investigations of representation in landscape and design, not merely in this project but also others that we have been involved with. Raising funds for a project as open-ended as this was a challenge and we are deeply grateful to colleagues at other institutions who not only wrote us letters of support but encouraged and advised us, including Anne Whiston Spirn, Adele Santos, James Wescoat, and Diane Karp. We also thank the Graham Foundation for the Arts for giving us the much needed financial support toward the production and reproduction of the visual material of the exhibition and book. The timely assistance of our students Shiau-Yun Lu, Ivan Rupnik, Te-Hsuan Liao, Hui Li, Maura Rockcastle and Christopher Junkin allowed us to keep to the schedule we had set for ourselves. We are thankful to the Department of Fine Arts at Penn for continued run of the screen printing facilities and to the staff of the computer labs of the School of Design and the Department of Landscape Architecture for their invaluable support.

Eventually the exhibition was held in the Glass House, a plant conservatory in the public garden of Lalbagh, a venue which we thought most apt not only because of its public nature but also because of Lalbagh's significant role in the construction of Bangalore's landscape. We are grateful to Dr G.K. Vasantha Kumar, Director of Horticulture, for considering it appropriate to have the exhibition in the Glass House and to Dr K. P. Krishnan, Managing Director, KUIDFC, Mr Chiranjiv Singh, Additional Chief Secretary and Developmental Commissioner, Govt. of Karnataka, Mr Mahendra Jain, Commissioner of Tourism, Govt. of Karnataka, Mr Jyothiramalingam, Commissioner, Bangalore Mahanagara Palike, and Mr Subash Chandra, Special Commissioner, Bangalore Mahanagara Palike, for their timely support in bringing the exhibition to the public. We were honoured to have Girish Karnad and Dr V. Radhakrishnan open the exhibition in October 2004. Behind the scene, a number of people believed in the work and helped us in many different ways from fund-raising to editing and installing — Nina and Mohan Bopiah, Sharukh and Renu Mistry, Venkatesh Babu, Mandira Kumar, Naresh Venkataraman, Asha Ghosh, Urvashi Jalali, Kaushik Ramanathan, Rohit Marol, Rajmohan Shetty, Edgar de Mello, Vatsala da Cunha, Alok Mathur, Suresh Jayaram, Anjali Venkataiah, Vikram Sardesai, Ramesh and Swati Ramanathan, and Rajeev Gowda.

We are grateful to our publisher Rupa & Co. for taking this work to publication with such enthusiasm and evident love for Bangalore; to his editorial staff for their assistance; and to Ram Sinam whose deep involvement and excellence in the craft of design is visible in the laying out of this book.

When the going gets tough, as it often did in this project, the brunt is taken by that mysterious institution called family. To Francis and Vatsala, Alok and Chandrika, Carmel and Gerard, Maria and Winston, Vincent and Indira, Alka and Nupur, and Anuradha's parents, Brijesh and Sardar Mathur, we can only ask to be taken for granted in return.

Lastly, there is a not-so-silent participant in this work whose cooperation was essential from the very beginning — our daughter Tara, who, at the age of three months, began travelling the Lower Deccan with us and at five, asserts herself as a co-author of this work.

We dedicate this work to Dilip's parents, the late Luis and Claudina da Cunha, who chose to make Bangalore their home and it is perhaps with them and their love for the place that this project began.

INTRODUCTION

Bangalore Prospects

In the early 1800s a number of European travellers referred to the heart of the South Indian peninsula where Bangalore is situated as a very *naked country*.[1] They were amazed by its open horizons. Looking back across the two centuries since, however, these individuals could very well have been referring to a place with a potential to be attired, perhaps in many different ways. Few cities in India today hold as many titles as Bangalore does — Silicon Valley of India, Infotech City, Biotech City, Horticultural Capital, Fashion Capital, and so on. These labels are as projective as they are descriptive, promoted by people's visions and ambitions for a place that evidently holds more potential for fabrication than it does for an identity.

One title, however, has taken firm root. It subtly frames the potential of Bangalore, directing new visions for the city as much as it contextualises memories. This title is *Garden City*. It was seeded by English ambitions for this land at the turn of the eighteenth century, ambitions that turned out more lasting, pervasive and extensive in the cultivation of its landscape than meets the eye. This cultivation had the backing of the East India Company, in transition at the time from a mercantile corporation to a territorial power. But it also had the force of a milieu known as the European Enlightenment when science and art were embracing measures of 'utility' and 'progress', measures that seduced as much as imposed themselves on cultures across the world.

The settlement that materialised from the intersection of these ambitions and forces is a place of parks, lakes, trees, tree-lined avenues, flower-planted traffic islands, and as one missionary in the 1840s put it, 'smiling bungalows . . . not a few bearing marks of horticultural taste'.[2] The title Garden City, which emerged formally in the early twentieth century, is reinforced by Bangalore's reputed climate which appeals to people today as it did to the English coming from the heat of the eastern coastal plains. Here, wrote a soldier in Lord Cornwallis' army, which captured the town in 1791 on behalf of the English East India

A number of amateur artists and army route surveyors during the 1791-92 War between Tipu Sultan and Lord Cornwallis captured the country that Lord Valentia in 1804 described as 'naked'. 'At six', he writes as he comes from the east, 'the celebrated town of Bangalore was in view. The country was more naked than any I had yet seen'.

TOP

Alexander Allan, 'View of Bangalore',
Views in the Mysore Country, 1794. [Yale Center for British Art, Paul Mellon Collection]

MIDDLE

Robert Home, *East View of Bangalore with the Cypress Garden,* 1792
Twenty Loose drawings. British Library, IOR WD 3775 5 [By permission of the British Library]

BOTTOM

Robert Home, *North View of Bangalore from the Pettah,* 1792
Twenty Loose drawings. British Library, IOR WD 3775 6 [By permission of the British Library]

Company, the climate is 'extremely temperate and salubrious' and 'the soil is fruitful, and produces the necessaries of life in great plenty'.[3] The century that followed this observation saw an aggressive cultivation of this land and toward the end of the 1800s Winston Churchill found Bangalore an exemplary cantonment. Like other cantonments built by the English in India, he observes, 'forethought and order have been denied neither time nor space' and planners had not held back in providing the 'considerable white communities' with 'splendid roads, endless double avenues of shady trees, abundant supplies of pure water'. In Bangalore, however, this generosity was rewarded more than elsewhere. Here, 'the roses of Europe in innumerable large pots attain the highest perfection of fragrance and colour. Flowers, flowering shrubs and creepers blossom in glorious profusion'.[4]

The frenzied pace of development that has come more recently with the pursuit of new titles, and the resulting loss of the substance behind the Garden City name such as trees, lakes, parks, and avenues, is a cause for worry amongst a growing number of residents. As far back as 1962 Prime Minister Jawaharlal Nehru was horrified that 'one of the most beautiful cities of India' had slums. He called for an immediate plan for Bangalore. 'Lack of a plan creates great difficulties... As the city is growing your plan must be in keeping with its pace, so that it may present a picture of a city of the future'.[5] Bangalore has had many plans since Nehru's visit, both comprehensive public endeavours and more specific, though as potent, private initiatives. All claim to enhance the Garden City's image even as they accommodate the infrastructure demanded by new titles for Bangalore.

The Garden City, however, is much more than the embellishment of a surface. Between the metropolis that is and the 'naked country' that the land was once perceived to be by 'outsiders', is a layer of enterprises that have cultivated various dimensions of the Garden City, dimensions by which it continues to be appreciated, communicated and transformed. These enterprises were initiated by individuals in the service of the East India Company at the turn of the eighteenth century who chose to see the land in terms of possibility, typical perhaps of colonisers. Their initiatives were instrumental in introducing new materials, ideas, images and skills. Their surveys, for example, gave Bangalore a spatial dimension, introducing topographical data, boundaries, categories of land-uses, and a tradition of maps; their sketches and paintings gave Bangalore a visual dimension, drawing out objects of significance from a background of ordinary life, and introducing an appreciation for the 'scene'; their plant studies gave Bangalore a material dimension which encouraged gardens, new introductions and hybrids that would transform sceneries, economies and cuisines. These endeavours are taken for granted today, their modes of inquiry and products embedded in disciplines, administration, plans, conversations and projections of Bangalore. In the late 1700s, however, when these individuals first took hold of this land, these endeavours were extraordinary pioneering ventures by amateurs who were operating, not merely on the Indian subcontinent, but in a global milieu of constructing 'useful knowledge'. They

LEFT

Bangalore enjoys many titles but one has taken root more firmly than others – 'Garden City of India'.

CENTRE

Lalbagh, which R. Venkataraman, former president of India, called the 'pendant in the necklace of Bangalore parks', has played a significant role in popularising Bangalore's title of Garden City of India, as well as in disseminating design vocabularies and plant material.

RIGHT

Bangalore's parks, lakes, tree-lined avenues, flower-planted traffic islands contribute to its image as a verdant and 'salubrious' place.

were formulating the methods and substances of disciplines while carrying out projects of global significance — measuring the curvature of the earth, devising plant classification schemes, documenting cultures, etc. These enterprises put Bangalore on the world stage even as they set it on a course to becoming the Garden City of India.

Of course, there was another side to these projects, the side that used the things they singled out and the knowledge that they constructed to administer a foreign land. Here surveys fixed boundaries and defined properties for the purposes of revenue; sketches and paintings were a means of statistical documentation; plant studies and introductions served the Company's economic objectives. These were colonial enterprises and they served not merely to exploit, but also to construct the land, its image, and its self-image.

Deccan Traverses is about these controversial enterprises, about the materials, ideas, images, skills, and modes of representation that they introduced and the landscapes that they constructed. But it is also about a land that exceeded their reach and exerted its own dimensions. This land beneath the 'naked country' confronted and eluded the inquiring and colonising ambitions of the eighteenth century and it continues in the guise of the 'ordinary' and 'everyday' to do the same with the disciplines, administrative divisions, and control measures that are the legacies of those ambitions. The Garden City presented here is thus as much a cultivated eye as it is a cultivated land; and it is as much the transformative trajectories begun by enterprising individuals as it is the embodied worlds of the Lower Deccan plateau.

Bangalore Gazetteer

In extending Bangalore's landscape to include its making, *Deccan Traverses* broadens, perhaps challenges, the tradition of the gazetteer, a mode of describing places for the purposes of governance and public administration. In its present form of divulging the history, geography, flora, fauna, geology, ethnography, industry, and so on of a place, the gazetteer tends to conceal, or at least underplay, the imagination that it took to give the land a vocabulary and make it conform to the demands of settlement and, importantly, of disciplines.

The gazetteer was developed as a tool in the mid-nineteenth century by 'rulers of India [who] had not been unmindful of the duty of placing information as to its history and resources within reach of the officials called on to administer it'.[6] It details descriptive information of particular places or more accurately of toponyms, i.e., 'proper nouns applied to topographic features'.[7] This particularity was compiled for districts and generalised for provinces and native states, eventually reaching the level of the subcontinent in Sir W.W. Hunter's 1881 *Imperial Gazetteer of India*. This work of nine volumes was, writes Hunter's biographer, Francis Henry Skrine, 'the sublimated essence of a hundred volumes of Statistical Accounts relating to the various provinces. . . . [Hunter] revealed the vast fabric [of India] to his countrymen, and enabled them to perform their trust under the guidance of the fullest knowledge'.[8]

The knowledge communicated by gazetteers was relatively new. It reached back to the same individuals and others like them at the turn of the eighteenth century who insisted on seeing the land of Bangalore, and indeed the entire peninsula of India, more in terms of potential than identity. They did not merely document places but sought a new beginning by declaring lands *terra incognita*. Such a beginning promised not merely a new way to look at things; it also promised new things to look at. It was the age of European Enlightenment, which Immanuel Kant, one of the most celebrated voices of that era, described as 'man's emergence from his self-imposed nonage. Nonage is the inability to use one's own understanding without another's guidance. . . . Dare to know! (Sapere aude.) "Have the courage to use your own understanding", is therefore the motto of the enlightenment'.[9]

Individuals who heeded the call of the Enlightenment had to not only devise ways of collecting knowledge but also had to transcend various forms of another's guidance in order to encounter a *terra incognita*. Barbara Stafford in *Voyage into Substance,* refers to these men as 'scientific explorer-artist-writers' who 'in trying to break from the limits of solipsism, custom, and habits of representation, strained to be extra-referential'. They were 'determined to break out of the metaphorical mode of simply "seeing as"'.[10] Such a break was easier away from home, particularly in lands that were changing from trading posts of European East India companies to territories possessed and in need of administration. It was a unique opportunity for men of the Enlightenment to provide an understanding that would become the basis of governance; men like Colin Mackenzie who would later recall the moment in the early 1780s when he first arrived on the plateau called the Deccan within the triangle of the South Indian peninsula. 'The Dekkan was in fact then a *terra incognita,* of which no authentic account existed, excepting in some uncertain notices and mutilated sketches of the marches of Bussy, and the travels of Tavernier and Thévenot, which by no means possess that philosophical accuracy demanded in modern times'.[11] Accounts by

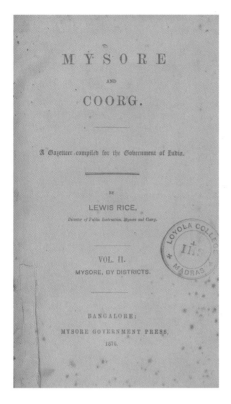

Lewis Rice, director of Public Instruction in Mysore and Coorg, was asked in 1873 to compile a gazetteer for Mysore. Collecting information, says Rice who was born in Bangalore in 1837, was a revelation as when he first joined the government service he was 'disappointed to be told, on inquiring from persons supposed to be acquainted with the subject, that Mysore had no history, was quite a modern State, and virtually unknown before the wars with Haider and Tipu brought it into prominence. As regards its language and literature, also, I was led to suppose that the language was merely a rude dialect of Tamil, and that literature it had none'. This was until he found the work of the men of the Enlightenment who came through Mysore in the 1790s and early 1800s. Of one of their works he says, 'Every page teems with valuable information'.

Mysore and Coorg: A Gazetteer compiled for the Government of India (Bangalore: Mysore Government Press, 1877)

Mackenzie and others like him evolved into gazetteers, but the enterprises that these individuals set in place in order to build their 'new' understanding of the land became the basis for new landscapes.

Deccan Traverses recalls the enterprises of the Enlightenment that did so much to pioneer and order the information communicated through the gazetteer but also through textbooks, guide books, maps, and other carriers of 'knowledge' to the public at large today. This recollection is not merely for the purpose of questioning this knowledge, but also to draw attention to the imagination and ambition necessary to devising an enterprise, i.e., 'daring to know without another's guidance', the motto that lies at the beginning of the gazetteer. It is also because Bangalore was a key point in emanating this daring on the Indian subcontinent. Its settlement — the making of the Garden City from what was perceived to be a 'naked country' — is inseparable from the transformative impact of the entrepreneurial flows that would generate here around 1800.

Traversing Bangalore

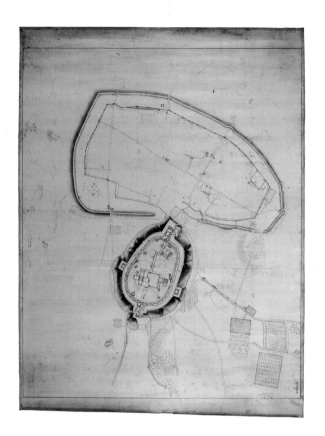

Plan of the Fortress of Bangalore, **1791. One of the earliest drawings of the Bangalore Pettah (town with an adjoining fort), highlighting the essential elements of Bangalore as a spatial entity — peripheral wall with gates, intersection of main roads at the centre, fort on the south.**

British Library, Add 18109-c [By permission of the British Library]

Bangalore is traced in the *State Gazetteer* as well as in popular accounts to a historic origin — a mud-walled town laid out in 1537 by an agricultural chieftain, Kempegowda I. It can also be traced to a point in early eighteenth century maps of the Indian subcontinent by European cartographers. This point first appeared in maps of southern India as one of many names in the interior of the peninsula. The name gradually gained prominence in later maps of India but also of Mysore, a native state which was first surveyed in the early 1800s. But even as the name Bangalore was growing in significance in maps of the peninsula and the region, it was beginning to command its own space, appearing in 1791 as an area, three miles in circumference, enclosed by a wall and a ditch and adjoined by an oval stone fort to the south. It was drawn as such by British surveyors during the Third Mysore War when it was occupied by Cornwallis's army. In 1807 this spatial entity developed a twin, a cantonment with the same name laid out by Lt. John Blakiston. The two settlements were tracked together thereafter as they evolved into a single administrative unit that today occupies one square metre at a scale of 1:25,000.

There is, however, another Bangalore, less defined, more material. It has its beginnings not in a cartographer's point but in the entrepreneurial ambitions of individuals who encountered a 'naked country' and proceeded to give it a vocabulary and language of transformation. This starting point is not necessarily in the past; it is rather buried beneath a weight of representations, physical interventions, and disciplines.

Deccan Traverses recounts our engagement with this less evident Bangalore, a place of potential rather than identity. It demands a shift in perception from seeing a place constrained by a timeline and held by the spatial limits of a municipality or metropolis, to seeing a gathering of materials and events each exerting its own presence, trajectory and ambition for a 'naked country'. It is not surprising that there is little written about this Bangalore. Our education and administration privilege the seeing of a defined if not physically demarcated entity (a city), and not an extended material terrain.

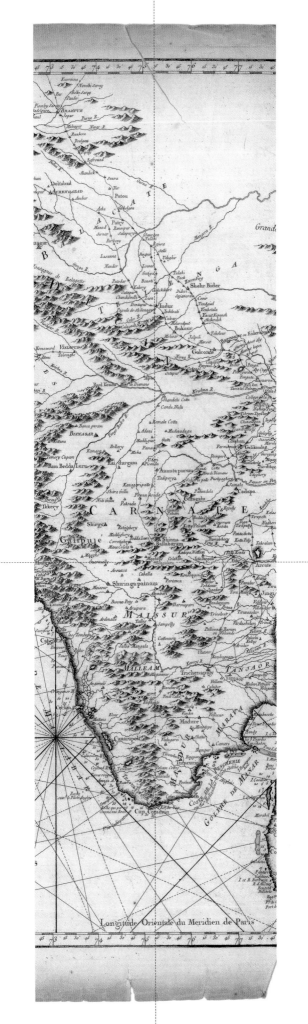

N

W   E

S

Jean Nicolas Bellin, Detail, *Carte reduite de la Presque Isle de l'Inde,* **1766. Bangalore as a point called Bengaluru amongst a field of names.**

Our engagement with this Bangalore began in an open field of conversations, photography expeditions, measured drawings, archival searches, and material investigations. The rich matter that we uncovered, not just within the municipal limits of Bangalore or the planning limits of its metropolitan area, but across the Lower Deccan plateau and further afield, revealed a place unhindered by boundaries. This open landscape, after many speculative orderings and radical re-orderings, gathered around four enterprises, each with an extensive reach into places and everyday practices — *surveying, triangulating, botanising, and picturing.* They were triggered by a fortuitous convergence in Bangalore of, on the one hand, individuals with an imagination steeped in the Enlightenment and, on the other hand, the immediate and local needs of a Company with colonising ambitions of a 'progressive' kind. According to Thomas Daniell, an English artist who came through Bangalore in 1792, it was a 'new era of civilization'.

'It was an honourable feature in the late century that the passion for discovery, originally kindled by the thirst for gold, was exalted to higher and nobler aims than commercial speculations. Since this new era of civilization, a liberal spirit of curiosity has prompted undertakings to which avarice lend no incentive, and fortune annexed no reward: associations have been formed, not for piracy, but humanity: science has had her adventurers, and philanthropy her achievements: the shores of Asia have been invaded by a race of students with no rapacity but for lettered relics; by naturalists, whose cruelty extends not to one human inhabitant; by philosophers, ambitious only for extirpation of error, and the diffusion of truth. It remains for the artist to claim his part in these guiltless spoliations, and to transport to Europe the picturesque beauties of these favoured regions'.[12]

Bangalore was a key disseminating point of this 'new era' and the four enterprises that we single out played a critical role in extending this point. They led in the construction of disciplined views of the land — geography, geodesy, botany, picturesque art, history, archaeology, architecture — and on their basis set in motion a profound material transformation of the peninsula. Their views and vocabularies were, however, not always accepted, and in moments and events of resistance and subversion one glimpses intersecting trajectories and ambitions. They provide us with points of departure and digressions, ultimately constructing a Bangalore that is as extraordinarily enigmatic as it is emergent.

This Bangalore cannot be merely written about. Nor can it be just photographed or mapped. Its representation has to be devised. The visual material in this book runs parallel to the text, the two relating to one another more analogously than convergently. The number of rare maps and drawings that we have uncovered are not only significant for their depiction of a place but also for the techniques and modes of recording a land that was being introduced to new measurements and portrayals. Our own 'map-prints' appropriate some of these found documents in the construction of layered silk screen prints that embed particular histories and geographies. The digital line drawings and photographs — often sequential, sectional and extended — suggest a mode of traversing these constructed terrains. Collectively they draw out material rhythms and contemporary issues of Bangalore's landscape.

Deccan Traverses is ultimately a platform for engaging Bangalore as an open terrain; for recovering the moments of wonder that make the ordinary extraordinary; for seeding new initiatives that cultivate fresh vocabularies and trajectories for future interventions.

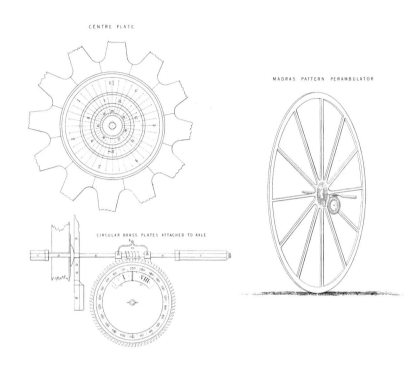

CENTRE PLATE

MADRAS PATTERN PERAMBULATOR

CIRCULAR BRASS PLATES ATTACHED TO AXLE

THE WAR

CAMP GROUND

PETTAH

ESPLANADE

LAST FRONTIER

August 27-1790

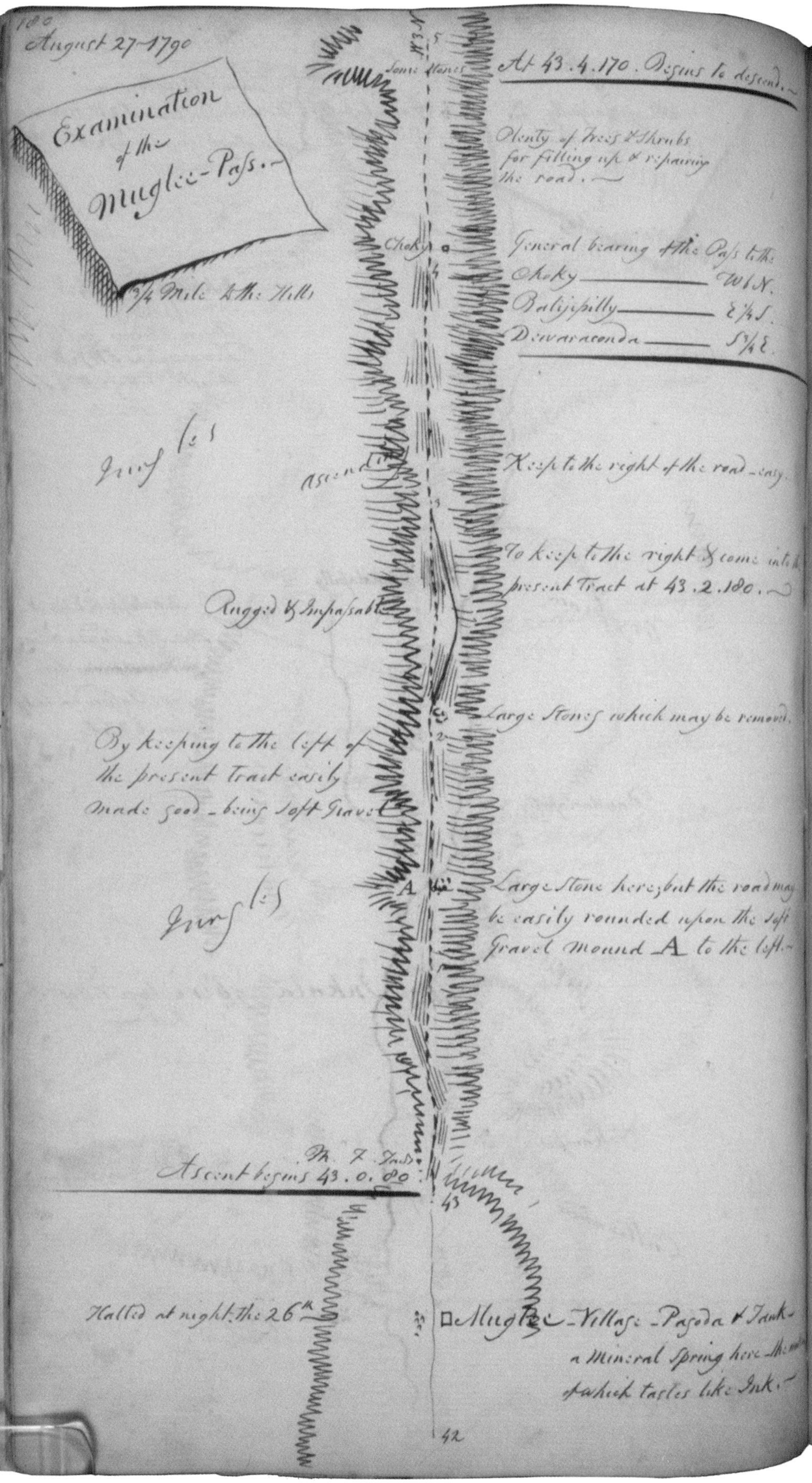
Examination of the Muglee-Pass.
3/4 Mile to the Hills
N 3 N
5
Some Stones
At 43.4.170. Begins to descend.
Plenty of Trees & Shrubs for filling up & repairing the road.
Choky
General bearing of the Pass to the
Choky — W b N.
Balijipilly — E ¼ S.
Dewaraconda — S ¼ E.
Jungles
Ascend
Keep to the right of the road - easy.
To keep to the right & come into the present Tract at 43.2.180.
Rugged & Impassable
Large Stones which may be removed.
By keeping to the left of the present Tract easily made good - being soft Gravel
Jungles
A
Large Stone here; but the road may be easily rounded upon the soft Gravel mound A to the left.
M. F. Yds.
Ascent begins 43.0.80
43
Halted at night the 26th
Muglee - Village - Pagoda & Tank - a Mineral Spring here - the water of which tastes like Ink.
42

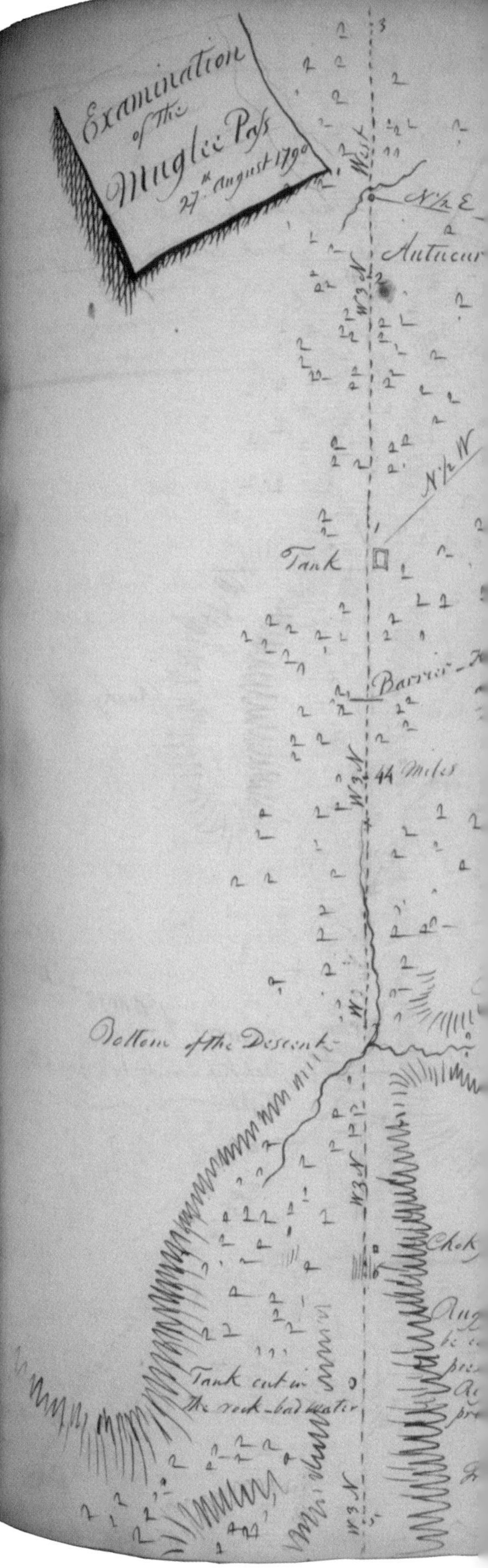
Examination of the Muglee Pass 27th August 1790
3
West
N ½ E
Autucur
W 3 N
N ½ W
Tank
Barrier
44 Miles
W 3 N
W
Bottom of the Descent
W 3 N
Choky
Tank cut in the rock - bad water
W 3 N

DECCAN TRAVERSES

THE WAR
CAMP GROUND
PETTAH
ESPLANADE
LAST FRONTIER

13

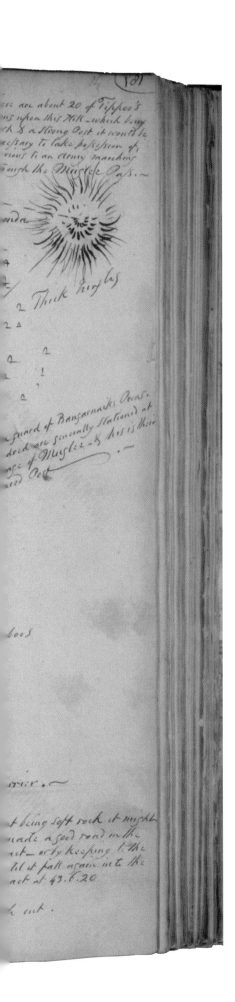

THE WAR

Geographers today know the Deccan Plateau as a trapezoidal high ground framed by the Vindhya Mountains on the north, the Eastern and Western Ghats that parallel the two coasts, and the Nilgiri Hills on the south. To men of the English East India Company, however, based in the east coastal plains or Carnatic, it was through most of the eighteenth century merely an 'interior', a land that lay beyond what Sir Walter Scott described as 'those tremendous mountain-passes . . . winding upwards among immense rocks and precipices . . . at one time completely overshadowed by dark groves of teak-trees, and at another . . . [passing] beside impenetrable jungles, the habitation of jackals and tigers'.[1]

Before the Company established its factories or fortified trading posts on the east coast in the early 1600s, this tract was largely absent in the renderings of European mapmakers who, with information provided by travellers to the region, made exquisite maps of the Indian peninsula. These travellers rarely ventured into the interior or, if they did, they did not report it. Marco Polo, who visited the Indian peninsula in the thirteenth century, writes of people who 'depict their gods and their idols black and their devils white as snow', yogis who live for 'as much as 150 or 200 years', and kings 'rich in treasure': but he admits no time for the interior. 'I have described only those provinces and cities that lie on the sea-coast. Of the inland regions I have told you nothing; for the tale would be too long in the telling'.[2]

It was eventually missionaries who would initiate and maintain a steady trickle of information from the interior. Thomas Jefferys, an English cartographer, comments on this in 1754: 'Europeans had but confused ideas of the inland and southern parts of the hither Peninsula of the Indies, before the missioners, especially the Romish, entered those countries to propagate their religion; and, as for more than a century none but they had visited them, none but they were able to give the world exact informations (sic) concerning them'.[3]

In the latter half of the 1700s, however, the trickle of information emerging from the interior would surge dramatically. The trigger was the Third Mysore War when Lord Cornwallis, appointed by the British parliament in 1787 as governor-general of the Company's possessions in

India, led a combination of the Company Army and the King's troops into the interior 'to bring the enemy to a decisive action in the field'.[4] The enemy was Tipu Sultan and the governor-general sought to end his 'raids' on the Carnatic conducted from the safety of his domain in the interior. Ten years before in America, Cornwallis had suffered the consequences of an elusive enemy. His army was weakened by men who fought as much through guerrilla tactics as through open battles. He was eventually made to surrender to George Washington at Yorktown, forcing the British government to give up their possessions to what, in 1776, had been declared the United States of America. That defeat was six years before he was made governor general of the East India Company's possessions in India, a position with powers of legislation and war instituted by the British Parliament to bring governing responsibility to a Company that was gaining territory largely by grants but increasingly by war.

The Carnatic was one place where the Company was initiating an entry into the peninsula. For half a century this terrain on the southeast, also known as the Coromandel Coast, had been crisscrossed by its army and political missions as the mercantile corporation was becoming increasingly involved in protecting its patrons in a turbulent region of rulers and sub-rulers with shifting alliances. The 'vicissitudes of their politics', writes Walter Hamilton of these native powers, 'and the perpetual fluctuation of their boundaries, rendered the most accurate account that could be given, only suited to the particular period in which it was written'.[5] It was not always clear as to who was a ruler and who a sub-ruler. 'Every deputy's deputy and the officer of every mud fort, or town', writes Mark Wilks, 'affected the fashionable designation of Nabob as the first step toward independence'.[6] The Nawab of Arcot, however, managed to do it more convincingly than others. The English East India Company paid him an annual rent of twelve hundred pagodas. His kingdom stretched, at least nominally, from the Krishna to the Coleroon (the north distributary of the Kaveri) and from the ghats to the Bay of Bengal. It was, nominally again, part of the Moghul Empire ruled through the 'Viceroy of the Dekhan' based at Aurangabad. But as the Moghul Empire weakened, their southern dominion was taken over by the Nizam, who was first based at Aurangabad and later at Hyderabad. This ruler blurred the line between emperor's representative and sovereign. His feudatories, in particular the Nawab of Arcot, did the same in a domino effect that extended to the local chieftains and Wilk's 'deputy's deputy'. Into this balkanisation – or more likely a land that always defied the distinction between tributary and sovereignty – were drawn the English and French Companies in search of gain or perhaps just a landlord. The rivalry of their nations in Europe set them against each other on the subcontinent. 'The war declared between Great Britain and France in 1744', writes Robert Orme, 'extended its operation to the settlements of the two nations in India . . . as allies to two Moorish Lords contending for the possession of the province of Carnatica'.[7] The 'Carnatic Wars', fought sporadically until 1760 between these nations, revolved around putting the right person on the thrones at Arcot and Hyderabad. The two places would eventually command kingdoms independent of each other but dependent on the English East India Company. Before this happened, however, the Company would seek to know these territories as they were never known before.

Jean-Baptiste Bourgignon D'Anville, 'Nouvelle Carte d'une Grande Partie de la Presqu'Isle des Indes en de ca du Gange'. This map was published in 1737 with information of the interior that was provided primarily by Jesuit missionaries. It was the basis for a number of other maps of the mid 1700s.

Jesuits, *Lettres edifantes et curieuses ecrites des missions etrangeres,* vol. 15, Nouvelle Edition (Paris: Nicolas le Clerc, 1781) [Annenberg Rare Book and Manuscript Library, University of Pennsylvania]

Thomas Jefferys, 'A Map of the Coast of Coromandel from the River Gadeveri to Cape Comorin' (in two parts). The 1740s and '50s saw the beginnings of route surveying in the coastal plains of the Carnatic primarily through the Carnatic Wars between the English and the French, each alongside their respective native allies.

Robert Orme *Historical Fragments of the Mogul Empire, of the Morattoes, and of the English Concerns in Indostan, MDCLIX* (London: C. Nourse, 1782). [Annenberg Rare Book and Manuscript Library, University of Pennsylvania]

This knowledge gathered around the most basic work of men known as route surveyors — the recording of roads taken by missions and marches. On the infrastructural network drawn by these men were hung 'military features; and a sketch of the ground, with explanatory references, together with a full and correct report of all the intelligence . . . from observation, or from such of the inhabitants as are most likely to be well acquainted with the localities, and most worthy of credence'.[8] This was a time when warfare was becoming a science communicated through the written word and the drawn line. Upon the route surveyor, it was often said, rested the fate of the army. Upon them also rested the future of maps and, to an extent, administrative knowledge. Maps of the Indian subcontinent in the latter half of the eighteenth century were disproportionately detailed and considered 'accurate' in areas infiltrated by route surveyors, prompting the leading mapmaker in Europe, Jean-Baptiste Bourgignon D'Anville, to comment: 'we might mention different parts of Europe, in which geography is less informed, than of many places in Coromandel'.[9]

Route surveyors worked with the bearings of compasses and distances recorded by perambulators (wheels, six to seven feet in diameter). These instruments made for a higher level of accuracy than the approximations of a day's journey and the rough directions of earlier travellers, although certain terrains like jungles and marshes and night marches forced them to abandon the perambulator and resort to estimating distance by the rate of the march. Robert Kelly, a prominent route surveyor in the Carnatic in 1770-80s states the minimum requirement: 'A pocket compass and watch are the sum of his apparatus, and if he guesses within half a point of the bearing, and half a mile of the distance, of one village or encampment from another, he is allowed to be very accurate in his observations'.[10] In addition to linear plotting of distances, features, and intelligence, many route surveyors did drawings of the horizon at various points to absorb and communicate their visual presence. These drawings ranged from simple line works to elaborate water colours. But it was their regular celestial observations that ultimately facilitated their routes and the objects along them to be assembled into maps used as much by the Company administration to base its knowledge as by historians to illustrate a 'seat of war' that was becoming a curiosity to people in Europe.

As much as the Company, however, desired all possible knowledge of the Carnatic, they would be increasingly drawn to its western boundary where the ghats were literally a thorn in the Company's (and Nawab's) side for the last four decades of the eighteenth century.

The word ghats is today popularly understood as the hill ranges along the east and west coast — the Eastern and Western Ghats. However, route surveyors in the 1700s found that it referred as much to the passes through which the interior was accessed. This ambiguity of a threshold — divider and unifier — captures the frontier-like milieu of route surveyors in the Carnatic. Their skill would be tested here between the Payenghat — land below the passes — and the Balaghat — land above the passes.[11]

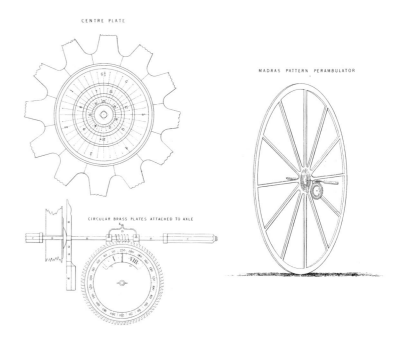

The Balaghat, the elevated tract beyond the ghats, had been in a transition in the 1750s from a lineage of Mysore Rajahs based in Seringapatam on the River Kaveri to a popular and ambitious soldier in his army, Hyder Ali. This man had distinguished himself in the Anglo-French wars of the Carnatic, where the Rajah, as a feudatory of the Nizam, had been summoned to assist the English and their Nawab's cause. The wars ended with the English as the firm victors and the Mysore army on the side of the French. But it was not until Hyder Ali assumed full power over the Rajah's dominion – the Balaghat – in 1761 that the English had cause for concern. His rule, followed by that of his son Tipu Sultan, was marked by a determination to eliminate the English from the peninsula. The shift in alliances and the changing power is written about in 1792 by Major James Rennell, a leading route surveyor and mapmaker revered by some as the Father of Indian Geography.[12] He recalls a time in the Carnatic wars four decades earlier 'when the Mysoreans were rabble, and their chief, Hyder Ali, an unpractised soldier. But such are the mutations in human affairs, that one of these parties, a handful of British troops, then in the capacity of auxiliaries to the Nabob of Arcot; became, in the course of a few years after, the arbiters of empire in India: and the other, their most powerful and determined enemy'.[13]

Getting onto the Balaghat from the Payenghat, involved a climb of over 500 metres. It was a formidable ascent demanding the negotiation of passes guarded by forts on top of hills. Here Cornwallis's army was led by Alexander Beatson, head of the Corps of Guides. This organisation, begun in 1777, accorded route surveying the recognition of a necessity carried out with focused expertise rather than an intermittent luxury undertaken by soldiers called away from the field. Beatson writes about how he devised routes in the interior and made 'sketch surveys' from information that he collected from natives well before he had marched those routes and well before he mapped them with compass and perambulator. He was, in a sense, always ahead of himself. 'By this means, I always could extend my Sketch Surveys considerably beyond the position of the Army which were very useful, on many occasions, in the regulation of its marches & Encampments'. The accuracy of his 'information routes', as he called the object of his speculative sketch surveys, always surprised him when checked against the actual survey done later.[14]

It was by information routes that Beatson found 'Sixty six Passes, between the River Kistnah & Cape Comorin', through the 'Western Frontier of the Carnatic'. When war was declared against Tipu Sultan in May 1790 he was prepared. The plan of the British campaign was for the Company army and its allies

The Madras Pattern Perambulator.

Colonel H.L. Thuillier and Lt. Colonel R. Smyth, *A Manual of Surveying for India detailing the Mode of Operations on the Trigonometrical, Topographical and Revenue Surveys of India* (Calcutta: Thacker, Spink and Co., 1875), Plate 2 and 12.

DECCAN TRAVERSES

THE WAR
CAMP GROUND
PETTAH
ESPLANADE
LAST FRONTIER

17

**Captain Charles Gold, 'An Artillery Elephant on Duty'.
In the accompanying text Gold writes: 'No Indian army
takes the field without a considerable number of
Elephants, which are employed in carrying camp
equipage, and in forwarding the heavy artillery up the
sides of mountains, and over bad roads. . . The scene
here represented is on the road ascending the Gauts
into Tippoo's country, which abounds in the bamboo
and other luxuriant shrubs, growing wild. Parties of the
Bengal and Madras artillery lascars, with a few Europeans, are assisting with drag-ropes. . . On the rise of the
hill are the leading bullocks of another gun and in the
distance below appears the Carnatic'.**
Oriental Drawings: Sketched between the years 1791 and 1798
(London: Bumey and Co., 1806). [Yale Center for British Art, Paul
Mellon Collection]

to consume the periphery of the Sultan's dominion on the southeast, west and north and then penetrate the interior, converging toward his capital of 'Seringapatam as to a common centre'. But Tipu Sultan could not be put in a defensive position. Until the end of the year, the English were occupied staving off a rampant Sultan in the Carnatic where, according to Rennell, he 'left marks of his savage barbarity, every where, along his march'.[15] It is at this time that Cornwallis decided to enter the interior. Feigning entry through a pass in the neighbourhood of Amboor by sending a battalion in that direction and seeing to it that Tipu Sultan expected him there 'by means of false intelligence, which a defected spy was compelled to give', Cornwallis went further north.[16] Here, on the advice of Beatson, he entered by the 'shortest and easiest' pass, the Moogly Pass connecting Chittoor and Palmaner. 'Several parts of it are steep; particularly the second and longest ascent, of about 500 yards; which, at the top, has rather a sharp turn to the left. The road was new, and well made; and neither rugged nor stony. The draft bullocks were not taken out of the yokes: and with the assistance of the troops at the drag-ropes; and the elephants, pushing from behind; the whole of the heavy guns were got up, in a few hours. Several other consider-able ascents, as well as descents, occurred, in going through the rest of the pass; which is all together about six miles through'.[17]

The pass was a considerable transition. 'As the army ascended at the Mugly pass in February, 1791, a change of climate much for the better was sensibly felt'.[18] Once through the pass, the army gathered on the eastern edge of what surveyors called the Mysore Tableland. This 'tract of elevated country (or Table Land, as it is commonly styled)', clarified Rennell at the time, was not an even surface. 'So far from this being the case, it has a vast number of lofty eminences on it: but these, in a general point of view, are nothing more than inequalities, on the top of a vast flat mountain'.[19] On this flat mountain he notes, 'The air was remarkably pure; and the nights very cold; from the greatness of the elevation'.[20] Here a grateful Cornwallis acknowledges the route surveyor: 'in justice to Captain Beatson, the Captain of the Guides, I must add that his exertions, and the accurate knowledge which he had obtained of the passes, were of essential service'.[21]

The accompaniment of an army made the route surveyor on the tableland a contrast to the lone missionary of the early eighteenth century, the surveyor's predecessor in providing information for maps. This army, according to Major Dirom, a senior participant in the war, comprised 14,000 'effective men', a significant number of which were mounted on horses, 27,000 bullocks, and 80 elephants. The attendants of these men and animals were estimated to number four times the fighting force. Added to their numbers were merchants with their own servants, 'palanquin and dooly-bearers for the conveyance of the sick', and the families of the native soldiers who insisted their kin travel with them. Then there were 'adventurers', men, 'with no other view than to plunder in the enemy's country; and even they far from being a nuisance, search for and dig up the pits of grain in the fields and villages, which would otherwise remain undiscovered, and bring in numbers of cattle that could by no other means be collected in the country'. The sight, he concludes, was less an army and more a nation. 'There are no towns to be depended upon for supplies; and an army in India, not only carries with it most of the means of its subsistence for several months, but also a variety of necessaries, which are exposed daily in the bazaars like merchandise in a fair: a scene altogether resembling more the emigration of a nation guarded by its troops than the march of an army, fitted out merely with the intention to subdue the enemy'![22] This moving nation was probably also a growing one. To supply the various wants of an army in India according to Robert Orme, 'dealers, pedlars, and retailers of all forts, follow the army, to whom separate quarter is allotted in which they daily expose their different commodities in greater quantities, and with more regularity than any fair in Europe'.[23]

With little or no resistance from local chieftains, Cornwallis's growing nation led by route surveyors would face its first resistance fourteen days later in Bangalore. Here it would be depleted sufficiently enough to have to settle in order to revive its strength.

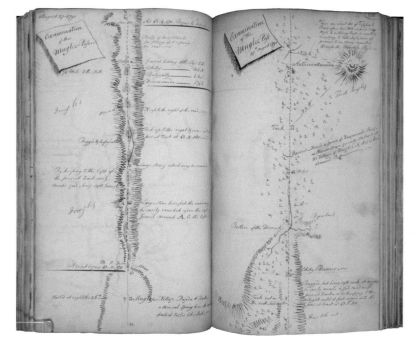

Major Alexander Beatson's survey of the Moogly Pass records the ascent of the army from the Payenghat at Palmaner. 'This line in the middle of the page', writes Beatson, 'represents the tract of the perambulator: upon which, are noted the distances measured; the bearings of the road by a pocket compass; the objects to the right and left, as hills, rivers, tanks or reservoirs of water, villages, forts, ravines, etc. are sketched in plan, to which are added short descriptions or remarks'.

Geographical observations on the Peninsula of India, vol. 1. British Library, Mss. Eur. D48 180 & 181. [By permission of the British Library]

DECCAN TRAVERSES

THE WAR
CAMP GROUND
PETTAH
ESPLANADE
LAST FRONTIER

19

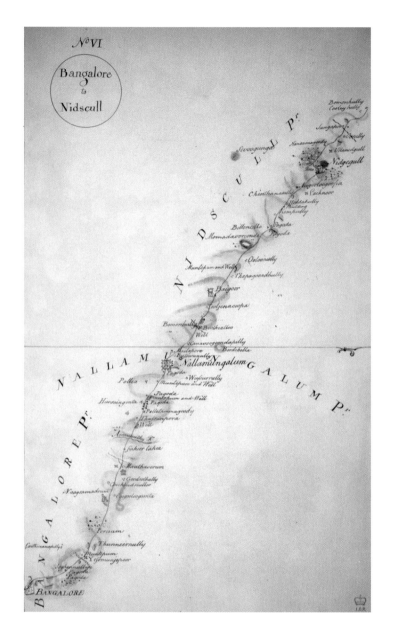

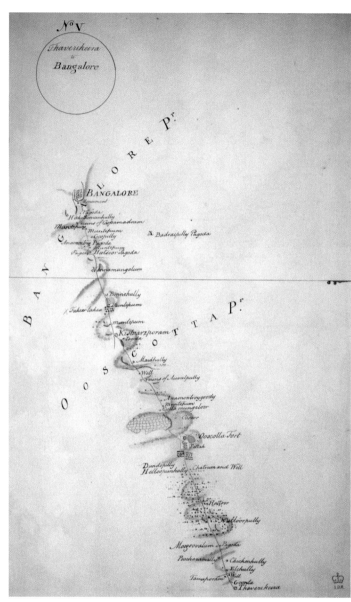

Route surveys, 1790s.

British Library, IOR X/2109/5 & 6 [By permission

of the British Library]

DECCAN TRAVERSES

THE WAR
CAMP GROUND
PETTAH
ESPLANADE
LAST FRONTIER

21

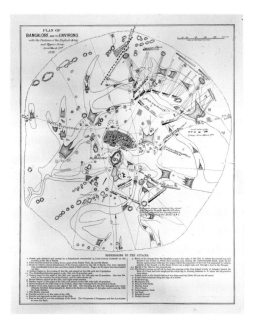

CAMP GROUND

Major Vibart, 'Bangalore and its Environs'. The map is a redrawing of the battle for Bangalore which took place within the 'bound hedge' and extended from 7 March when the pettah was captured to 21 March when the fort was taken. Surveyors distinguished between low grounds of water collection and high grounds for positions and camps.

The Military History of the Madras Engineers and Pioneers, From 1743 up to the Present Time, vol. I, (London: W.H. Allen & Co., 1881)

Once through the Moogly Pass and on the Mysore Tableland route surveyors sped Cornwallis's army to Bangalore. This town was originally intended to be merely a step on the way to Seringapatam, which they sought to reach before Tipu Sultan mobilised his army from the passes to the south where he had been deceived into waiting for Cornwallis and his men. But the Sultan realised his folly sooner. 'Astonished when he found himself so egregiously duped, and learnt, that the British forces, having without interruption surmounted the formidable barrier opposed by nature to their progress, were rapidly penetrating into his dominions; he found himself compelled to abandon his purpose, and repair with speed to the protection of his own country'.[24] He caught up with the governor-general near the centre of the peninsula, both armies converging on Bangalore, one from the east-north-east, the other from the east-southeast. As Lt. Roderick Mackenzie records the events of 5 March 1791, the enemy literally emerged from the mist. 'Thick fog', writes Mackenzie, 'concealed the Mysoreans for some time after sun rise; but clearing up as the day advanced, their whole force was discovered in motion toward Bangalore. Orders for marching were immediately issued in the British camp, and the two powers moved for some time parallel to each other, separated by a piece of low swampy ground'.[25] The Sultan's forces apparently 'made a show of offering battle; but Lord Cornwallis, not deceived by this feint, opposed to him his left wing only, while the right, covering the battering train, baggage, and stores, pursued its march. The enemy began a cannonade at a great distance; which, as they did not advance, was not returned'.[26] The governor-general refused to be distracted but he now had to contend with the Sultan's army, which had evidently arrived to make a stand in Bangalore.

Route surveyors record the meeting of 5 March as occurring just outside the 'bound hedge' of Bangalore. The Bound Hedge, according to Major Dirom, was, 'A broad strong belt of planting, chiefly the bamboo tree, the prickly pear, and such other trees and shrubs as form the closest fence. Most of the forts and villages are surrounded with such a hedge; and the large forts have a bound hedge that encloses a circuit of several miles, as a place of refuge to the inhabitants of the adjoining country against the incursions of horse'.[27] This planting ran in a circle of about eight to ten kilometres in diameter. It defined the

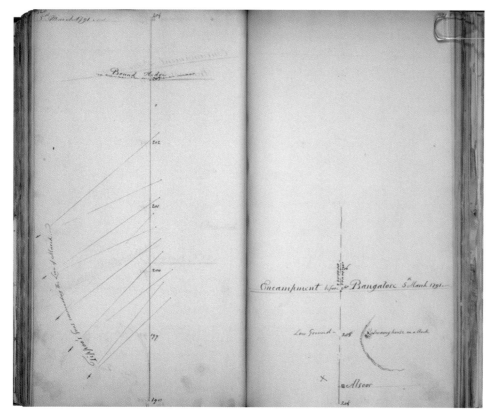

LEFT

Major Alexander Beatson's record of the marches of 5 March 1791 show the exchange of artillery fire between Cornwallis's and Tipu's armies just before they reach the Bound Hedge of Bangalore.

Geographical observations on the Peninsula of India, vol. 1. British Library, Mss. Eur. D48 320 & 321 [By permission of the British Library]

BELOW

Claude Martin, 'Plan of the Fort of Bangalore from Sights, without Measurement'. Writing in *The European Magazine and London Review,* 1792, Martin describes the fort: 'This fort is about a mile in circumference, and shaped like an egg. There are two entrances to it: one at each end, lying to the north and south. The northern entrance is called the Delhi gates; they are five in number, and are strong, large and elegantly finished. The southern entrance is called the Mysore gates; they are low, and far inferior to the Delhi gates, and are four in number'.

Published by J. Sewell. British Library, IOR P255 [By permission of the British Library]

BOTTOM

A plaque commemorating the British victory in the battle for the Bangalore Fort, 21 March, 1791

territory of the first battle of the war on the Mysore tableland, the battle for Bangalore, which comprised a pettah and fort located near the centre of the circle. The pettah itself was less than a kilometre across with its own mud wall and beyond that 'an excellent ditch with an intermediate berm, if such it may be called, of near one hundred yards wide, planted with impenetrable and well-grown thorns'.[28] From the time the two armies penetrated the hedge on 5 March 1791, the fifty-odd square kilometre area between ditch and hedge was to become the site of manoeuvres, charges, assassination attempts, bombardments, defences but perhaps most importantly and extensively, encampments.

Surveyors were quick to record the high and low grounds within this enclosure for the purpose of siting encampments and defence positions. They sought the higher ground to the northeast for settling the 'Grand Army' – comprising Company troops, King's troops, Nizam's men and the Marathas – while Tipu Sultan's men camped to the southwest. It was a polarity within the Bound Hedge that would be tested with skirmishes until Cornwallis's men stormed and occupied the pettah on 7 March, attacking it before the adjoining fort 'as the only means of procuring forage for the cattle and materials for the siege [of the fort]'.[29] Two weeks later, on the night of 21 March, the fort, weakened by batteries of guns positioned in the pettah, was taken.

'The reduction of Bangalore', writes Mackenzie, 'whilst it afforded the British force a firm establishment, and fixed the war on a solid foundation, in the heart of Tippoo Sultaun's dominions, was at the same time attended with the very best consequences to the several operations of our allies. The capture of so important a fortress, disheartening the Mysoreans wheresoever besieged, operated to the advantage of the confederates in all directions.

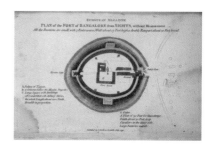

DECCAN TRAVERSES

THE WAR
CAMP GROUND
PETTAH
ESPLANADE
LAST FRONTIER

23

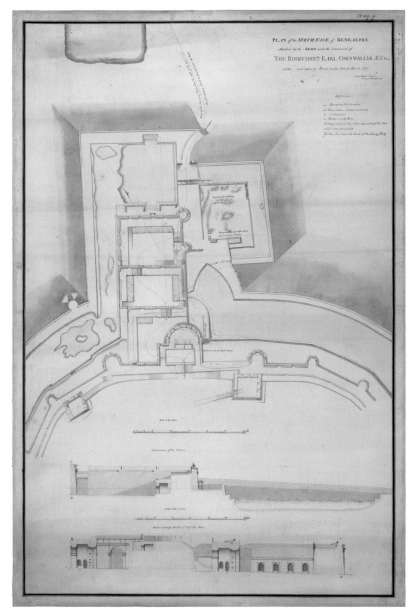

Joseph Stokoe, *Plan of the north face of Bangalore taken by Storm 21 March 1791*. Lt. Roderick Mackenzie describes the mood in the British camp when the assault of the fort began: 'Whilst the troops destined for the assault, advanced to their several stations, with awful stillness, the garrison both in the fort and outworks, as if wearied with incessant exertion, were equally lull; a bright moon, at times obscured by a passing cloud, shone against the battered precipices over which the assailants had to pass; from the heavens there came not a breath of wind; nothing disturbed thought; and gallant corps, after bestowing in reflection a soldierly and affectionate tribute on their fair friends, bade adieu to all worldly concerns, and riveted their minds to death or victory'.

British Library, Add 18109-g [By permission of the British Library]

Robert Home, 'North View of Bangalore from the Pettah, shewing the Curtain & Bastions that were breached'.

Select Views in Mysore, The Country of Tipoo Sultan from Drawings taken on the spot with Historical Descriptions (London: Bowyer, 1794).

Polligars of all descriptions transferring their allegiance to the superior power, in order to testify attachment at an early period, flocked with provisions to the British camp'.[30] Despite the new allegiances, however, resources were too strained and support too limited to move on in war, and instead of being a step to Seringapatam, Cornwallis was forced to make Bangalore a primary campground. Through the rest of the year, the Company army stationed here made expeditions all around the Bound Hedge, subduing chieftains loyal to the Sultan. More often than not these men were stationed on droogs located in all directions around Bangalore. The droog, one surveyor writes, is 'a hill, or rather a mountain, standing by itself in a plain, or so unconnected with its contiguous chain as to be out of reach of annoyance from that quarter. It is also such as to be, from its declivity, or the scarped nature of its sides, particularly difficult of ascent'.[31] The expeditions to overcome these fearsome outcrops and the forts on the relatively flat terrain between them inscribed and re-inscribed the centrality of the Bound Hedge of Bangalore on the Mysore Tableland. After each of these forays, Dirom writes, the soldiers returned to a place that they 'looked forward to as their home'.[32]

Eventually, nearly a year after they entered the Bound Hedge of Bangalore, Cornwallis, at the head of a 'Grand Army', stormed Seringapatam in Feburary 1792 to bring the Sultan to the treaty table.

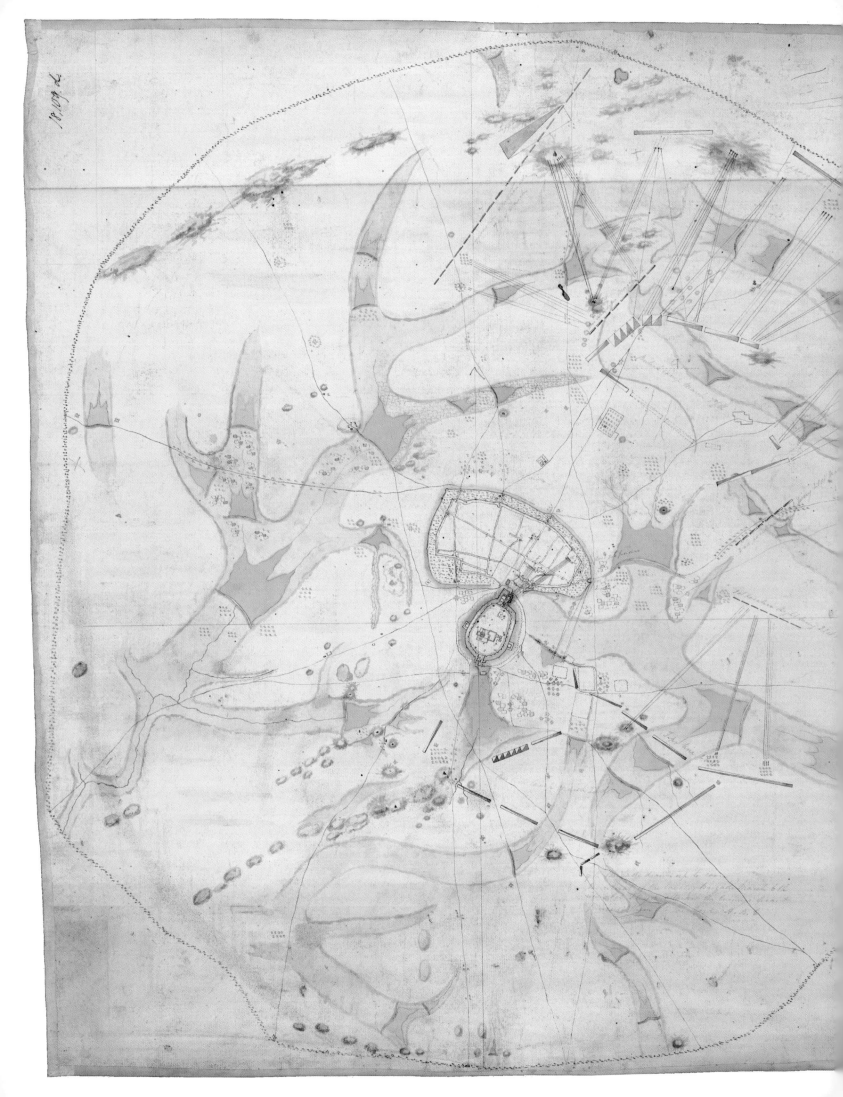

DECCAN TRAVERSES

THE WAR
CAMP GROUND
PETTAH
ESPLANADE
LAST FRONTIER

25

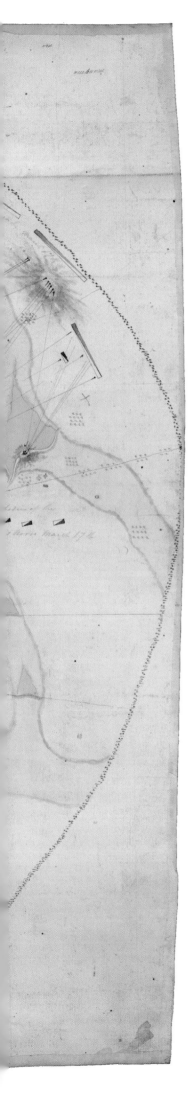

***Plan showing the position of the British
Troops round the Pettah, March 1791.***
**Surveyors during the Third Mysore War
gave the name Bangalore to the Bound
Hedge that surrounded a number of
settlements, Bangalore or Bengaluru
being perhaps the most significant. This
Hedge marked the limits of the battle
for Bangalore in March 1791.**

British Library, Add 18109-d   [By permission of
the British Library]

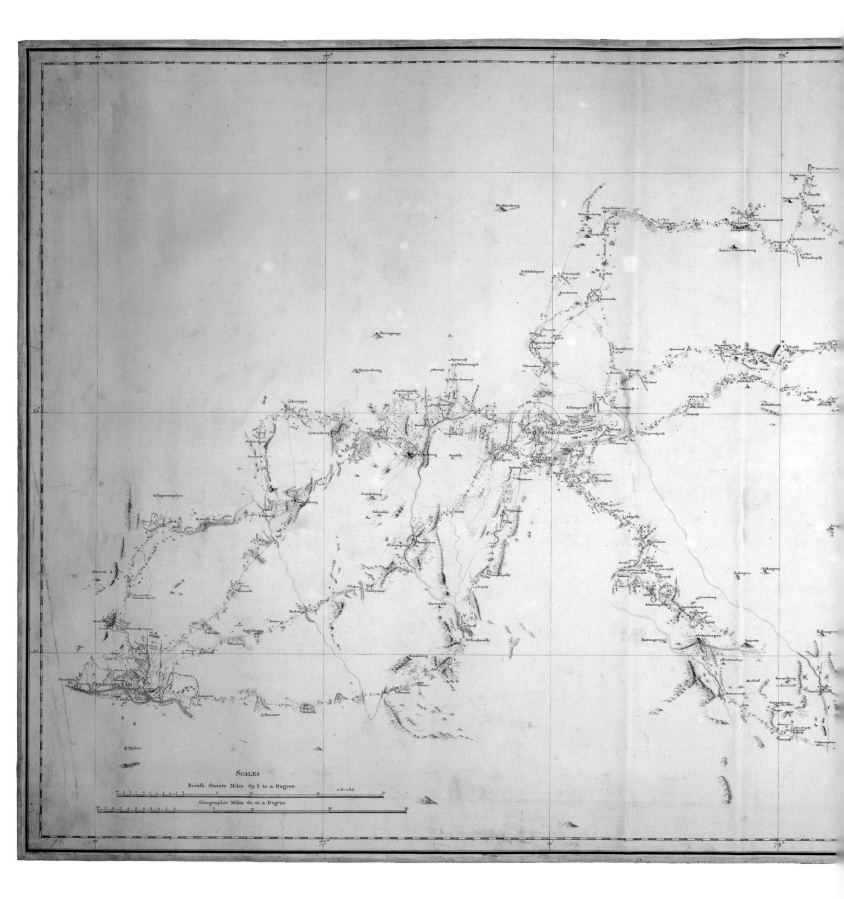

SCALES
British Statute Miles 69 ½ to a Degree.

Geographic Miles 60 to a Degree.

DECCAN TRAVERSES

THE WAR
CAMP GROUND
PETTAH
ESPLANADE
LAST FRONTIER

27

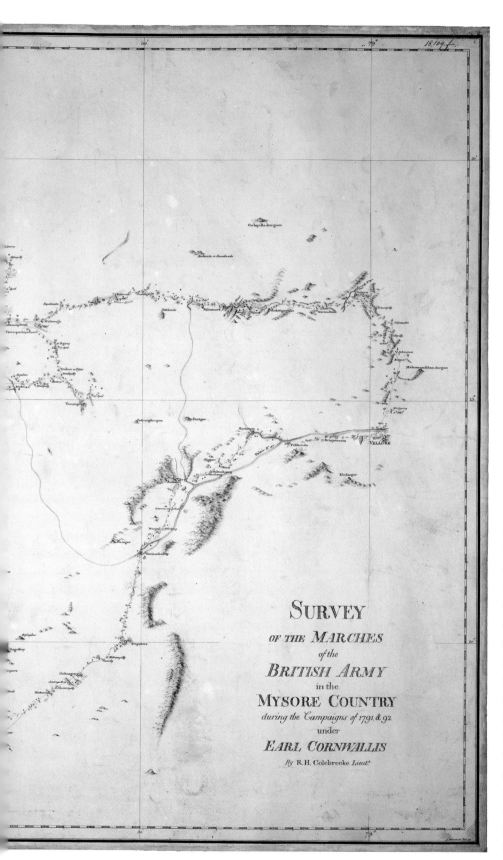

Lt. Robert Colebrooke, *Survey of the Marches of the British Army in the Mysore Country during the Campaign of 1791 & 1792 under Earl Cornwallis.* The map is a compilation of the many routes taken by Cornwallis's army in 1791-92, routes which enforced Bangalore's strategic position on the Mysore Tableland. 'In marching', Colebrooke writes of his surveys during the war, 'the direction and turnings of the road were observed with a pocket compass, and whenever a village, tank, or any conspicuous object occurred, or road altered its direction, the distance given by the wheel was carefully noted down. The same was done whenever the theodolite was used. Separate Protractions of each day's march, upon a scale of one mile to an inch, in which, besides what was allowed for crooked roads, a reduction of 1/30 was made for the inequalities of the ground and the unsteadiness of the man who drove the wheel, enabled me to ascertain nearly the direction or horizontal distances, which, being then corrected, were applied as Bases in the protraction of the map'.

British Library, Add 18109-f [By permission of the British Library]

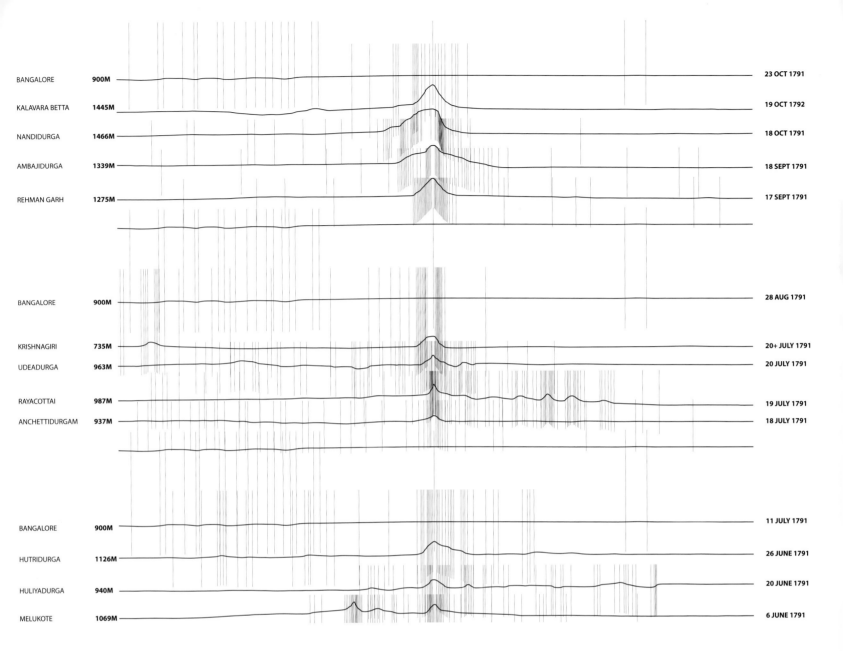

BANGALORE	900M		23 OCT 1791
KALAVARA BETTA	1445M		19 OCT 1792
NANDIDURGA	1466M		18 OCT 1791
AMBAJIDURGA	1339M		18 SEPT 1791
REHMAN GARH	1275M		17 SEPT 1791
BANGALORE	900M		28 AUG 1791
KRISHNAGIRI	735M		20+ JULY 1791
UDEADURGA	963M		20 JULY 1791
RAYACOTTAI	987M		19 JULY 1791
ANCHETTIDURGAM	937M		18 JULY 1791
BANGALORE	900M		11 JULY 1791
HUTRIDURGA	1126M		26 JUNE 1791
HULIYADURGA	940M		20 JUNE 1791
MELUKOTE	1069M		6 JUNE 1791

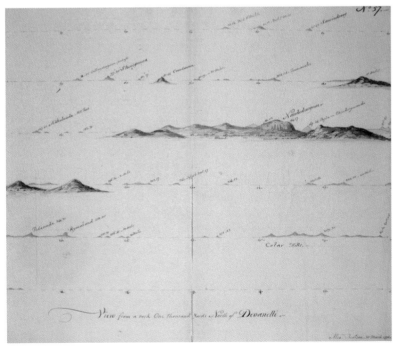

A calendar of Cornwallis's expeditions from Bangalore from March 1791 when they entered the Bound Hedge to February 1792 when they stormed Seringapatam. These expeditions primarily involved the capturing of fortified hills called droogs. Each of these 'immense masses of naked stone' loomed 200 to 500 metres above the tableland. Following each expedition, Cornwallis's men returned to their camp in Bangalore, a place they called 'home'.

LEFT

Major Alexander Beatson's record of horizons from Devanelli (Devanahalli, twenty-five miles north of Bangalore).

Geographical observations on the Peninsula of India, vol. 1. British Library, Mss. Eur. D48 9 [By permission of the British Library]

DECCAN TRAVERSES

THE WAR
CAMP GROUND
PETTAH
ESPLANADE
LAST FRONTIER

29

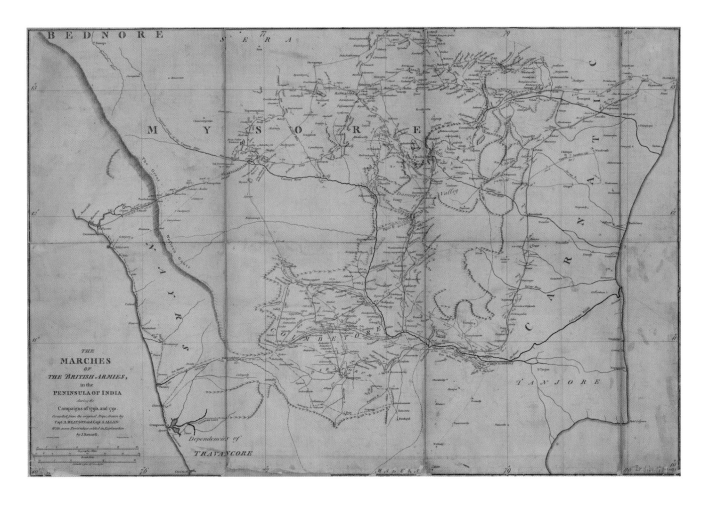

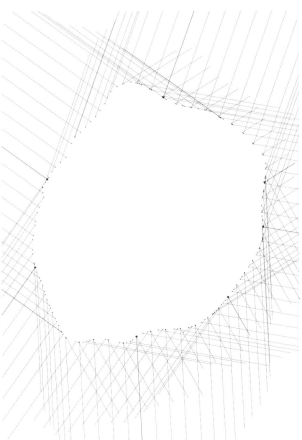

James Rennell, *The Marches of the British Armies in the Peninsula of India, during the Campaigns of 1790 and 1791.* **The Mysore Tableland between the Eastern and Western Ghats unfolded in its detail as a 'theatre of war' through the routes taken by Cornwallis's army.**

[New York Public Library]

LEFT

The Bound Hedge of Bangalore, enclosing a portion of the tableland, posed a barrier to the front of an invading army. As enclosure and barrier the Hedge did not last through the 1800s. It has, however, left its traces — the toll stations on the major highways, the same roads by which Cornwallis's army entered and exited each time they undertook an expedition from their base in Bangalore.

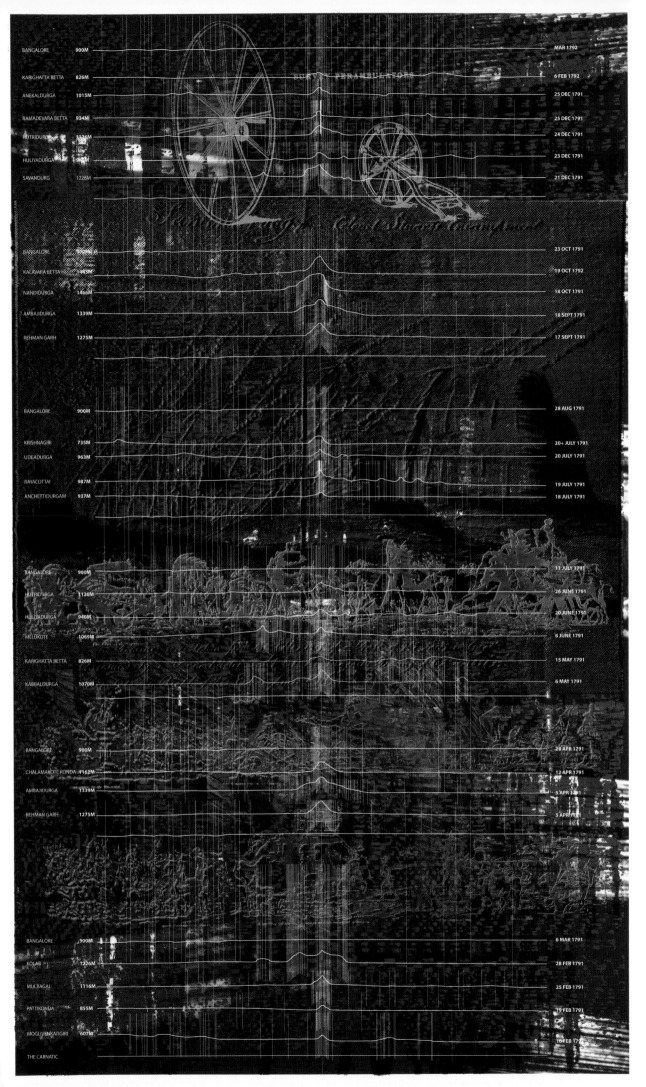

Camp Ground 1

Screen Print on paper, 22"x30" + Digital Plot

Camp Ground 2

Screen Print on paper, 22"x30" + Digital Plot

DECCAN TRAVERSES

THE WAR
CAMP GROUND
PETTAH
ESPLANADE
LAST FRONTIER

33

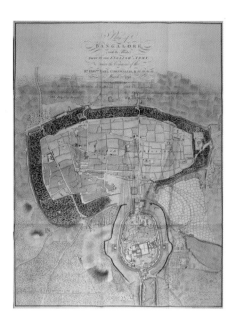

PETTAH

Robert Home, 'Plan of Bangalore (with the attacks) taken by the English Army under the command of the Rt. Honble Earl Cornwallis, K. G. etc. etc. March 22ⁿᵈ 1791'. The route surveyor's drawing was as much a recording of events as it was a geographic display; as much a document of the past as a lesson for future warfare.

Select Views in Mysore, The Country of Tipoo Sultan from Drawings taken on the spot with Historical Descriptions (London: Bowyer, 1794).

The day before Cornwallis's army stormed the Bangalore pettah at the heart of the Bound Hedge on 7 March 1791, route surveyors reconnoitred it, searching for ways to penetrate its 'three-mile circumference' which was fortified with a lofty mud wall, a thick hedge of bamboo, thorny bushes and prickly shrubs nearly a hundred yards wide, and a dry ditch. They found four entrances with strong gates, bastions and guns. They were aware that 'Many years ago these defences, on repeated occasions, baffled the whole Maratta force'.[33]

The surveyors chose to attack the north entrance of this secure entity. It comprised two gates separated by a passage 'narrowed so much by a thick jungle on either hand, that the troops, unable to extend their front, had scarcely room to advance'. The half-hour sequence of the fall of the inner gate is Company legend — the failed attempt by lesser guns to blow it down, the fall of Col. Moorhouse, the hole made by the iron eighteen-pounder that had to be ordered in, the crawling through that hole of Lt. Ayre to the sound the general's command of 'support the little gentleman', and the scaling of the ramparts. Once within, route surveyors recorded the 'many streets laid out with much regularity, and of great width; few towns in Hindostan can boast of better houses, or of richer inhabitants, if credit can be given to appearances'.[34]

Surveyors' records within the pettah were not simple linear progressions anymore but complex ones involving a fanning from, and a returning to, key points and main roads. They were following the enemy who 'fled from the gate, but continued firing from the houses for some time. Parties were sent in different directions to dislodge them; and before nine we were in complete possession of the place'.[35] The hills, reservoirs, and trees of the 'vast flat mountain' that they had crossed on the march from the Moogly Pass were replaced by walls of houses in which were found 'bales of cloth, with immense quantities of cotton and grain; . . . [I]ndeed the booty dug up by individuals, out of concealments and deserted houses, strongly indicated ease, comfort, and happiness in former times'.[36]

The surveyor's drawing of the pettah records an event as much as a spatial entity, registering elements of resistance, lines of access, even lines of fire. It was a historical event of considerable significance

according to Robert Colebrooke. 'If the circumstances attending the siege', he writes, 'be considered, that the enemy were in full possession of the open country, so as to preclude the possibility of our getting supplies, that during our operations in the Pettah, we had but a small force in the camp to withstand the attack of their whole army, and that our stock of provisions and ammunitions was nearly exhausted, the capture of Bangalore may be deemed one of the greatest achievements of the British arms in India. To Tippoo it was a blow which threw him into such a state of distraction at the time that he is said to have wept'.[37] The event made it a household name in England and led to an East India Company ship being named after Bangalore. But it also gave Bangalore a new prominence in maps, singling it out from the field of settlements shown in earlier maps of the interior.

However, it was as a geographic place more than a historic event that the surveyor's map would be immortalised – the walled town at the centre of the Bound Hedge. When historians would later seek the origin of this town, they would find it in the life of Kempegowda I, a chieftain whom they say laid out the town in 1537 as a 1.5 square kilometre entity divided by two intersecting roads into quarters, the whole bound by a wall and opened through gates. These quarters, they say, were further compartmentalised or perhaps grew into economically homogeneous neighbourhoods or (smaller) towns – taragupet (grain market), halipet (cotton market), etc. The image used in this depiction of Kempegowda's creation is the route surveyor's map of 1791. It assumes that Kempegowda designed the walled entity that surveyors encountered two and a half centuries later. It also assumes that Kempegowda conceived Bangalore in spatial terms as city planners do cities today.

It would not surprise route surveyors, who were all too conscious of the event that defined the space of their maps, that the origin of the pettah is recorded in folklore, not as a spatial entity but as an auspicious event. The story goes that at a favourable moment at a place

DECCAN TRAVERSES

THE WAR
CAMP GROUND
PETTAH
ESPLANADE
LAST FRONTIER

35

VIEW of the PETTAH GATEWAY, where COLONEL MOORHOUSE fell.

Published as the Act directs by R. Bowyer, Historic Gallery, Pall Mall, London, & W. Sharp, Madrass, Feb.y 1794.

LEFT

Robert Hyde Colebrooke records Cornwallis's march between Kristnaporum (Krishnarajapuram) through the Bound Hedge of Bangalore to the encampment northeast of the pettah. It records the exchange of fire outside the Hedge between the two armies and an initial sketch of the pettah and fort. [National Archives of India, New Delhi].

Robert Home, 'View of the Pettah Gateway, where Colonel Moorhouse fell'. 'The point of attack was a gateway of considerable strength on the north face', notes Roderick Mackenzie, **'The first barrier was soon carried. . . but whilst the field pieces played on the inner gate, without effect, as it was barricaded with stones, a brick fire from a mud bastion, from turrets, and from roofs of houses, made considerable slaughter amongst the Europeans. It was here that the gallant Moorhouse fell'.**

Select Views in Mysore, The Country of Tipoo Sultan from Drawings taken on the spot with Historical Descriptions (London: Bowyer, 1794).

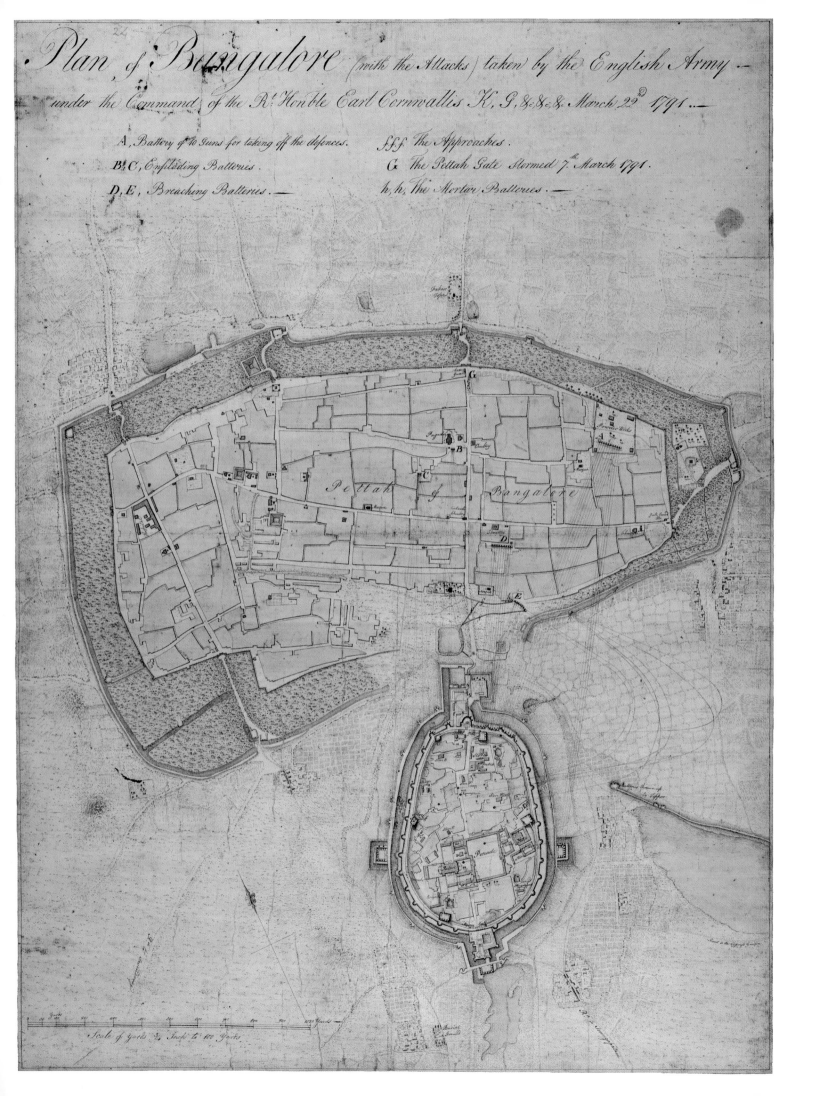

Plan of Bangalore (with the Attacks) taken by the English Army —

under the Command of the Rt. Honble Earl Cornwallis K. G. &c.&c.&c. March 22nd 1791 —

A, Battery of 10 Guns for taking off the defences.

B, C, Enfilading Batteries.

D, E, Breaching Batteries. —

f, f, f, The Approaches.

G, The Pettah Gate Stormed 7th March 1791.

h, h, The Mortar Batteries. —

Pettah of Bangalore

Scale of Yards ½ Inch to 100 Yards

DECCAN TRAVERSES

THE WAR
CAMP GROUND
PETTAH
ESPLANADE
LAST FRONTIER

37

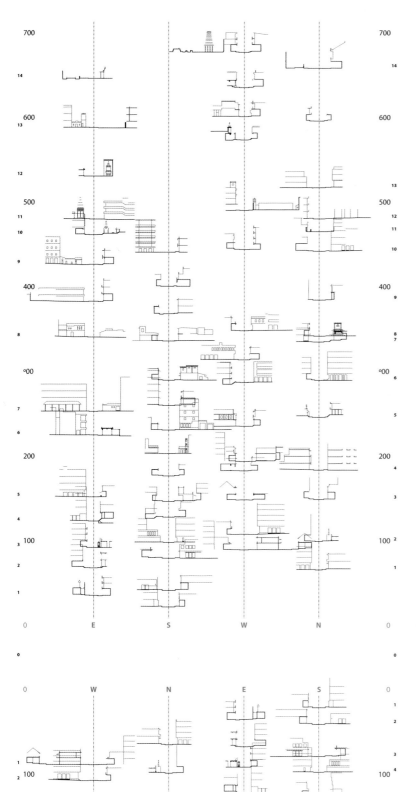

FAR LEFT

Plan of Bangalore (with the attacks)
taken by the English Army under the com-
mand of the Rt. Honble Earl Cornwallis,
K, G. etc. etc. March 22nd 1791. Cornwallis's army arrived at a point on a map
on 5 March 1791 but left in the summer
of 1792 from a spatial entity drawn by
surveyors during that period — a mud-
walled town surrounded by a ditch and
an 'egg-shaped' stone fort to its south.
The plan records the battle for the fort
on 21 March, two weeks after the pettah
was captured. 'Few towns in Hindostan',
observed a soldier, 'can boast of better
houses, or of richer inhabitants, if credit
can be given to appearances'. Indeed, he
continues, 'the booty dug up by individuals, out of concealments and deserted
houses, strongly indicated ease, comfort,
and happiness in former times'.

British Library, Add 18109 [By permission of the
British Library]

LEFT

Route surveyors found
four entrances to the
pettah, each leading to a
centre that they described
as an intersection of
main roads or a chowk.
Folklore, however, would
turn this view around,
portraying this centre not
as an intersection but a
starting point, the site
of an auspicious event
orchestrated by Kem-
pegowda I to begin the
settlement of Bangalore.
At this point he is believed
to have let four bullocks
harnessed to ploughs fur-
row four ways, east, west,
north, and south. This
place of beginning is even
today a divergent moment
rather than a convergent
form, calling for move-
ment outward along four
streets that gather an
open landscape rather
than consolidate a bound
entity.

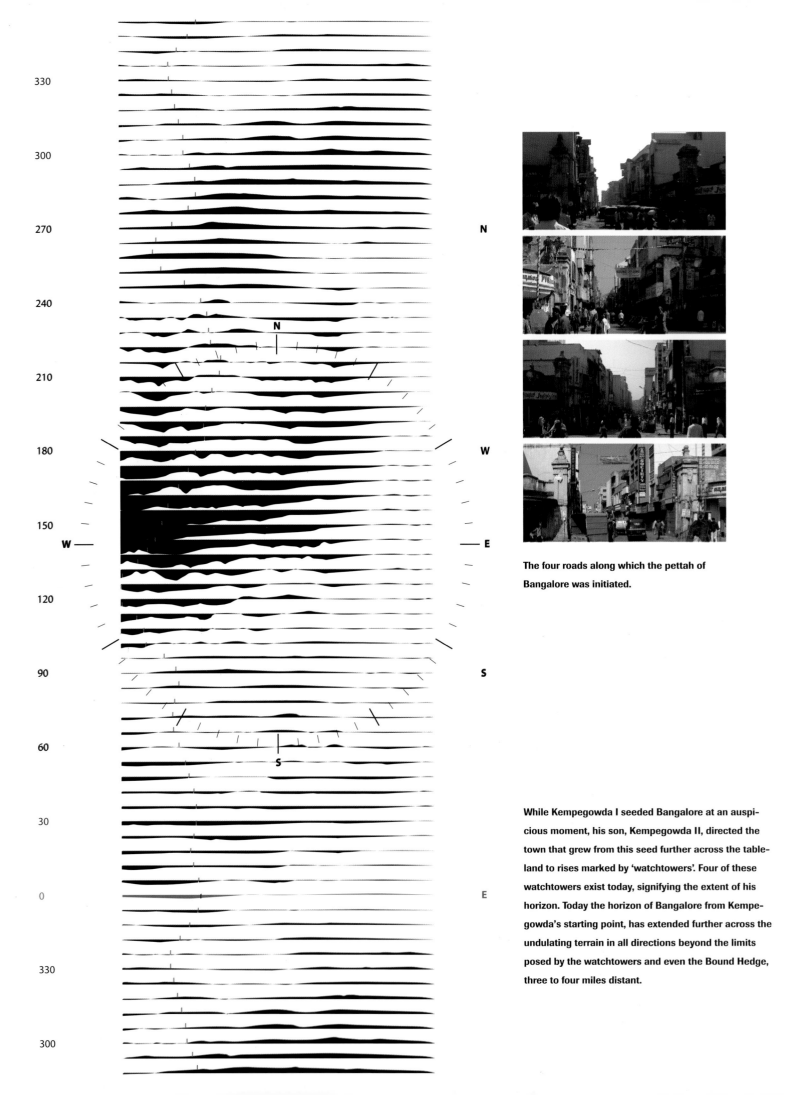

The four roads along which the pettah of Bangalore was initiated.

While Kempegowda I seeded Bangalore at an auspicious moment, his son, Kempegowda II, directed the town that grew from this seed further across the tableland to rises marked by 'watchtowers'. Four of these watchtowers exist today, signifying the extent of his horizon. Today the horizon of Bangalore from Kempegowda's starting point, has extended further across the undulating terrain in all directions beyond the limits posed by the watchtowers and even the Bound Hedge, three to four miles distant.

DECCAN TRAVERSES

THE WAR
CAMP GROUND
PETTAH
ESPLANADE
LAST FRONTIER

39

where in a dream he saw a hare chase a dog, Kempegowda I pointed 'four milk white bullocks . . . harnessed to four decorated ploughs' in four directions and let them furrow the streets.[38] Mud walls with gates are merely moments in the playing out of this emergent event, probably moments celebrated in their own right and in their own time.

The pettah as an emergent event (rather than spatial entity) is apparently one of many initiations attributed to Kempegowda I. He is credited with temples, agricultural tanks, and agraharas (schools for priests) in the vicinity of the pettah and within the Bound Hedge. These starting points spawned settlements of their own, settlements that are easily taken for spatial entities in maps. If one allows for the assumption that Kempegowda I was not on virgin terrain given the many inscriptions found in the vicinity of the pettah, which date back many centuries before him, then one may assume that those who preceded and followed him did likewise, viz. initiated events and as a consequence, settlements. Those that followed him include his descendents, the governors of the Sultans of Bijapur and the Mughals, the Wodeyars, the Tigers of Mysore (Hyder Ali and Tipu Sultan).

Today Bangalore can be seen as the continued unfolding of the trajectory of Kempegowda's starting point intersecting the trajectories of numerous other initiations, each evolving by its own rhythms.

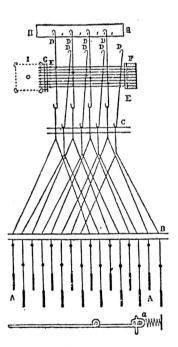

Some streets of the pettah today work to the rhythms of the Jacquard loom and its successors. These looms, programmed by a slot card are forerunners of the computer. The sounds of their shuttles emerge from behind veils of secrecy that mark the competition of the silk industry.

Pettah 1

Screen Print on paper, 22"x30" + Digital Plot

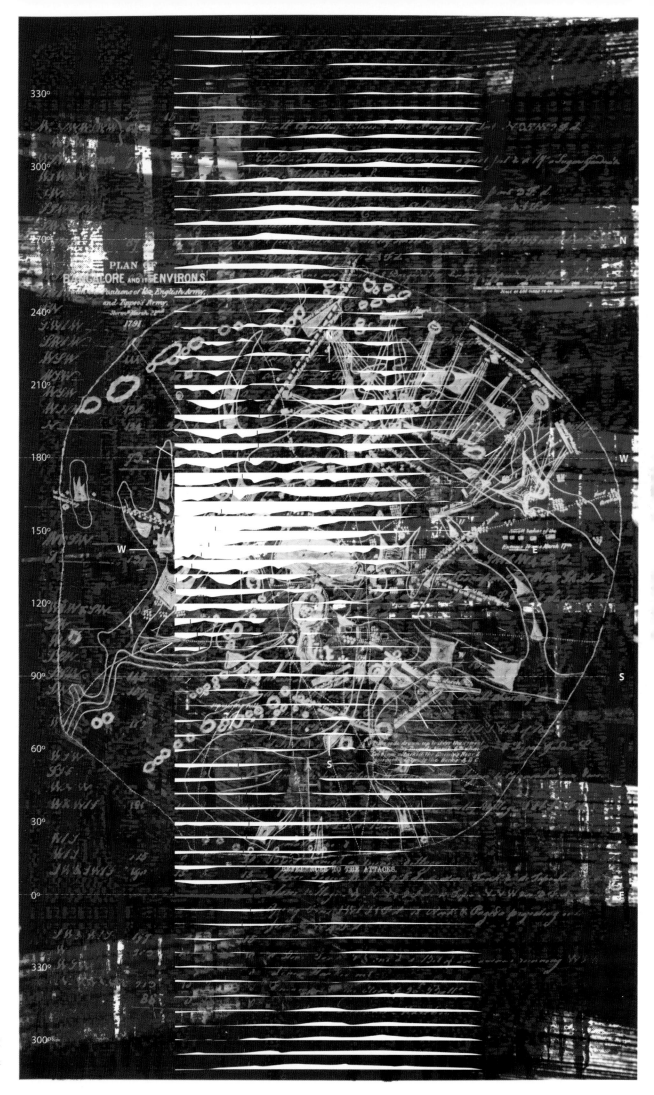

Pettah 2

Screen Print on paper, 22"x30" + Digital Plot

DECCAN TRAVERSES

THE WAR
CAMP GROUND
PETTAH
ESPLANADE
LAST FRONTIER

43

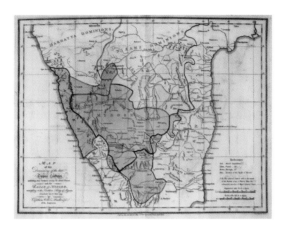

ESPLANADE

Eight years after Bangalore was returned by the treaty of 1792 to Tipu Sultan, the English returned to the Mysore Tableland to fight the Fourth Mysore War. This war was more decisive, ending in the defeat and death of Tipu Sultan. Unlike the previous war in which it took Cornwallis a year to subdue the Mysore country, this one was brief, perhaps because the land was known. 'This last and conclusive war against Tipu gave little scope for survey operations; for the purposes of the rapid advance on Seringapatam, the surveys already collected were sufficient'.[39] Bangalore is not mentioned in this war, General Harris's army approaching Seringapatam through the passes in the southeast. Bangalore, however, was to return to the centre as a terrain that would relegate Seringapatam to a fabled place of Tipu's last stand in paintings and plays in Europe.

Following this decisive war, much of the Mysore Tableland was placed in the hands of the Wodeyars from whom Hyder Ali was believed to have usurped power, though some places like Seringapatam were tenured for garrisoning Company troops. Bangalore was discounted, as the buildings there were inadequate to house the troops and new barracks were deemed too expensive. Instead it was made a tented station for troops 'if it be only to preserve tranquillity in the adjacent districts some of which connect with the Nizam's Frontier while others are infested by robbers'.[40] In 1807, however, the new governor of Madras, William Bentinck, would reconsider making a more permanent settlement in Bangalore. It followed concern for the quality of life (of the Europeans in particular) at places on the tableland where troops were cantoned, some of which were proving more unhealthy and expensive to maintain than others. But the issue was becoming also one of centralising troops on the peninsula, perhaps because the task of enforcing the transition and keeping the peace on the tableland had been accomplished. Seringapatam was a primary contender, its case made earlier on by Colonel Arthur Wellesley, famous in the defeat of Tipu Sultan but more famous in the defeat fifteen years later of the man who had desired to come to the Sultan's aid, Napoleon Bonaparte. His support for the island capital centred on 'the general opinion of its power, the means which experience has proved it possesses of equipping an army, its superior convenience as a depot

for the Malabar coast'. The other contenders were 'Bangalore, Chittledroog [Chitradroog], Sera, Nuggur [Bednore], Colar'. They were all 'nearly, if not equally populous with Seringapatam: some of them are places of great trade and riches'.[41]

When it came to health, however, one place was far ahead of the field, Bangalore. Situated toward the crest of the Mysore Tableland, two hundred meters above Seringapatam, its climate was deemed 'additionally salubrious'.[42] In 1807 Bentinck ordered the centralisation of European regiments in a new cantonment here.

Lt. John Blakiston, engineer and route surveyor with the Madras army writes of being 'ordered up to Bangalore to fix on a site, and prepare plans, for a new cantonment about to be established there on a large scale'.[43] He chose a site a few kilometres east of the pettah. It was the place where Cornwallis's army had first camped when they came within the Bound Hedge on 5 March 1791. This was no ordinary camp ground; it was the edge of a terrain, moments before the gently undulating surface that the army had marched across from the ghats transitioned into a more rugged one. The transition divided the camps of the warring sides; Tipu opted for the rugged terrain southwest of the fort while Cornwallis settled on the gently undulating terrain to the northeast.

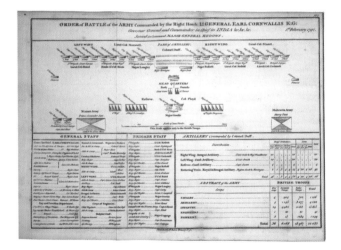

Major Dirom, 'Order of Battle of the Army Commanded by the Right Honb. Lt. General Earl Cornwallis K:G: Governor-General and Commander-in-Chief in India &c. 1st February 1792'. The army generally camped in the order of battle.

A Narrative of the Campaign in India which terminated the war with Tipoo Sultan in 1792 (London: W. Bulmer and Co., 1793). [Annenberg Rare Book and Manuscript Library, University of Pennsylvania]

DECCAN TRAVERSES

THE WAR
CAMP GROUND
PETTAH
ESPLANADE
LAST FRONTIER

45

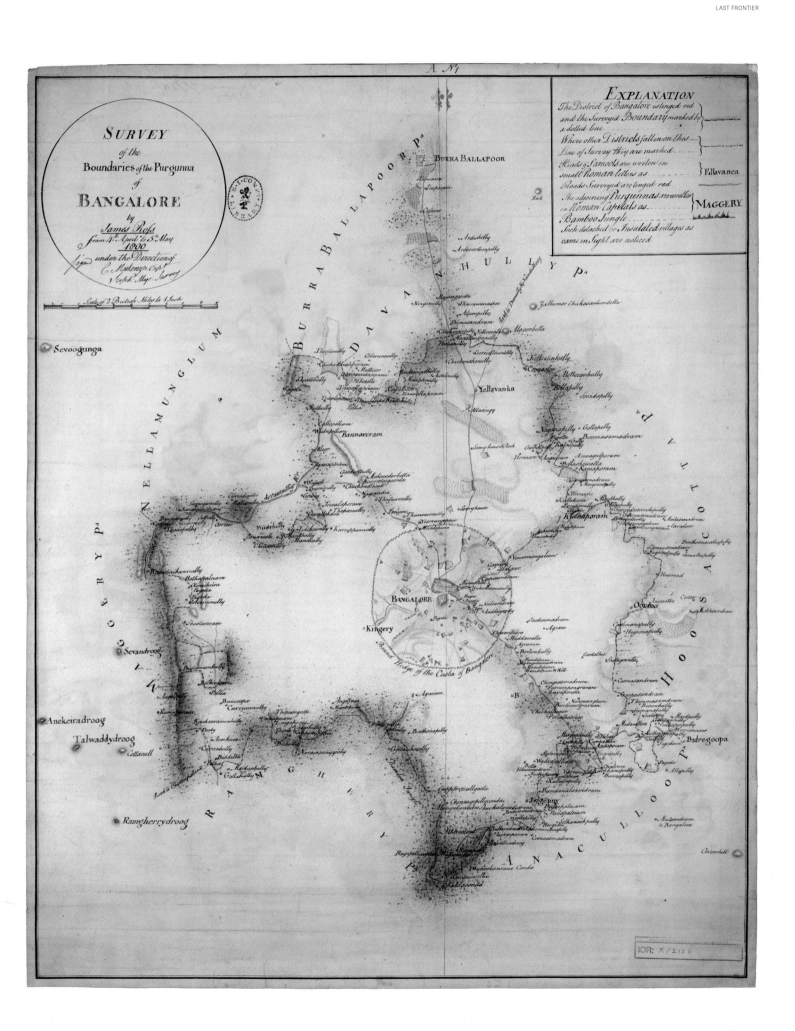

SURVEY
of the
Boundaries of the Purgunna
of
BANGALORE
by
James Ross
from 1.st April to 5.th May
1800
under the Direction of
C. Mackenzie Cap.t
Supt. Mys.r Survey

Scale of 2 British Miles to 1 Inch

EXPLANATION
The District of Bangalore is tinged red
and the Surveyed Boundary marked by
a dotted line
Where other Districts fall in on this
Line of Survey they are marked
Heads of Samools are written in
small Roman letters as ⎤ Yellavanca
Roads Surveyed are tinged red
The adjoining Purgunnas are written
in Roman Capitals as ⎤ MAGGERY
Bamboo Jungle
Such detached or Insulated villages as
came in Sight are noticed

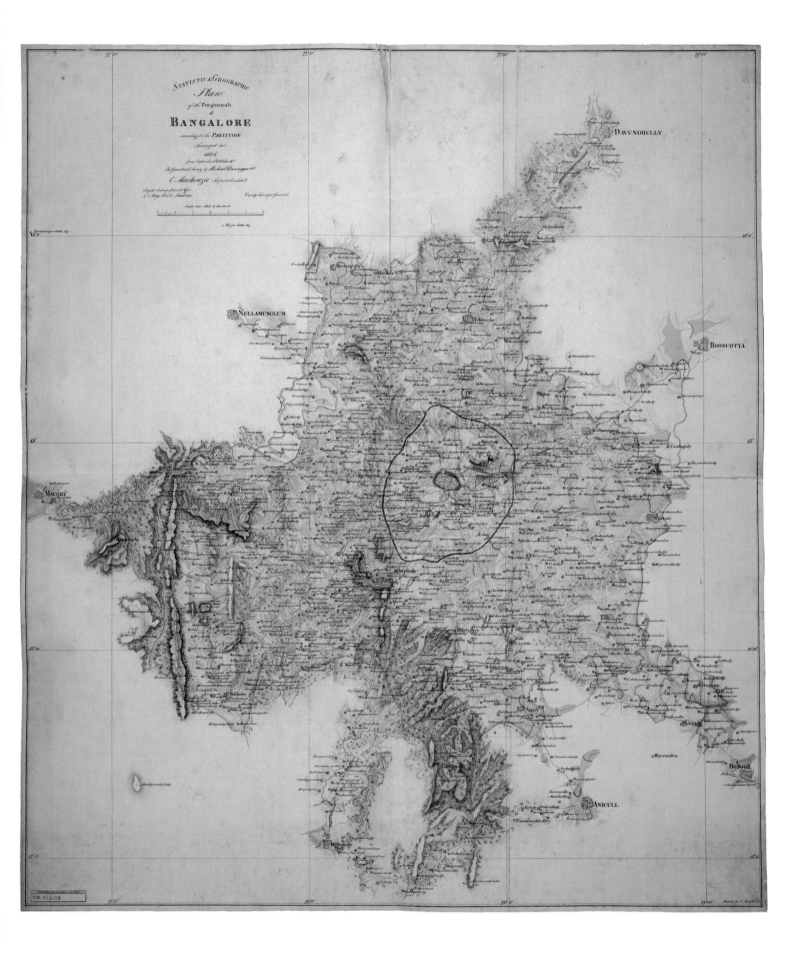

STATISTIC & GEOGRAPHIC
Plan
of the Purgunnah
of
BANGALORE
according to the PARTITION
Surveyed in
1806
from September to October &c.
In Geodetical Survey by Michael Donnigan &c.
C. Mackenzie Superintendant.

Deputy Surveyor Generals Office
1st May 1832. Madras   Deputy Surveyor General

Scale One Mile to the Inch

DECCAN TRAVERSES

THE WAR
CAMP GROUND
PETTAH
ESPLANADE
LAST FRONTIER

47

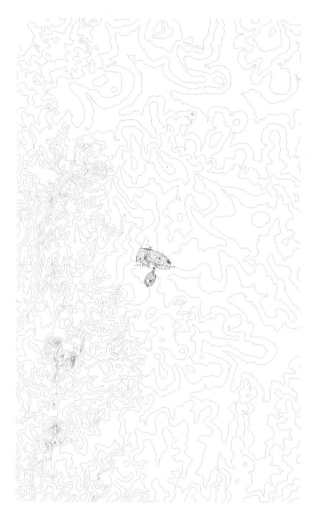

Lt. John Blakiston chose the site of Cornwallis's camp on 5 March 1791 for the Bangalore Cantonment. Coming from the east as Cornwallis did, the camp was pitched a moment before the gently undulating terrain transitioned into a more rugged one. The transition divided the camps of the two sides at war in 1791 as it would divide the cantonment from the 'native town' for a century and a half.

LEFT

Statistic & Geographic Plan of the Purgunnah of Bangalore according to the Partition Surveyed in 1806 from September 8th to October 16th. **In 1807 the Cusba of Bangalore became the 'obvious' place for a cantonment that would centralise the troops of the Company and British Armies on the southern peninsula. 'Bangalore possesses many advantages', wrote a Major of Engineers in a report to the Madras government, 'which render it exceedingly well calculated for a central military depot and fortress of the first class. It is situated in a healthy and fertile country with a temperate climate particularly favourable to the European constitution and where all the necessaries of life are cheap and abundant. It has good and safe communications with the Malabar Coast, the Ceded Districts, the Nizam's Dominion, the Southern Maharatta Country, and Trichinopoly and our Southern Provinces. . . . The communication with the Presidency is also extremely good and convenient and the distance moderate'. The map, evidently made to identify the land for the Bangalore Cantonment in 1806, was updated in 1832 and shows the laying out of the cantonment in its early stages.**

British Library, IOR X/2127 [By permission of the British Library]

Geologists describe the distinction between the two camp grounds as 'strikingly contrasting geomorphic zones'. Toward the west is a 'younger terrain' that is rugged, the soil cover is thin, and the drainage pattern is dendritic and fine-textured. Runoffs here quickly turn into streams and rivers. Toward the east is an 'ancient land surface' with slopes that rarely exceed ten degrees, a soil cover that is extensive, and a drainage pattern that is coarse-textured, which is to say the soil is more permeable.[44] Blakiston chose the latter side, the more level traces of Cornwallis's camp.

Blakiston had little experience with cantonments, but a lot with camps, having been on numerous marches across the peninsula since arriving in India in 1802. The cantonment, to Blakiston, was a longer lasting camp, more an event than a settlement, more a moment than a town. Its organising element was the esplanade, a perfection of the Mysore Tableland, a purposefully levelled ground across which the army could march and perform if only in simulations. Oriented east-west, the esplanade was, as William Arthur, a missionary, describes it, 'more than a mile long, and of

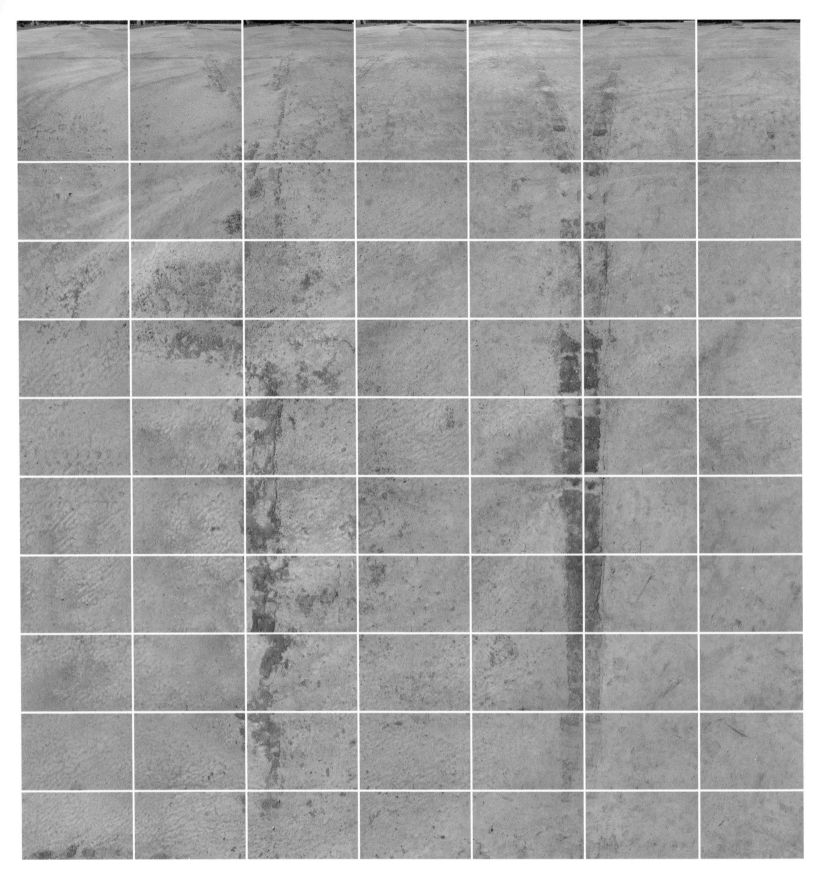

The Parade Ground in Bangalore today is a segment of Blakiston's mile-long esplanade. It was a tank that was filled by Blakiston to the level of the bund that ran along its southern edge (the raised walk on the north side of Mahatma Gandhi Road today). Since then this levelled ground has borne many marks – the 'brilliant manoeuvring of the hussars,' 'mock mud-forts,' 'bazaars,' 'public amusements,' games, sports, barracks, besides parades.

DECCAN TRAVERSES

THE WAR
CAMP GROUND
PETTAH
ESPLANADE
LAST FRONTIER

49

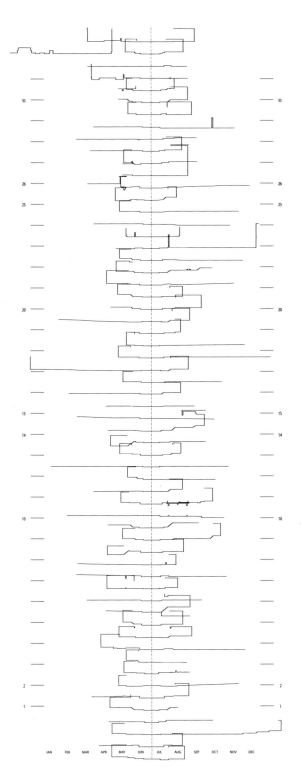

Blakiston's esplanade, the centre of the Cantonment, was also the camp's exemplar temporal ground, modulated by events, seasons and rhythms — marches, exercises, bazaars, games, and 'public amuse-ments'. Today with the fencing off of the esplanade into a parade ground, a stadium, a park, a club, etc., this temporal ground has shifted to the street, working to the rhythms of festivals and events. Here traffic weaves through celebrations, entertainment, marches, drying agarbathis (incense sticks), vendors, bazaars.

considerable breadth. Each of its sides is skirted by an avenue of trees, with a fine broad road. Along the right-hand road extends a series of barracks. . . . The opposite road is lined with compounds, as the garden-plots in which houses stand are invariably called'. Unlike in Bombay or Calcutta where the esplanade was a cleared distance between fort and native settlement, here it was the centre of the cantonment. In the early years of the cantonment it was occurrences rather than expanse that impressed Blakiston's esplanade upon the visitor — the 'brilliant manoeuvring', sepoys turned into 'huge automatons and performing rapid evolutions', 'brown lads' being made not into awkward recruits but 'veterans of tactics, if not in campaign', the sounds of 'angry artillery, practicing its thunders on mock mud forts'.[45] Bangalore, Major Bevan writes, is 'famous for a constant routine of military duties, drill, etc.'[46]

But Blakiston's creation fast settled into a town as the general's call to march became only an impersonation, the theatre of war a distant backdrop, and the esplanade a parade ground. Colonel James Welsh, who had stopped within the Bound Hedge in 1803 on his way to fight the Marathas, came through again six years later and was taken aback by what he saw. 'On the 24th June we reached the cantonment of Bangalore, distant twenty-six miles, and here, as if by magic, had arisen a large military town, about three miles from the fort'.[47] In less than a year Blakiston had 'completed barracks for two regiments of Europeans, five regiments of natives, and a proportion of artillery, besides hospitals and other requisites'. His creation acquired the name of Bangalore from the pettah that already carried it. By 1809 the cantonment had 'grown into the first military station on the Madras establishment; while its climate, situation, and productions, contributed, with its extensive society, to render it by far the pleasantest and most agreeable residence on the peninsula'. Nearly two decades later, Blakiston notes that 'Since I left the country, it has increased both in size and beauty, and may now be considered one of the largest and finest cantonments in India. The reader will excuse me for indulging in a little garrulity on the subject of this my architectural offspring. I consider myself, in fact, a little Romulus'.[48] Even its designer had begun to believe its permanence.

Esplanade 1

Screen Print on paper, 22"x30" + Digital Plot

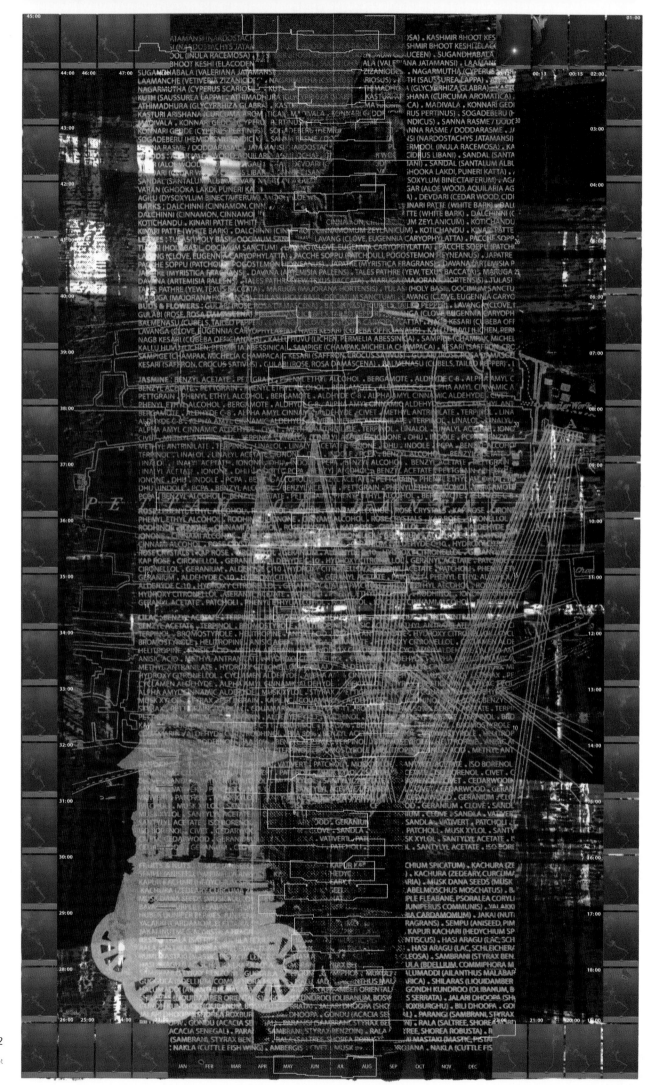

Esplanade 2

Screen Print on paper, 22"x30" + Digital Plot

Geological Survey of India

GEOLOGICAL MAP SHOWING THE DISTRIBUTION OF COMMERCIAL GRANITES

IN PARTS OF RAMANAGARAM AND MAGADI TALUKS, KARNATAKA

INDEX

Quarry

Grey porphyritic granite

Pink porphyritic granite BR = Bevan Rose

IR = Imperial Red ; TP = Tumkur Pink

Grey granite (MG = Magadi grey)

Hornblende granite

Pink granite (FR = Flash red;

RP = Rosy pearl ; CR = Chilly red)

Pink migmatite (Category I) JP = Juphana

Pink migmatite (Category II) SM = Sannoks

Pink migmatite (Category III) ET = English

Pink migmatite

Leuco granite (OW = Ocean white)

Peninsular Gneissic Complex

PREPARATION SURFACE FINISHES & TOOLS

DECCAN TRAVERSES

THE WAR
CAMP GROUND
PETTAH
ESPLANADE
LAST FRONTIER

53

LAST FRONTIER

The line of hills to the west of Bangalore is as imposing today as it was to route surveyors in the 1790s. Initially a barrier, it eventually served as a threshold in the siege of Seringapatam that ended the war in 1792.

The younger terrain to the west of Bangalore gets younger. It becomes what Major Dirom calls a 'difficult country'. After the battle for Bangalore, this difficult country would emerge as a barrier between the Mysoreans and the British. 'Between the River Maddoor and Bangalore', writes Dirom, 'there is a tract of country full of hills, and very woody, extending all the way from Shevagunga to the north bank of the Caveri, and forms a strong barrier between Bangalore and Seringapatam. Through this difficult country there are three roads. . . . On each of these roads, and throughout the whole extent of this tract of country, many of the hills are fortified, and were formerly the castles and possessions of rajahs and polygars, the petty princes and chiefs of the Gentoo people; but they are now all subject to Tippoo and garrisoned by his troops'.[49] By the end of 1791 when all but Seringapatam was taken by Cornwallis, this difficult country or as Lt. Roderick Mackenzie referred to it, 'the wilds which separate Seringapatam from Bangalore', would become the 'last frontier' of the Third Mysore War.[50]

The hills in this tract are arranged in what Bruce Foote, whom some consider the father of South Indian geology, called a line and not a chain. 'The expression line of hills', says Foote, 'is used in preference to the term chain as there is little continuity of high ground, the hills being mostly quite detached and separated in some parts by considerable spaces'.[51] The line, in other words, is a potential concentration of the autonomous and fearsome droogs that characterised the Mysore Tableland. Geologists give this line of conflict a rich material quality. They see it as relatively young igneous rock sandwiched between two older gneiss terrains. Averaging twenty kilometres across, this rock, they say, extends further north from the battlefields of the Third Mysore War to Vijayanagar on the Tungabhadra. Two billion years ago this was a fiery line variously conceived today by geologists as a collision, accretion, shear, rift, and horst, depending on how they see the line operating and the nature of the event/s that framed this operation.

The material of this line of hills is a pink porphyritic granite also known as Closepet Granite after the town of Closepet, now Ramnagaram. Like other granites, the magma from which it begins has cooled slowly enough for its minerals to form crystals that can be seen with the naked eye. It suggests a plutonic (netherworld) rather than a volcanic beginning, the latter leading to more fine-grained and even non-crystalline rock

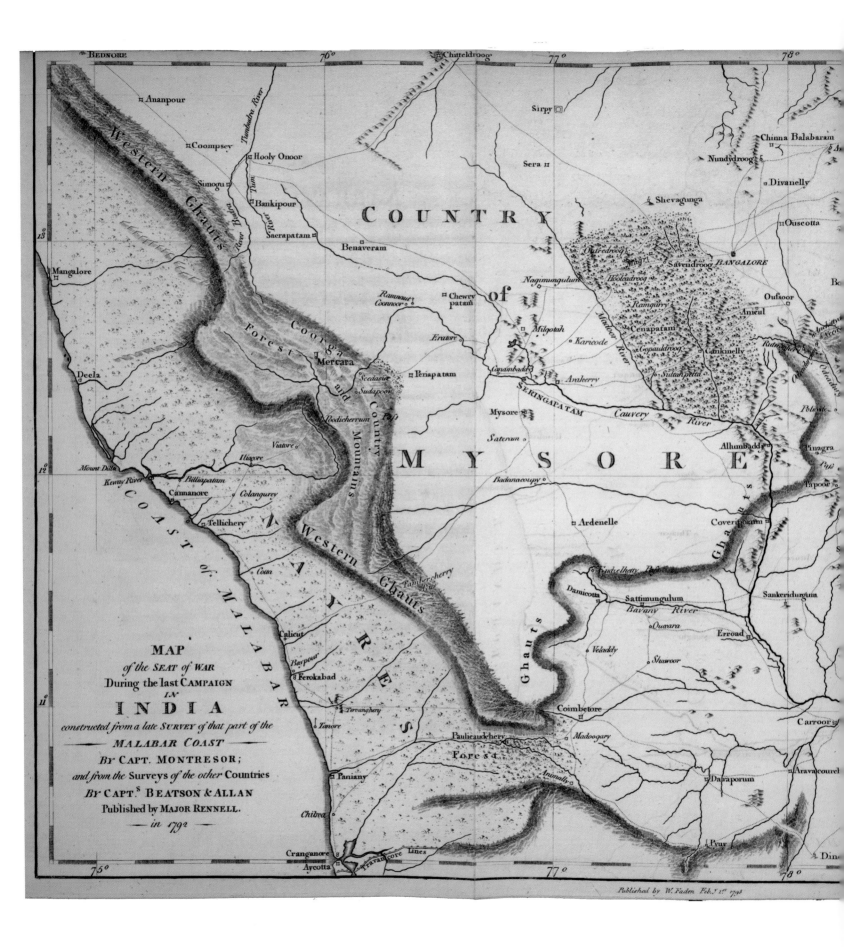

MAP
of the SEAT of WAR
During the last CAMPAIGN
IN
INDIA
constructed from a late SURVEY of that part of the
◄— MALABAR COAST —►
BY CAPT. MONTRESOR;
and from the Surveys of the other Countries
BY CAPT.S BEATSON & ALLAN
Published by MAJOR RENNELL.
—◄ in 1792 ►—

BEDNORE

Ananpour

Coompsey

Hooly Onoor

Simogu

Bankipour

Saerapatam

Mangalore

Deela

Mount Dilla

Kenny River

Billiapatam

Cannanore

Colangurey

Tellichery

Coin

Calicut

Baypour

Ferokabad

Tervanghery

Tanore

Chitwa

Cranganore

Aycotta

Paniany

Western Ghauts

Coorga Forest

Mercara

Seedasia

Sudapoor

Noodicherrum

Viatore

Iliagore

A I R E S

Western Ghauts

Country and Mountains

Tamlercherry Pass

Chitteldroog

COUNTRY

of

MYSORE

Benaveram

Ramnout Coonnoor

Chewry patam

Eratore

Periapatam

Canambadda

Mysore

Saterun

Badanacoupy

Ardenelle

SERINGAPATAM

Cauvery River

Anakerry

Sirpy

Sera

Shevagunga

Nagimungulum

Milgotah

Karicode

Nundydroog

Divanelly

Ouscotta

Outredroog

Hooladroog

Savendroog

BANGALORE

Ramgurry

Cenapatam

Gopauldroog

Cankinelly

Sultanpetta

Anicul

Oufsoor

Chinna Balabaram

Poliate

Pinagra Pass

Tapoor

Alhumbaddy

Coveriporum

Ghauts

Sankeridurgum

Sindzelhety Pass

Damicotta

Sattimungulum

Bavany River

Quavara

Erroad

Veladdy

Shawoor

Coimbetore

Paulicaudchery

Madoogary

Daraporum

Carroor

Aravancourel

Forest

Animally

Pyur

Coast of Malabar

Travancore Lines

Din

Published by W. Faden Feb.y 1.st 1793

DECCAN TRAVERSES

THE WAR
CAMP GROUND
PETTAH
ESPLANADE
LAST FRONTIER

55

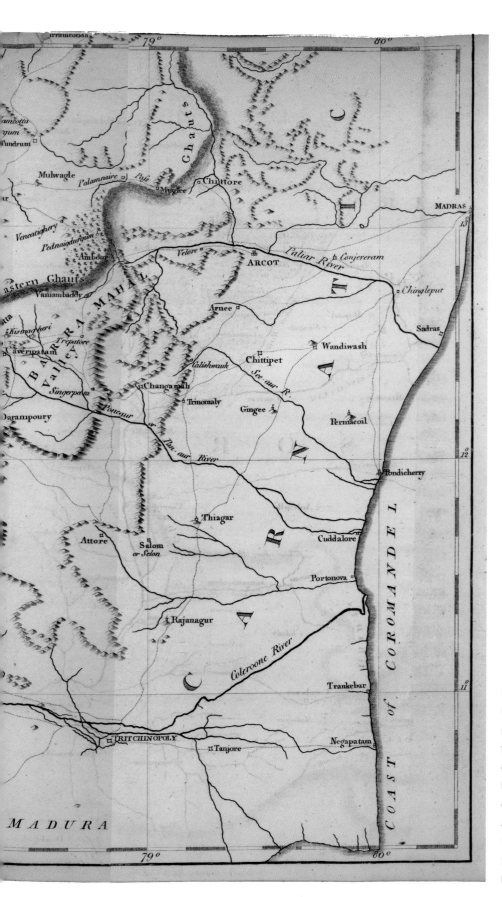

Major Dirom, 'Map of the Seat of War during the last Campaign in India constructed from a late Survey of that part of the Malabar Coast by Capt. Montressor; and from the Surveys of the other Countries by Capts. Beatson & Allan'. The map indicates the 'wild country' between Bangalore and Seringapatam that impeded the progress of Cornwallis's army.

A Narrative of the Campaign in India which terminated the war with Tipoo Sultan in 1792, (London: W. Bulmer and Co., 1793).

[Annenberg Rare Book and Manuscript Library, University of Pennsylvania]

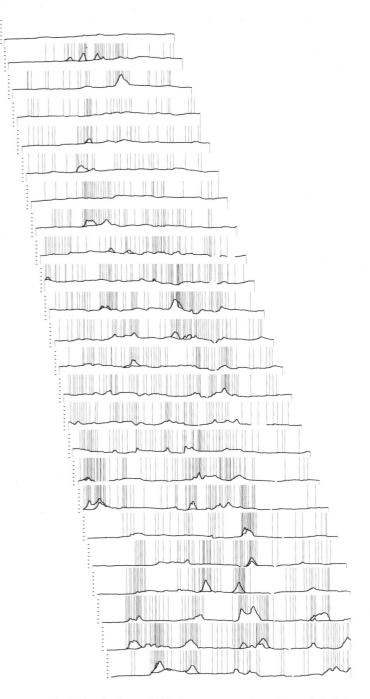

The distinct horizons of hills that weave together to form a belt that separated English in Bangalore from the 'Mysoreans' in Seringapatam in 1791 runs between the seats of two former empires — the Gangas on the Kaveri and the Vijayanagar rulers on the Tungabhadra. The belt provided the stones for the many monuments of both capitals — Talakad and Hampi — that today stand ruined but not abandoned.

On the surface, the belt that stalled Cornwallis and today nestles Chamrajsagar Reservoir and the Arkavati River, is topographically distinct from the 'featureless plains' on either side. Geologically, however, the transition beneath is less obvious. The magma of this belt that cooled into granite, geologists say, is not necessarily fresh from the earth's mantle but may be the result of partial melting of gneiss as two continental plates slipped against each other. The result is a transition from gneiss (existent metamorphic rock) on either side to granite (new igneous rock) at the heart of the belt where the melt was almost complete.

DECCAN TRAVERSES

THE WAR
CAMP GROUND
PETTAH
ESPLANADE
LAST FRONTIER

57

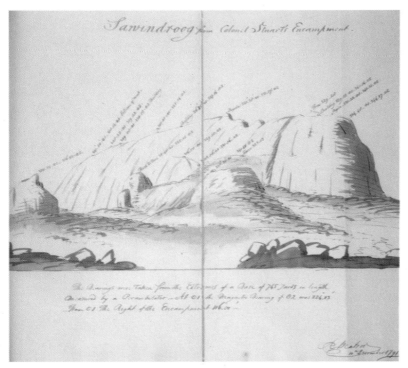

Major Alexander Beatson, 'Savendroog from Colonel Stuart's encampment'.

Geographical observations on the Peninsula of India, vol. 1. British Library, Mss. Eur. D48 36 [By permission of the British Library]

because exposure to the atmosphere cools it down quickly. The vastly different crystal sizes of this granite, however, suggests that the cooling of Closepet Granite was uneven, the result perhaps of the magma moving from hotter to cooler locations. This could merely signify a rise of the magma from the hotter earth's mantle to the cooler earth's crust or it could imply as geologists believe today, a partial melting of the gneiss as two plates of the earth's crust slipped against each other. There is, they say, a clear transition from gneiss to granite to gneiss.[52]

The gneiss on either side of the granite is amongst the oldest rocks on the planet. The Geological Survey of India declared it a national monument in 1975. But it is the granite that is more coveted for stone. 'At a small temple', writes Francis Buchanan in 1800, 'I observed, for the first time, the rock of red granite. It is a handsome variety, consisting of bright red feldspar, a small quantity of glassy quartz, and a very minute proportion of black mica. I had before seen many detached masses of it in buildings; so that it is probably common in the country. It is a most elegant stone'.[53]

Today, the Closepet belt is a source of 'ornamental stone' in contrast to the 'ordinary stone' quarried from the gneiss on either side. Gneiss is used for compound walls, sidewalks, drains, foundations, roofs, etc. Granite is exclusive: it is used in fine buildings, sculptures and 'polished' surfaces. Unlike gneiss, which remains local, granite is largely exported well beyond the edge of the Dharwar craton — the tectonic unit that encompasses much of the tableland. It is an instability powered by economies rather than plate tectonics.

In the immediacies of war in 1791, however, the distinctive pink porphyritic granite was hardly noticed. This was merely 'a country which from the ruggedness of its surface, occasioned the loss of several carts and much baggage . . . a country every where broken by deep ravines into rugged precipices'.[54] It was also a jungle through which troops had to 'cut their way with such infinite labour', and it was a land of droogs led by Savendroog, or the Rock of Death, 'no less famed for its noxious atmosphere, occasioned by the surrounding hills and woods, than for its wonderful size and strength'.[55]

By January 1792, however, the route surveyors had made this wild territory a haven. 'The strong hilly country between Bangalore and Seringapatam, which, studded with hill forts, had posed such serious inconvenience to the operations of the army, now increased the security of the convoys, and gave the most promising hopes of success in the attack of the last and main object of the war'.[56] The conquered droogs would become prospects and the forest would become a refuge. It was here on 25 January 1792 that 'the armies of Earl Cornwallis, Secunder Jaw, and Hury Punt formed one extensive encampment' before leaving for Seringapatam in three columns for the final assault on that island capital which was taken on 6 February to bring the war to an end.[57]

North View of Ramgaree.

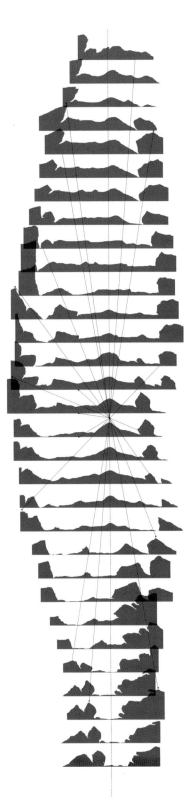

TOP

Robert Home, 'North View of Ramgaree'. This droog gives its name to the town of Ramnagaram and the village of Ramgarh in the film *Sholay*.

Select Views in Mysore, The Country of Tipoo Sultan from Drawings taken on the spot with Historical Descriptions (London: Bowyer, 1794).

ABOVE

Gabbar Singh's (dacoit from the film *Sholay*) den at the foot of Ramgiri.

LEFT

Sections disclose the enclosure of Gabbar's den within the plutons of granite circled by lookouts on rocks. It brings out the two sides of the igneous belt encountered by route surveyors in 1791 — refuge and prospect; the low rock at the centre on which Gabbar Singh is in command and the high rocks on the periphery from which his men maintained lookouts.

1000 M

Robert H. Colebrooke, 'North View of Sewandroog shewing the Attack in December 1791'. This 'vast mountain of rock' wrote Major Dirom, makes hills 'low only from the proximity of the huge mass behind them' and 'afforded such harbour to the enemy, that there was scarcely a possibility of a convoy passing it unmolested'.

Twelve Views of Places in the Kingdom of Mysore (London, 1794). [Yale Center for British Art, Paul Mellon Collection]

900 M

840 M

850 M

DECCAN TRAVERSES

THE WAR
CAMP GROUND
PETTAH
ESPLANADE
LAST FRONTIER

59

LEFT

The summit, slope and bare rock surface of Savandroog assert their presence at every stage of a circuitous 400-metre climb as it perhaps did on Cornwallis's men. 'Lord Cornwallis thinks himself fortunate, almost beyond example', wrote a soldier in December of 1791, 'in having acquired, by assault, a fortress of so much strength and reputation . . . as Savendroog, without having to regret the loss of a single soldier on the occasion. He can only attribute the pusillanimity of the enemy, yesterday, to their astonishment, at seeing the good order, and determined countenance, with which the troops who were employed in the assault entered the breach, and ascended precipices that have hitherto been considered in this country as inaccessible'.

Nearly two centuries after the 'Grand Army' marched across the last frontier, this territory would be recalled in both its dimensions of that war — a wildness and a refuge. In the 1970s it was made familiar to millions as the domain of the dacoit, Gabbar Singh, in G.P. Sippy's blockbuster *Sholay*, a name with fiery origins that appears to refer as much to grand passions and heroic confrontations that rocked Hindi cinema as it does to the once magmatic geo-suture. The fugitive's den within the massive plutons of pink granite circled by lookouts on rocks made the 'difficult country' a source of terror and extortion to the villagers of Ramgarh in the adjoining plains. It required heroes from elsewhere to brave this terrain, both in the film and the making of the film. The director and his crew from Bombay, a contemporary writer remarks, 'were like pioneers heading out to the Wild West; warriors fighting for a just cause. They selected a barren landscape in South India, inhabited it, transformed it against mind-numbing odds to suit their vision, and created a compelling work of art'.[58]

In the 1980s, the difficult country reached a wider audience as the land of E.M. Forster's alluring and disorienting Marabar Caves in David Lean's rendition of *A Passage to India*. With their sense of 'infinity, eternity and vastness' on the one hand and confusion, isolation, and 'double vision', on the other, the caves in Forster's novel are a site of an event clouded in mystery and uncertainty that would fuel both sides of empire. The caves in the film are set on Savandroog, the 'vast mountain of rock' which Dirom had said made hills appear 'low only from the proximity of the huge mass behind them' and 'afforded such harbour to the enemy, that there was scarcely a possibility of a convoy passing it unmolested'.[59] This droog provided Lean with the material grandness and firmness against which the caves' darkness and uncertainty were magnified in the way that the unseen in these 'wilds' must have been to Cornwallis's men. It was something that he did not find in the Marabar Hills of Bihar where Forster set his story. He found it in the fiery line of nether-formed rock that once made an army pause long enough to make Bangalore 'home'.

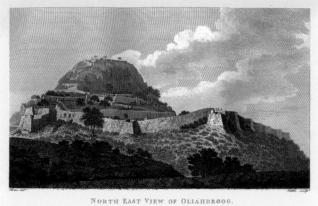

NORTH EAST VIEW OF OLIAHDROOG.

Robert Home, 'North East View of Oliahdroog'. It was at the foot of this droog in the midst of the 'difficult country' that the Grand Army assembled before the final siege of Seringapatam in February 1792.

Select Views in Mysore, The Country of Tipoo Sultan from Drawings taken on the spot with Historical Descriptions (London: Bowyer, 1794).

Last Frontier 1

Screen Print on paper, 22"x30" + Digital Plot

Last Frontier 2

Screen Print on paper, 22"x30" + Digital Plot

Fire 1

Screen Print on paper, 22"x30" + Digital Plot

Fire 2

Screen Print on paper, 22"x30" + Digital Plot

THE SURVEY

BASELINE

BUND

TANK

THOUSAND TANKS

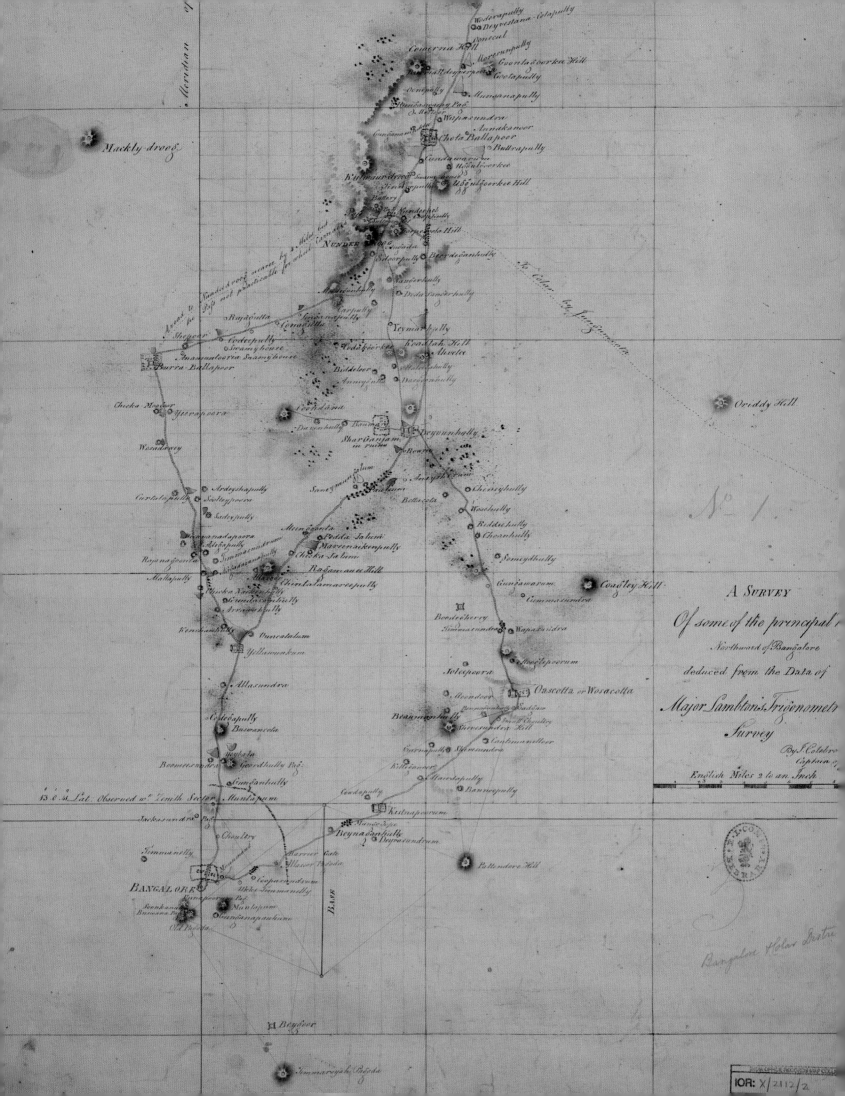

A SURVEY
Of some of the principal
Northward of Bangalore
deduced from the Data of
Major Lambton's Trigonometr
Survey
By J.Colebro
Captain &
English Miles 2 to an Inch

Mackly droog

Meridian

Coverna Hill
Woderapully
Deyvestana Cotapully
Donecul
Morconpully
Goontadoorkee Hill
Cootapully
Bettalldepurpoor
Oonepully
Munganapully
Rundaswamy Pas
S. Madhoor
Wapasundra
Annakanoor
Gundanara
Chota Ballapoor
Bullrapully
Gundawarum
Hoonloorkee
Killmaurdroog
Simonylowel
Uboonloorkee Hill
Nindipully
Battery
Narodachel
Coopfully
NUNDEE DROOG
Emida
Gonyoola Hill
Sedoorpully
Beerdedanhully
Kundarkully
Maddeconhully
Doda manserhully
Carpully
Rajagutta
Sonicepully
Congidilla
Yeymarhully
Shepoor
Codepully
Swamyhouse
Kvadah Hill
Anamulooria Snamylowse
Todadoorkee
Alewtee
Burra-Ballapoor
Biddeloor
Malicahully
Anneyhully
Dacoonhully
Chicka-Mooloor
Meerapoora
Coondana
Oriddy Hill
Wosadroey
Dacoonhully
Beaum
Sharganjam in ruins
Deyunnhully
Howry
Ardeyshapully
Sane ymanalium
Ootyel Crum
Curtatapully
Scotteypoora
Gundarum
Chineyhully
Sadexpully
Bettacota
Wosehully
Riddehully
Jenganatapoora
Meengunta
Attapully
Pedda Jaloni
Choanhully
Jimmasundra
Mareenaikenpully
Rajanagoonta
Chicka-Jaloni
Someydhully
Mallapully
Moolca
Ragamaree Hill
Chinta Jamareepully
Gundawarum
Coagley Hill
Chicka Nacksenhully
Cimmasundra
Gundacasahully
Arrinahully
Boodocherry
Wenchashully
Simmasundra
Wapasundra
Ouncatalum
Yellawunkum
Anegtepoorum
Jolepoora
Allasundra
Abondoo
Oascotta or Wosacotta
Cootedapully
Beaumanahully
Saesll Chaultry
Buswancota
Karesundra Hill
Cantimanelloor
yeykata
Curnapull
Abondoo
Goordhully Pas
Cimsanhully
Mungdepully
Bannepully
Boomeesundra
Killeannoor
13.0" Lat. Observed w.th Zenith Sector Muntapum
Cowdapully
Jackasundra Pas
Kistnapoorum
Mange Jape
Chaultry
Beynadonhulle
Timmanelly
Barrier Gate
Deyvasundrum
Monument
Allasor Pagoda
Pettendore Hill
BANGALORE
Ucket Timmanelly
Jeepasundrum
Yimnapooria Pas
Swonkanda Pas
Muntapum
Buswana Pas
Goondanapaulium
Old Pagoda
BASE

N.o 1

Bendoor

Timmarayah Pagoda

To Colar by Jangamcotta

Bangalore Kolar District

IOR: X/2112/2

THE SURVEY

By 'the late glorious campaign', wrote Major William Lambton in *Asiatic Researches* in 1803, 'a district of country is acquired, which not only opens a free communication with the *Malabar* coast, but from its nature affords a most admirable means of connecting that with the coast of *Coromandel* by an uninterrupted series of triangles, and of continuing that series to an almost unlimited extent in every direction'.[1] Lambton, a Brigade major who participated in the storming of Seringapatam in 1799, was presenting his idea of a trigonometrical survey of the southern peninsula to the Asiatic Society 'instituted in Bengal for inquiring into the history and antiquities, the arts, sciences, and literature of Asia'. This august group — which included men such as William Jones, founder of the Society and Henry T. Colebrooke who would initiate the Royal Asiatic Society in London in 1823 — suggests that this was no ordinary survey. It was, in fact, no ordinary trigonometrical survey and it would eventually gain Lambton recognition by both the French Academy of Science as well as the Royal Society of London for the Improvement of Natural Knowledge.

At the time of publishing the article in *Asiatic Researches* — the first of four on the subject that he went on to write over a period of fifteen years — Lambton had already begun the series of triangles 'in the neighbourhood' of Bangalore, 'on account of its being a centrical situation'.[2] Although largely in the hands of the Rajah, there was a strong presence of Company and King's troops garrisoned across the Mysore Tableland to ensure the transition of power as well as to collect topographical information considered necessary for administration. Lambton saw this as an opportunity to address two concerns. The first was to place 'the great geographical features of a country upon correct mathematical principles'.[3] The second was to evolve the surveyor's practice that had hitherto worked 'upon a series of plane triangles and to suppose the surface on which they made their surveys to be flat, thinking the curvature of the Earth of too little consequence to be taken into consideration, and the only mode of correcting was by observing Jupiter's satellites, occultations of the stars, etc'.[4] Both concerns hinged on one unknown, the curvature of the earth. Geographical positioning and surveying, to Lambton, were inadequate without geodesic reasoning and the unique aspect of his survey was that it was going to determine both the curvature of the earth and positions of features and objects on it through the same process of triangulation.

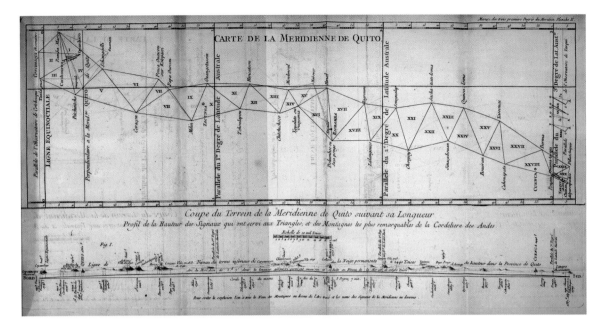

Profil de la Hauteur des Signaux qui ont servi aux Triangles, et des Montagnes les plus remarquables de la Cordeliere des Andes

Lambton was following up on a debate that had raged in Europe in the first half of the eighteenth century regarding the shape of the earth which Isaac Newton among others had declared was not a perfect sphere. Newton himself believed it to be flat at the poles (an oblate spheroid). Jacques Cassini, a member of the famous Cassini family who held the directorship of the Paris Observatory for four generations, found reason to believe that it was compressed at the equator (a prolate spheroid). To resolve the issue, the French Academy of Science sponsored two expeditions in 1735, one to Lapland (Sweden) and the other to Peru, seeking to compare the length of a degree of latitude at the equator with that near the earth's pole. The findings confirmed Newton's view. The question of the earth's precise form, however, was still open. A handful of men would contribute to this computational pursuit in the mid to late 1700s with measures of arcs – i.e., a series of triangles – along an axis of longitude in France, North America, England, Russia and South Africa. The computed distance between two points on this arc was treated as the length of a chord of a circle, the radius of which was ascertained through observations at these points of stars moving on a celestial arc assumed to be on a sphere. It provided the length of a degree along the meridian, i.e., a degree of latitude. But as much as these points fixed the earth, they were also fixed by the earth. As such, while the curvature of the earth was determined at 'primary' points or stations, these stations could anchor an extended network of triangles. More importantly, these primary triangles allowed for 'secondary' and 'tertiary' triangles to fix less significant points in what was, theoretically at least, interminable detail.

Lambton's hero in integrating the causes of geodesy and surveying was General William Roy, largely credited with originating the Ordnance Survey in England. As early as 1766 Roy had proposed 'carrying on the Series of Triangles . . . to trace one grand Meridian line, thro' the whole extent of Island, marked by obelisks from distance to distance'. Such an arc of the meridian would begin with a measurement of a 'great base of the first triangle'. This base would be 'six or eight miles in length, measured with the utmost exactness on the Sands of the Sea Shore, or in one of the open level Countries . . . and afterwards reduced to the Level of the Sea'. It would then extend through other series 'along the Coast, and along the remarkable Ridges of Hills and principal Rivers'. In this way 'the Situations of all the material points would be truly fixed with regard to one another, and thence the Great Outlines of the Country would be truly determined'.[5]

In 1787, Roy, eager to see the measurement of the earth's curvature undertaken in as many places as possible, recommended that the Company undertake 'the measurement of five degrees of latitude on the coast of Choromandel' and that 'two degrees of longitude, at each extremity of this arc, should likewise be measured'.[6] His suggestion was taken seriously but shelved because of expense, until Lambton

Charles-Marie La Condamine and Pierre Bouguer's triangulation across the Andes in the Spanish occupied territory of Peru was the first measurement of the earth's curvature. The Quito Line computed the length of a degree of latitude between two baselines, one at Yarouqui near Quito and the other at Tarqui near Cuença (1736-39).

Charles-Marie La Condamine, *Mesure des trois premiers degrés du méridien dans l'hémisphere austral: tirée des observations de Mrs. de l'Académie royale des sciences, envoyés par le roi sous l'équateur* (A Paris: De Imprimerie royale, 1751). [Annenberg Rare Book and Manuscript Library, University of Pennsylvania]

DECCAN TRAVERSES

THE SURVEY
BASELINE
BUND
TANK
THOUSAND TANKS

71

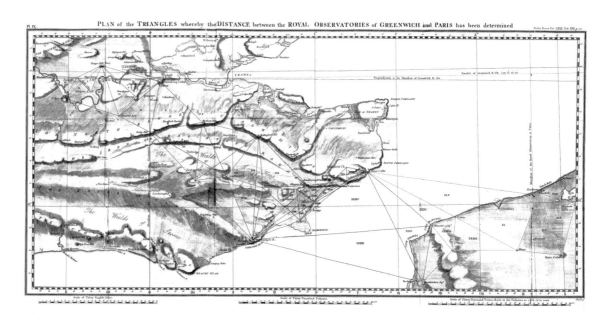

PLAN of the TRIANGLES whereby the DISTANCE between the ROYAL OBSERVATORIES of GREENWICH and PARIS has been determined

Major-General William Roy began a project in 1783 to determine the relative positions of the Royal Observatories in Paris and Greenwich. It led to the measurement of a base line on Hounslow Heath, southwest of London, and a series of triangles across southern England and the English Channel.

Major-General William Roy, 'An Account of the Trigonometrical Operation, whereby the distance between the Meridians of the Royal Observatories of Greenwich and Paris has been determined', *Philosophical Transactions of the Royal Society* 80, 1790, Pl. IX.

re-issued Roy's geodesic ambition in 1800, saying 'I shall rejoice indeed if it should come within my province to make observations tending to elucidate so sublime a subject'.[7] But he also re-issued Roy's survey ambition, arguing that his arcs would lay the foundation for determining 'the exact position of all the great objects that appeared best calculated to become permanent geographical marks, to be hereafter guides for facilitating a general survey of the Peninsular and particularly the territories conquered by the British Arms. . . . The surveyors of particular districts will be spared much labour when they know the positions of some leading points to which they can refer because when these points are laid down in the exact situations in which they are upon the globe, all objects of whatever denomination, such as towns, forts, rivers, etc., which have a relation to those points, will also have their situations true in latitude and longitude'.[8]

The land available to the Company now was not just the plains of the east coast but virtually the entire peninsula. The Company sanctioned Lambton's proposal to measure an arc across the peninsula, with the potential of extending it in a network as well as of intersecting it with an arc of the meridian. However, his attention, initially at least, had to focus on the newly opened territory of Mysore. His project was to parallel yet assist the 'mathematical' aspect of the Mysore Survey being undertaken by Captain Colin Mackenzie.[9]

In 1799 the governor-general, Richard Wellesley, had ordered Mackenzie, an engineer in the Madras Army and an accomplished route surveyor in his time, to conduct 'a survey on an extensive scale of the territories lately subjected to the Company and to the Rajah of Mysoor. Such a survey is in the first place absolutely necessary to the accurate settlement of our frontier; it will also tend to augment our knowledge of Indian Geography, and to produce immediate and important benefits in establishing and conducting our government in the conquered provinces'.[10] Mackenzie's plan for the survey was ambitious. He proposed two 'great leading objects, Mathematical and Physical'. The first comprised a survey that would mark the boundaries of provinces and 'inferior divisions', and position 'every Town, Fort, village . . . rivers and their courses, the roads, the Lakes, Tanks, Defiles, Mountains, and every remarkable object, feature, and property of the Country' by a process of laying out 'Triangles connected by Bases to be carefully measured'. The physical part of the survey would include 'all remarks, facts, and observations that can be conducive to the improvement of Natural History'. This included diseases, medicines, remedies, air, climate, seasons, soil, modes of cultivation, tenures of land, classes of natives, customs, languages, and so on.[11] It was, according to Major Reginald Phillimore, eminent historian of the Survey of India, 'the first completely organized survey expedition to take the field in India'.[12]

Between 1800 and 1808, with many interruptions due to inclement weather and the loss of men to illness and duties elsewhere, Mackenzie surveyed the Mysore country. Topographical maps of the territory provided the ground upon which he recorded information in the 'branches of Botany, Mineralogy, and Natural History', having native artists draw plants, animals, implements, etc. He also records facts in the fields of religion, history and archaeology. His collections of 'scattered fragments which exist of true history' were coveted by the Directors of the East India Company for their Oriental Museum in London. They noted the breadth, significance, and pioneering nature of Mackenzie's work. 'The actual survey upon geometrical principles of a region containing above 40,000 square miles, generally of an extremely difficult surface, full of hills and wildernesses . . . never before explored by European science in a climate very insalubrious, is itself no common performance and . . . the masterly execution, upon a large scale, of the general map and its striking discrimination of different objects . . . form altogether an achievement of extraordinary merit adding most materially to the stores of Indian geography, and of information useful for military, financial, and commercial purposes'.[13]

However, even as Mackenzie's work was being applauded, Lambton was casting the topographical aspect of his survey in doubt. Both surveys fell in the genre of trigonometric investigations, which computed, rather than physically measured, distances between points by invoking triangular relationships. The only distance physically measured in this kind of survey is what Roy had called the 'great base of the first triangle'. After that measure of seven to eight miles carried out carefully using a chain, the surveyor moved from point to point, recording horizontal angles between points with a theodolite and calculating distances with trigonometric formulae. The measurement of the baseline was carried through the survey in computations until a check was deemed necessary. At this time, which was often 100-150 miles down a series of triangles, the closing side of the last triangle – a base of verification – was measured and checked against its computed length. Besides the initial and final baseline, the survey literally touched down only at points or stations, doing away with the ground measurements so central to the work of route surveyors.

Mackenzie's survey was the kind that Lambton was seeking to reform through geodesy. Besides shared stations and observations there was little common ground, the two surveys ultimately presenting very different terrains. To Mackenzie, their difference mattered little, particularly 'on the scale of common maps'.[14] To Lambton however, one was a terrain that extended seamlessly over the earth; the other was a jointed flat surface, each component corrected for curvature. Eventually, in a milieu directed toward higher accuracy and certainty, Lambton's survey would relegate Mackenzie's work to the archives.

Lambton, however, was soon questioning his instruments – the chain, the theodolite, etc. They were accurate enough for Mackenzie's Mysore Survey but not for the 'higher' demands of geodesy. 'Though this is not a work that I wish to be considered as executed with mathematical precision, yet I am not without confidence that when I come to verify the principal points with a more powerful instrument than I have at present, I shall not find them out, either in Latitude or Longitude, more than five or six seconds. . . . My intention is now to return to the eastward . . . and, if possible fix upon some points to connect the country above the Ghauts with the Carnatic, which will much facilitate my plan of crossing the Peninsula'.[15] In 1802 he began again in Madras, choosing his baseline there carefully in the same latitude as his line in Bangalore. 'Having in the year 1800, measured a Line of near 7½ Miles in length, a little to the Eastward of Bangalore, its Northern extremity being nearly in the Latitude of 13°, I was

Colin Mackenzie, 'Map of the Territories of the Rajah of Mysore together with Canara & Punganoor etc. belonging to the E.E.I. Company from The Survey of Mysore, 1808'. R.H. Phillimore, ed., *Historical Records of the Survey of India,* vol. II, (Dehradun: Survey of India, 1950), Plate 11.

DECCAN TRAVERSES

THE SURVEY
BASELINE
BUND
TANK
THOUSAND TANKS

73

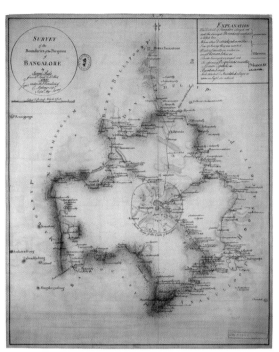

James Ross, *Survey of the Boundaries of the Purgunna of Bangalore from 4th April to 5th May 1800*. Part of Colin Mackenzie's Mysore Survey (1799–1808).
British Library, IOR X/2126 [By permission of the British Library]

desirous of finding an extent of Country which would admit of a line similarly situated, with respect to latitude, and bearing with the Meridian as my intention has always been to proceed as nearly in the same parallel of Latitude as circumstances would admit in carrying the principal series of primary points to the Malabar Coast and I have been so fortunate as to make the Northern extremity of this line fall within five seconds of the Northern extremity of the Base near Bangalore, and both these Lines take nearly the same direction and within a few Minutes of the Meridian'.[16]

In 1806, at Bangalore, Lambton began his project to realize a 'grand meridian line' for India, reaching Cape Comorin in 1808. Beginning again in Bangalore that year, he extended this arc north. He died near Nagpur in 1826 and George Everest took on his ambition. The Great Indian Arc of the Meridian – as the line came to be called – would eventually reach across 21° 22' of latitude or 2,250 kilometres. It was, Clements Markham would say in 1878, 'one of the most stupendous works in the whole history of science'.[17]

Lambton's triangulation became a framework for the survey of India. In 1826 John Philippart wrote, 'Though the measurement of the arc of the meridian was the principal object of the labours of Col. Lambton, he extended his operations to the east and west, and the set of triangles covers great part of the peninsula of India, defining with the utmost precision, the situation of a very great number of principal places in latitude, longitude, and elevation, and affording a sure basis for an amended geographical map'.[18] Lord Hastings declared 'there was no other solid basis on which accurate geography can so well be founded. The primary triangles thus spread over this vast country establish almost beyond error a multitude of points, and the spaces comprehended within these when filled up by the details of subordinate surveyors, will afford . . . to the world, a map without a parallel, whether in the relation to its accuracy, to its extensiveness, or to the unity of the effort by which it will be achieved'.[19]

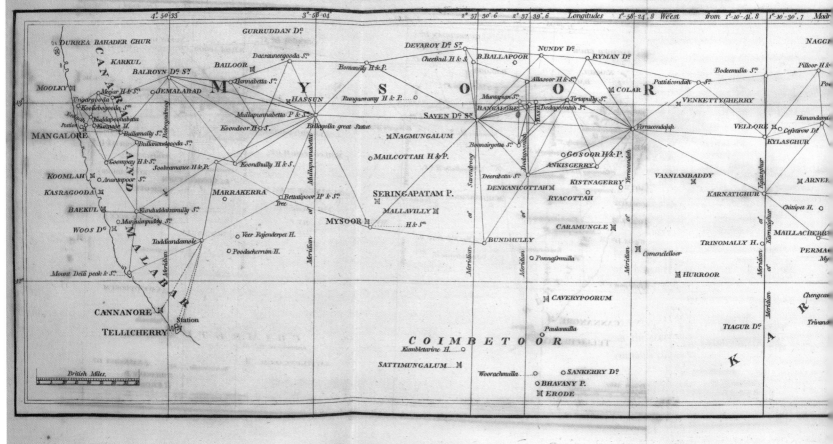

In the 1860s much of Lambton's measurements on the tableland would be revised with more sophisticated equipment. But his method remained dominant, its certainty and geodesic reality making sure that the maps of the tableland by Mackenzie were shelved almost as soon as they were completed and those of early travellers were relegated to 'tales' and to 'fancy'. 'The presence in India', Phillimore observes, 'of a man of Lambton's genius and character, knowledge of mathematics, and interest in geodesy, was entirely fortuitous. So also was his service in Mysore with the Grand Army, which impressed on him the vastness of an area that was practically unknown to geography, and the futility of trying to survey it without the aid of geodetic science'.[20]

The Great Trigonometrical Survey (GTS), as Lambton's project came to be called, extended across the space of the peninsula; it also extended across the time of this peninsula. From the 'permanent geographical marks' of Lambton's project, 'surveyors of particular districts' did not only mark secondary and tertiary points, they also surveyed periodically to record changes in the less permanent elements of the land — the boundaries of settlements, the fluctuations of water bodies, etc. In other words, the GTS was not just a reading of the land; it was an infrastructure that facilitated updates, holding rhythms and aberrations as it held stations and movement. The Survey of India, formed in 1878, took over this infrastructure, recording the changes in the peninsula thereafter.

William Lambton began the Madras Longitudinal Series with the Bangalore Baseline measured between October and December 1800. However, he reworked most of his measurements beginning in Madras in 1804 on a section of coast chosen to be in line with the baseline in Bangalore.

'General Plan of Triangles' in William Lambton, 'An Account of the Trigonometrical Operations in crossing the Peninsula of India, and Connecting Fort St. George with Mangalore', *Asiatic Researches*, vol. X, 1811, Pl. 4. [Annenberg Rare Book and Manuscript Library, University of Pennsylvania]

DECCAN TRAVERSES

THE SURVEY
BASELINE
BUND
TANK
THOUSAND TANKS

75

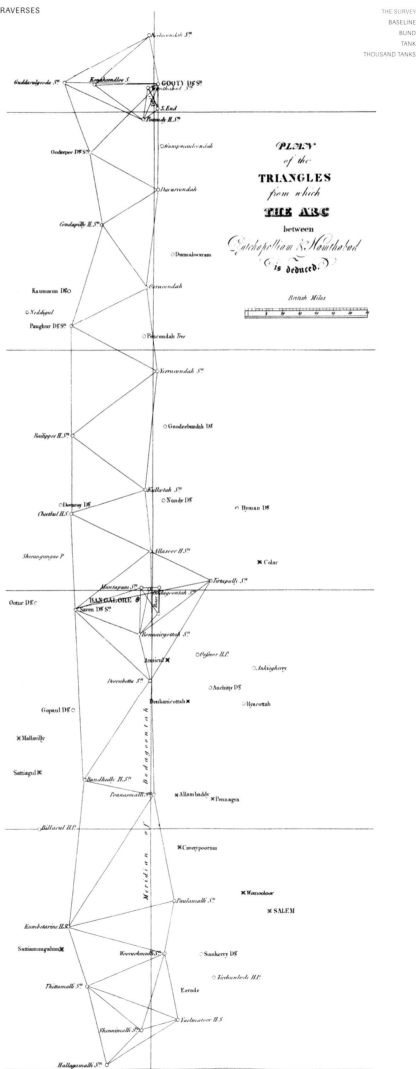

'Plan of the Triangles from which the Arc between Putchapolliam & Namthabad is deduced'. Clements Markham in *A Memoir of the Indian Surveys* writes of the importance of this arc. 'The measurement of an arc in the peninsula of India was, in a purely scientific point of view, of the highest importance. By it the exact figure of the earth was to be ascertained; and it should be remembered that this was not, as has been asserted, an object of mere curiosity.
It affects some of the tables used in navigation, especially all those of which the moon's parallax is an element, and is therefore an investigation of the greatest practical consequence to the whole civilized world'.

William Lambton, 'An Account of the Measurement of an Arc on the Meridian, extending from Latitude 10° 59' 49" to 15° 6' 65" North', *Asiatic Researches,* vol. XII, 1818. [Annenberg Rare Book and Manuscript Library, University of Pennsylvania]

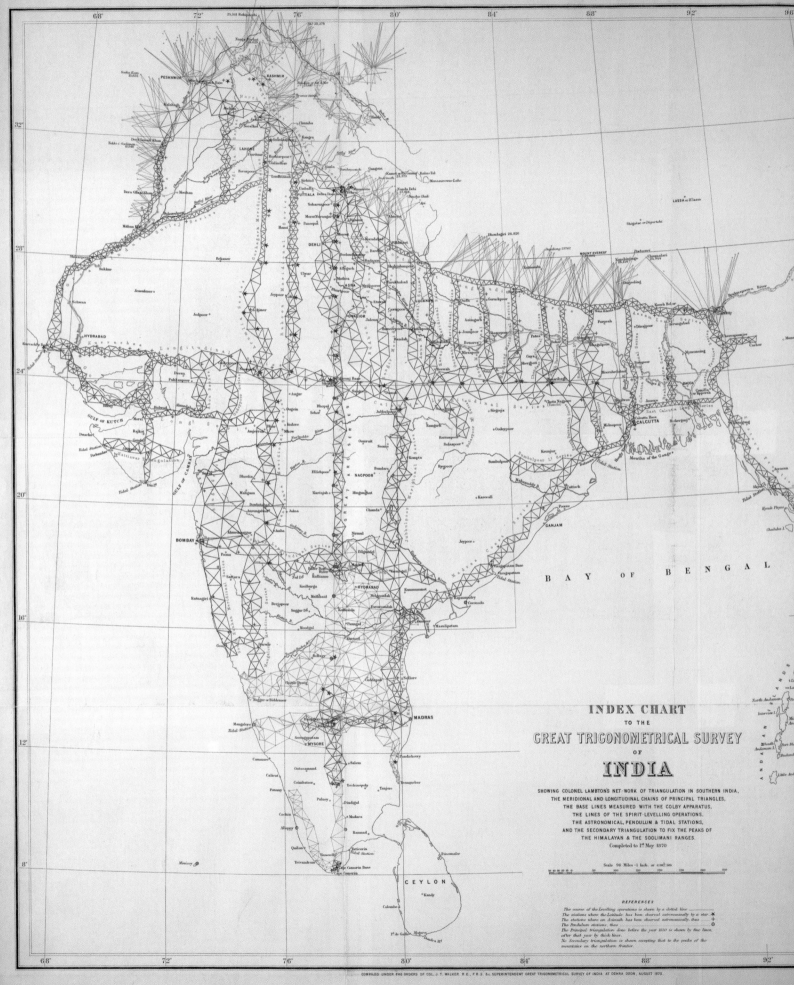

INDEX CHART
TO THE
GREAT TRIGONOMETRICAL SURVEY
OF
INDIA

SHOWING COLONEL LAMBTON'S NET-WORK OF TRIANGULATION IN SOUTHERN INDIA,
THE MERIDIONAL AND LONGITUDINAL CHAINS OF PRINCIPAL TRIANGLES,
THE BASE LINES MEASURED WITH THE COLBY APPARATUS,
THE LINES OF THE SPIRIT-LEVELLING OPERATIONS,
THE ASTRONOMICAL, PENDULUM & TIDAL STATIONS,
AND THE SECONDARY TRIANGULATION TO FIX THE PEAKS OF
THE HIMALAYAN & THE SOOLIMANI RANGES.
Completed to 1st May 1870

Scale 96 Miles =1 Inch or c36ʳ⁄₁₀₀

REFERENCES

The course of the Levelling operations is shown by a dotted line
The stations where the Latitude has been observed astronomically by a star
The stations where an Azimuth has been observed astronomically than
The Pendulum stations, thus
The Principal triangulation done before the year 1830 is shown by fine lines,
after that year by thick lines.
No Secondary triangulation is shown excepting that to the peaks of the
mountains on the northern frontier.

BAY OF BENGAL

CEYLON

COMPILED UNDER THE ORDERS OF COL. J. T. WALKER, R.E., F.R.S. &c. SUPERINTENDENT GREAT TRIGONOMETRICAL SURVEY OF INDIA AT DEHRA DOON, AUGUST 1870.

Engraved at the Surveyor General's Office.
Calcutta Novʳ 1870.

DECCAN TRAVERSES

THE SURVEY
BASELINE
BUND
TANK
THOUSAND TANKS

77

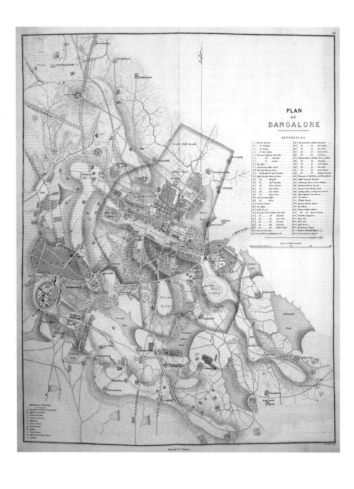

'Index Chart to the Great Trigonometrical Survey of India, showing Colonel Lambton's net work of triangulation in Southern India, the meridional and longitudinal chains of principal triangles, the base lines measured with the Colby apparatus, the lines of the spirit-levelling operations, the astronomical pendulum & tidal stations, and the secondary triangulation to fix the peaks of the Himalayan & the Soolimani Ranges. Completed to 1st May 1870'. The project began with the measurement of a baseline in Bangalore in 1800.

Account of the operations of the Great Trigonometrical Survey of India, vol. I, (Dehradun: Office of the Great Trigonometrical Survey, 1870).

One of the first maps to place Bangalore on the globe measured by William Lambton.

The Atlas of the Southern Part of India including the Plans of all the Principal Towns & Cantonments reduced from the Grand Trigonometrical Survey of India. Pharoah & Co. 1854. Plate 48. [Annenberg Rare Book and Manuscript Library, University of Pennsylvania]

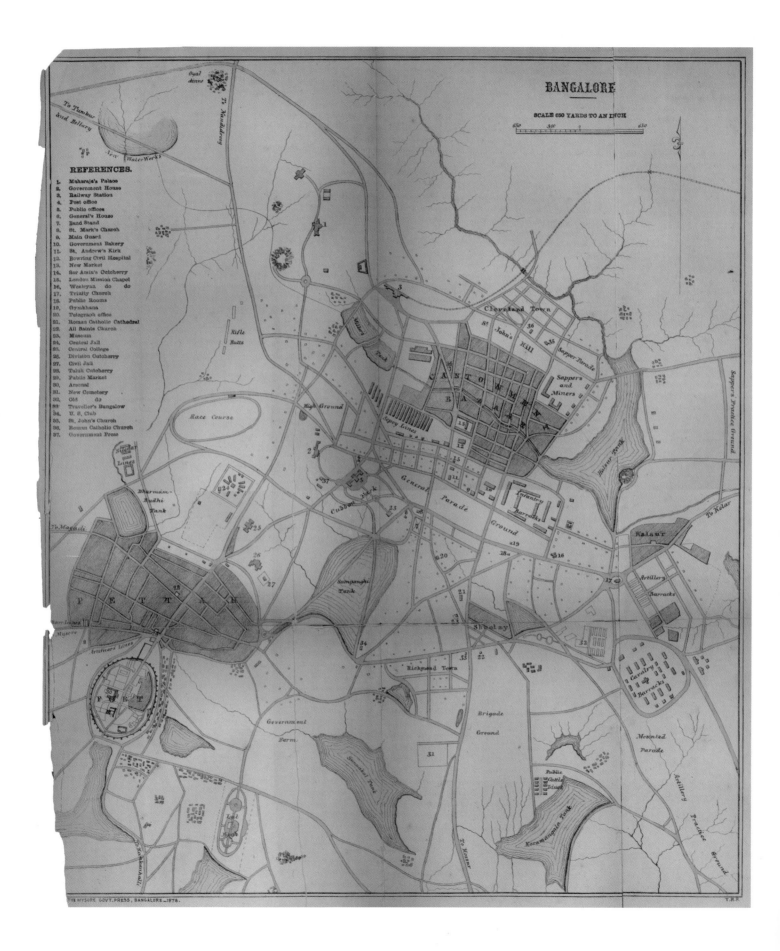

BANGALORE

SCALE 880 YARDS TO AN INCH

REFERENCES.

1. Maharaja's Palace
2. Government House
3. Railway Station
4. Post office
5. Public offices
6. General's House
7. Band Stand
8. St. Mark's Church
9. Main Guard
10. Government Bakery
11. St. Andrew's Kirk
12. Bowring Civil Hospital
13. New Market
14. Sar Amin's Cutcherry
15. London Mission Chapel
16. Wesleyan do do
17. Trinity Church
18. Public Rooms
19. Gymkhana
20. Telegraph office
21. Roman Catholic Cathedral
22. All Saints Church
23. Museum
24. Central Jail
25. Central College
26. Division Catcherry
27. Civil Jail
28. Taluk Cutcherry
29. Public Market
30. Arsenal
31. New Cemetery
32. Old do
33. Traveller's Bungalow
34. U. S. Club
35. St. John's Church
36. Roman Catholic Church
37. Government Press

DECCAN TRAVERSES

THE SURVEY
BASELINE
BUND
TANK
THOUSAND TANKS

79

Lewis Rice, 'Bangalore'.

Mysore and Coorg: A Gazetteer compiled for the Government of India (Bangalore: Mysore Government Press, 1877).

Lewis Rice, 'Bangalore'. The Bound Hedge that was centred on the pettah of Bangalore in maps of early surveyors is replaced by an abstract 'Four Miles Circle' centred on the (British) Residency. Toward the end of the century the dividing boundaries of these two settlements would recede to make room for an extended surface. A century later, in maps by the Survey of India the two settlements would be barely distinguishable.

Mysore: A Gazetteer compiled for the Government of India (Westminster: Archibald Constable and Company, 1897).

THE GREAT TRIGONOMETRICAL SURVEY OF INDIA

PRINCIPAL TRIANGULATION

THE SOUTHERN TRIGON

THE SIMULTANEOUS REDUCTION

AND THE DETAILS OF COMPONENT SERIES

THE GREAT ARC MERIDIONAL SEC... AND THE BOMBAY LONGITUDINAL.

PREPARED ... DIRECTIONS OF

LIEUT.-COLONEL S. STRAHAN ... OR GENERAL, TRIGONOMETRICAL BRANCH

PUBLISHED ... ORDERS OF

COLONEL H. R. THUILLIER, ... URVEYOR GENERAL OF INDIA

NORTH END OF BANGALORE BASELINE

SALEM LINE

MADRAS LINE

OLD MADRAS ROAD

H.A.L LINE

N BIMANAGAR MAIN ROAD

AIRPORT ROAD

BANGALORE AIRPORT

KEMPAPURA ROAD

NORTH END OF BANGALO

SALEM LINE

MADRAS LINE

OLD MADRAS RO

H.A.L LINE

JIVAN BIMANAG

AIRPORT ROAD

BANGALORE AIR

KEMPAPURA RO

DECCAN TRAVERSES

THE SURVEY
BASELINE
BUND
TANK
THOUSAND TANKS

81

BASE LINE

Alexander Allan, 'Sawen-Droog from the S'.
Views of the Mysore Country, London, 1794.
[Yale Center for British Art, Paul Mellon Collection]

The Mysore Tableland was peculiarly suited to the demands of a trigonometrical survey. The massive rock outcrops that James Rennell referred to as 'lofty eminences' on a 'vast flat mountain' made ideal primary stations. They provided the extended views necessary to connect stations with a theodolite. Some of these outcrops were part of ranges but many were isolated hills, 'seemingly dumped at random . . . like trophies gathered from afar by some forgotten race of megalithic hoarders'.[21] They certainly appeared to fit the demands of 'permanent geographic marks, to be hereafter guides for facilitating a general survey of the Peninsular' that Lambton called for in his proposal to the governor. Few terrains offered such prospects and permanence. When triangulating in the coastal plains of the Carnatic for example, Lambton was often led to use the top of temple structures and when the Survey reached the Gangetic Plains of North India, George Everest designed sixty-foot masonry towers to do what the rock outcrops of Mysore did.

While rock outcrops made the perfect trigonometrical stations to extend Lambton's enterprise, a land as flat as possible was required to begin. 'The first operation for obtaining a datum in this mode of survey-ing', wrote Lambton, 'is by the measurement of a base line which being reduced to the level [of the sea] becomes a part of a great circle on the surface of the Earth'.[22] It was imperative that this line, the only material measure of distance for hundreds of square miles, be accurately determined. The chain, the instrument used at the time to measure length, had to be watched carefully for expansion and contrac-tion; its alignment from one extremity of the baseline to the other had to be maintained rigorously; and its horizontality at all times during measurement was crucial.

It was this critical and painstaking start to the GTS that Lambton sought to make in Bangalore as General William Roy had done in Hounslow Heath. If the busy Heathrow airport came to that heath at about the same time that the Bangalore airport came to the country that Lambton chose for his baseline, it was because Lambton and Roy were looking for the level ground that an aircraft pilot would appreciate. Lambton required a stretch of open country of about seven miles in length, as close in direction to the meridian as possible (i.e., North-south) and 'clear of the tanks and cultivated grounds'. The ends had

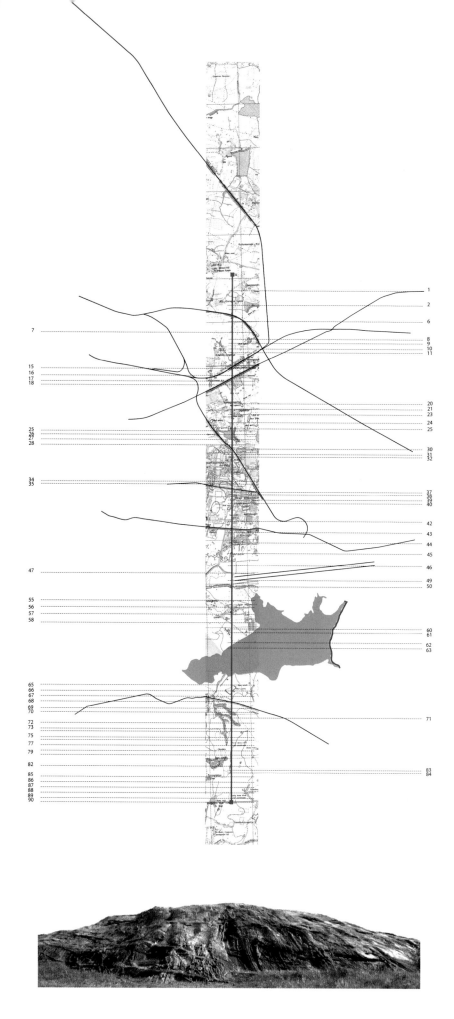

to command a prospect besides, of course, being in view of one another and viewing the terrain in between. In addition, he had to locate a third point a good distance away from the line but as close as possible to the latitude of one of the ends. The distance between this point and the baseline did not have to be measured; it formed the 'first' triangle and its distance from the ends of the baseline could be computed. Lambton, therefore, was looking to position a first triangle – three commanding apexes in view of each other and the country around.

It took a month after his arrival in Bangalore on 8 September to identify this first triangle, having decided that it 'should be in the neighbourhood of [Bangalore] on account of its being a centrical situation, and whose meridian would answer for the present as the principal meridian to my survey. . . Both extremities of the

A drawing of the ninety stages of the measurement of the Bangalore Baseline. At each stage, which was anywhere between 100 and 2,000 feet, Lambton noted the height of the commencement above or below the termination of the preceding stage, the elevation or depression made with the horizon, and the mean of five thermometer readings. When Lambton's survey was reworked in 1867, the line could not be re-measured as a number of obstacles had come in the way – rail embankments, military and private territory, highways, buildings, nullahs. Today, the obstacles include the runway of the Bangalore airport.

The south end of the baseline is called M.E.G. Rock today. Lambton describes it in 1801: 'The South extremity of the Base is to be found near the village of Agram, a mile northward of the road from Bangalore to Oosoor. It is marked by a piece of masonry about 4 foot square and 2½ feet high having in the centre a large picket hooped at the top with iron about two inches of this hoop appears above the masonry. There is a step on the south side to ascend by and it is railed round to preserve it from the cattle'.

DECCAN TRAVERSES

THE SURVEY
BASELINE
BUND
TANK
THOUSAND TANKS

83

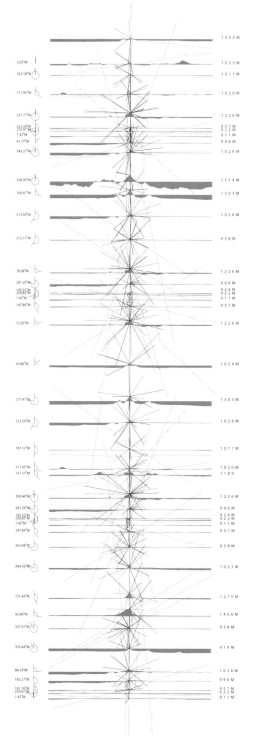

A sequential plotting of a portion of Lambton's triangulation around the Bangalore Baseline. Lambton triangulated east, west, north and south, moving from point to point, 'fixing' the location of objects that he considered permanent. Each point was related by a 'bearing' with the previous point and one other point, following a convergent path even as it constructed a divergent network of triangles. His points on the tableland were primarily the 'lofty eminences' called droogs, kondas or bettas.

Rock outcrops like Savandurg, which a visitor likened to 'tea-cups here and there reversed on its surface' made ideal stations for Lambton's survey. They provided sight lines ranging across many miles.

The mound marking the primary station (in the foreground) on top of Savandurg, 400+ metres above the surface of the tableland.

Table containing the particulars of the measurement of a baseline near Bangalore, commencing in latitude 12° 54' 64"N. and extending 7.4321 miles N. Easterly, making an angle with the meridian 0° 57' 7".

William Lambton, 'An Account of a Method for extending a Geographical Survey across the Peninsula of India', *Asiatic Researches*, vol. VII, 1803, Table 1. [Annenberg Rare Book and Manuscript Library, University of Pennsylvania]

base were upon very commanding ground from which might be seen a prodigious extent of country and these extremities were clearly distinguished from each other'.[23] The north end was near the 'village of Banaswaddy about a mile to the northward of the great road from Bangalore to Ooscottah' at about the place outside the Bound Hedge where Cornwallis's men and Tipu Sultan's troops rubbed shoulders in the fog of 5 March 1791 at the start of the Third Mysore War on the tableland. The south end was 'near the village of Agram, a mile northward of the road from Bangalore to Oosoor' where Cornwallis's Grand Army camped for much of the war. The two ends were separated by what was at the time a busy thoroughfare involving the movement of armies, supplies, and embassies that crossed this terrain to and from the Carnatic. The extraneous third point was on the 'Muntapum Hill', a rise north of the pettah from where nine years previously Tipu Sultan's men had troubled Cornwallis's camp, at that time located to its east.

Lambton began the measurement of his baseline across this terrain on 14 October 1800. Using a 100-foot chain of blistered steel made of 40 links, he covered the distance in 90 stages. At each stage, which was anywhere between 100 and 2,000 feet, he noted the height of the commencement above or below the termination of the preceding stage, the elevation or depression made with the horizon, and the mean of five thermometer readings. Five twenty-foot coffers of wood held the chain during measurement. The coffers were supported by three-inch diameter wooden pickets shod with iron. They were driven into the ground and their height adjusted so that the coffers placed on them were horizontal. But it was soon found 'in the course of practice that tripods with elevating screws in the center answered much better . . . as a very great part of the ground was hard and stony'. To prevent the wear of the chain, Lambton 'allotted twenty

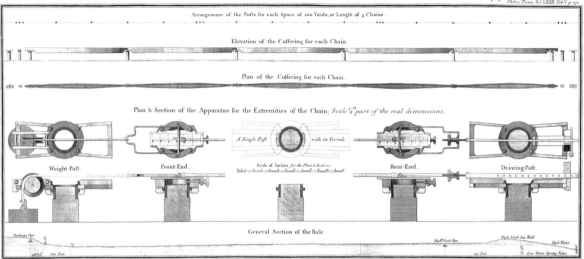

Arrangement of the Posts for each Space of 100 Yards, or Length of 3 Chains.

Elevation of the Coffering for each Chain.

Plan of the Coffering for each Chain.

Plan & Section of the Apparatus for the Extremities of the Chain; *Scale ¼th part of the real dimensions.*

A Single Post   with its Ferrule.

Weight-Post.   Front-End.   Scale of Inches *for the Plan & Section.*   Rear-End.   Drawing-Post.

General Section of the Base.

coolies, that is one to every two links, whose sole business it was to lift out the chain and lay it on the ground whilst the coffers were moved forward, and then to replace it when they were ready. All this was done with the greatest care, and always by the word given them, that the motion might be as trifling as possible'.[24] Completed on 10 December, the line measured 7.437 miles after corrections for temperature (62° F deemed the temperature at which the chain was free of expansion/contraction errors) and reduction to sea level.

From the Bangalore baseline, Lambton triangulated east, west, north and south, moving from point to point, 'fixing', as he promised, the 'great geographical features of the country', primarily the granite hills referred to today with suffixes of droog, konda and betta. This baseline was relegated temporarily to a 'base of verification' when Lambton revised the project to begin from a baseline measured in the coastal plains of the Carnatic with new and better instruments that had arrived from England in 1802. But this premier line on the tableland, re-measured in 1804 at 7.19 miles, would return to its pioneering position in 1806. 'After having crossed the Peninsula', wrote Lambton in 1802, 'I would then commence again from the Base near Bangalore on account of its being nearly half way from sea to sea and proceed as nearly north as circumstances would admit. From the same base another series might be extended to a certain distance southerly'.[25]

At the time, this operation – known today as the Great Indian Arc of the Meridian – was to Lambton an arc on the Dodagoontah meridian, named after a settlement within the Bound Hedge of Bangalore. Lambton deemed this meridian 'nearly in the middle of the Peninsula'. 'I have considered it', he notes of this place, 2° 37' 40" west of the Madras observatory or 77° 38' 50" east of Greenwich, 'as the properest meridian to which all latitudes and relative longitudes should be referred'.[26] The triangles on the Dodagoontah meridian crept south from Bangalore to Cape Comorin and north to the Dehra Dun every so often spawning a longitudinal arc across the width of the peninsula (e.g., the Coimbatore series, the Bombay series, the Calcutta series). 'That the whole of India will be eventually covered with triangles may be looked for as a result almost as certain as any future can be', declared George Everest.[27]

Lambton's baseline remained active until 1867. At this time it was deemed necessary to rework much of his survey. 'Owing to his instrumental appliances having been far less complete than at present, his work, though executed with the greatest care and ability, admitted of being improved in every part'. Orders were issued to re-measure the Bangalore baseline. But in the six decades since Lambton's measurement 'the surface of the country was much changed'. The east-west movement that marked this terrain in his time was formalised in infrastructure that was difficult to cross. 'Irrigation tanks as well as a lofty railway embankment, now cross Colonel Lambton's baseline. Hence the necessity for a new site'[28]

DECCAN TRAVERSES

THE SURVEY
BASELINE
BUND
TANK
THOUSAND TANKS

85

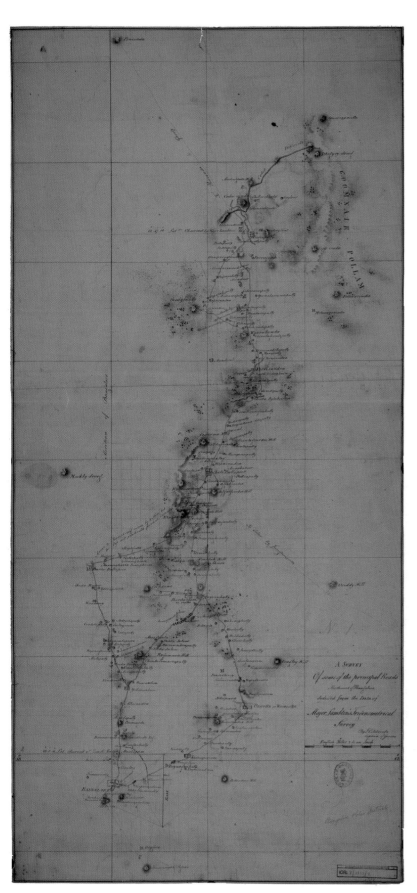

The terrain of the first triangle today as already in 1867, is hardly the naked country that it was in Lambton's time. There is little evidence to suggest its presence except perhaps the M.E.G. Rock at the south-end, which holds traces of Lambton's mark. Yet the baseline is everywhere. Beginning in the maps of the Survey of India, which would not be without the 'permanent geographical marks' that Lambton's line pinned down, the baseline is embedded in revenue surveys, topographical surveys, site surveys, and from there it enters taxation, building, city plans, disciplines, education, and administration.

James Colebrooke, *A Survey of some of the principal Roads Northward of Bangalore deduced from the Data of Major Lambton's Trigonometrical Survey.* This is a rare drawing showing the original baseline of Bangalore before Lambton began a re-measurement of his triangulation from Madras in 1802.

British Library, IOR X/2112/2 [By permission of the British Library]

The rock outcrops that Lambton saw becoming 'permanent geographical marks' are being weathered by quarrying. Bethalsur is one of them, a prominent participant in both the longitudinal arc series across the peninsula and the Great Indian Arc of the Meridian. In a report dated 24 June 1801, Lambton describes the outcrop as a 'remarkable hill of solid rock about halfway from Bangalore to Nundydroog . . . This and the station on Shevasandra hill will serve for taking in a great extent of country to the NE most of Deonelly district may be surveyed from these two points'.

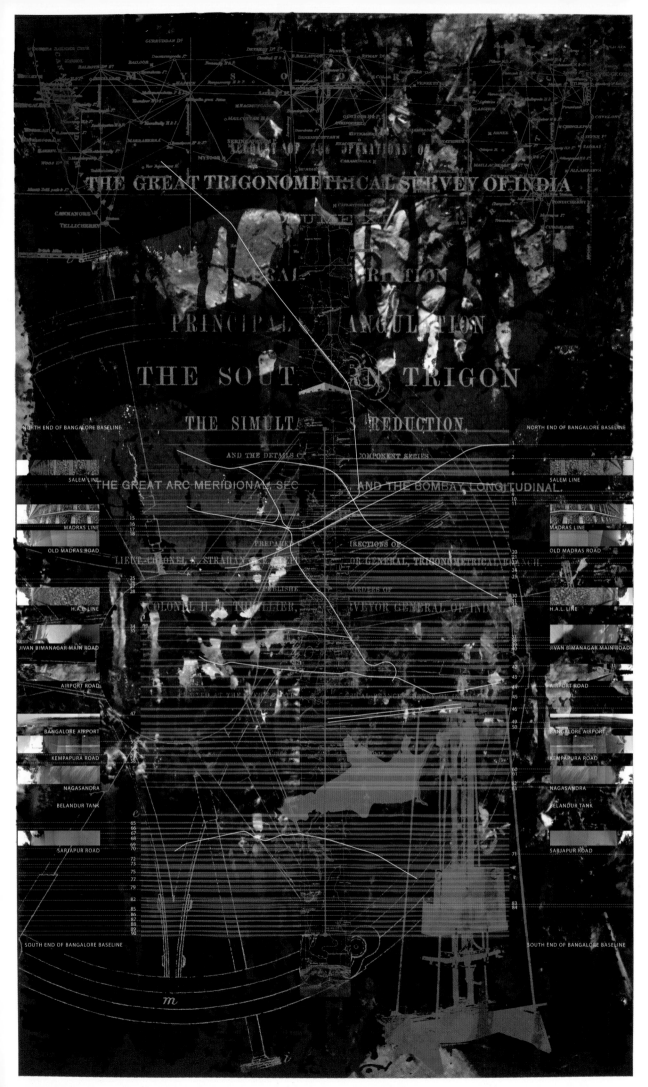

Baseline 1

Screen Print on paper, 22"x30" + Digital Plot

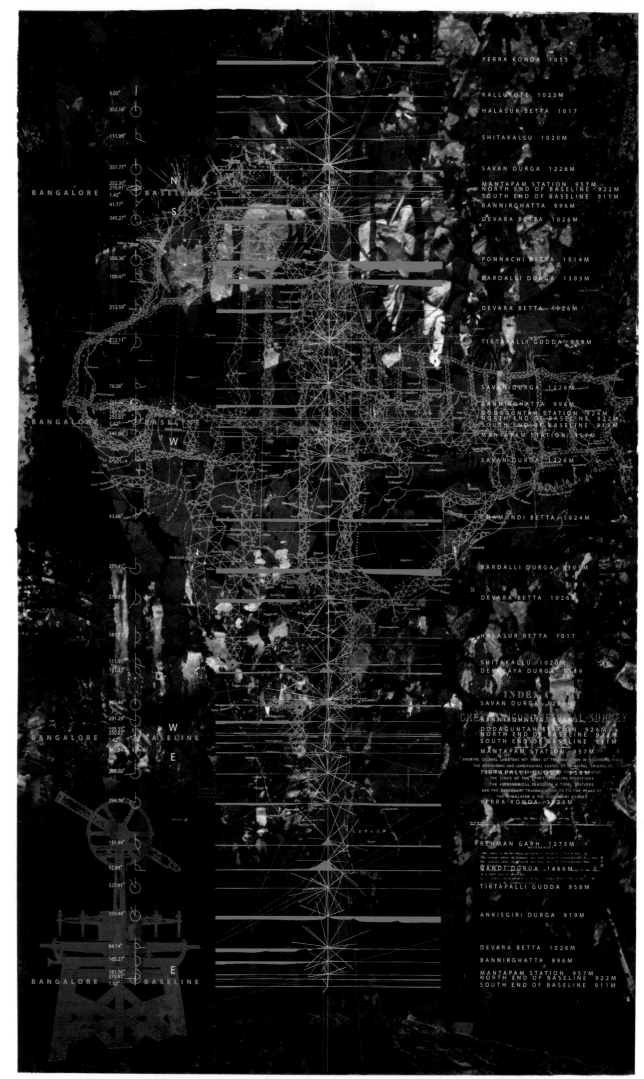

YERRA KONDA 1055

KALLUKOTE 1023M
HALASUR BETTA 1017

SHITAKALLU 1020M

SAVAN DURGA 1226M
MANTAPAM STATION 957M
NORTH END OF BASELINE 922M
SOUTH END OF BASELINE 911M
BANNIRGHATTA 996M

DEVARA BETTA 1026M

PONNACHI BETTA 1514M

BARDALLI DURGA 1303M

DEVARA BETTA 1026M

TIRTAPALLI GUDDA 958M

SAVAN DURGA 1226M

BANNIRGHATTA 996M
DODAGUNTAH STATION 924M
NORTH END OF BASELINE 922M
SOUTH END OF BASELINE 911M
MANTAPAM STATION 957M

SAVAN DURGA 1226M

CHAMUNDI BETTA 1024M

BARDALLI DURGA 1303M

DEVARA BETTA 1026M

HALASUR BETTA 1017

SHITAKALLU 1020M
DEVARAYA DURGA 1189

INDEX CHART
SAVAN DURGA 1226M
GREAT TRIGONOMETRICAL SURVEY
BANNIRGHATTA 996M
DODAGUNTAH STATION 924M
NORTH END OF BASELINE 922M
SOUTH END OF BASELINE 911M
MANTAPAM STATION 957M
TIRTAPALLI GUDDA 958M

YERRA KONDA 1023M

REHMAN GARH 1275M

NANDI DURGA 1466M

TIRTAPALLI GUDDA 958M

ANKISGIRI DURGA 919M

DEVARA BETTA 1026M
BANNIRGHATTA 996M
MANTAPAM STATION 957M
NORTH END OF BASELINE 922M
SOUTH END OF BASELINE 911M

Baseline 2

Screen Print on paper, 22"x30" + Digital Plot

This hypothenuse is computed, but may be measured during the dry season. From the excessive rains that had fallen, the arm of a large tank had extended a considerable way across the line, the angles for computing this distance, as well as those of the oblique directions, were the mean results of three different observations with the circular instrument, the rate was level, while something is computed, but may be measured

DECCAN TRAVERSES

THE SURVEY
BASELINE
BUND
TANK
THOUSAND TANKS

89

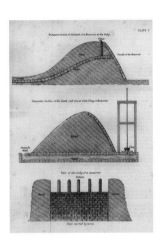

BUND

Francis Buchanan's 1800 sections through two kinds of sluices of a bund – an overflow sluice marked by stone pillars and an underflow sluice manned by a plug.

A Journey from Madras through the countries of Mysore, Canara, and Malabar (Madras: Higginbotham and Co., 1870), Vol. I, Plate 1

Lambton was apparently untroubled by the movement of armies, supplies and embassies across his baseline. They were events that could be scheduled, perhaps redirected. But one particular crossing was as uncontrollable as it was unexpected. It would disrupt the measurement sufficiently to shake Lambton's confidence already weakened by inadequate instruments.

Two-thirds of the way and six weeks along, Lambton notes in his table of measurements, 'From the excessive rains that had fallen, the arm of a large tank had extended a considerable way across the line'.[29] He was forced to triangulate around the incursion, i.e., compute rather than measure it. It was not something Lambton liked to do with the only material measure upon which stations across hundreds of square miles of territory depended for the accuracy of their location. There was, however, little that he could do. 'This hypotenuse is computed', he notes in the margins of his field book, 'but may be measured during the dry season'.

The tank that crossed Lambton's path was part of the terrain of the Belandur bund, an embankment linking high grounds of the same elevation across a land that dips. Bunds were a common feature on the Mysore tableland just as they were in the Carnatic. Francis Buchanan, who on his journey across the peninsula ahead of Lambton's Longitudinal Arc Series tended to compare everything with his home base of Bengal, writes of the first tank he came across: 'It has not been formed by digging, like those in Bengal; but by shutting up, with an artificial bank, an opening between two natural ridges of ground'.[30] The shutting up, of course, was not total and sluices controlled the flow through the bund into the fields beyond or into canals that bypass fields to the next tank. The Great Trigonometrical Survey would eventually reach back down from the primary stations in the vicinity of the baseline to 'fix' the direction, width, height and openings of the Belandur bund and the many other 'artificial banks' on the tableland together with the other objects that surveyors

DECCAN TRAVERSES

THE SURVEY
BASELINE
BUND
TANK
THOUSAND TANKS

91

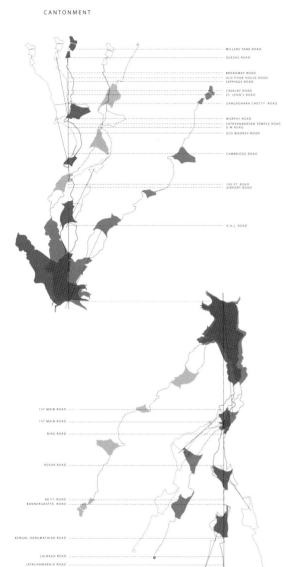

CANTONMENT

MILLERS TANK ROAD
QUEENS ROAD

BROADWAY ROAD
OLD POOR HOUSE ROAD
SEPPINGS ROAD
CAVALRY ROAD
ST. JOHN'S ROAD
GANGADHARA CHETTY ROAD

MURPHY ROAD
SATHYANARAYAN TEMPLE ROAD
D M ROAD
OLD MADRAS ROAD

CAMBRIDGE ROAD

100 FT. ROAD
AIRPORT ROAD

H.A.L. ROAD

1ST MAIN ROAD
1ST MAIN ROAD
RING ROAD

HOSUR ROAD

80 FT. ROAD
BANNERGHATTA ROAD

KENGAL HANUMATHIAH ROAD

LALBAGH ROAD
JAYACHAMARAJA ROAD

NARASIMHARAJA ROAD

CITY

Belandur Bund gathers two terrains: the first extends from the Bangalore Pettah, also called the City, and the second from the Bangalore Cantonment that in 1881 became known as the Civil and Military Station. Observers would describe these settlements as vastly different — 'a native town almost exclusively Kanarese in origin' and 'a heterogeneous assemblage of people of various nationalities and speaking several languages'. Belandur Bund, however, united them in the soil that it gathered from these settlements via two series of tanks.

Today Belandur bund is a meeting ground of urban and rural worlds, urban soil and agricultural fields.

deemed worthy of recording. But the edge of the waters that collected against these bunds would always elude them as it eluded Lambton himself. Despite the care that Lambton took to locate the extremities of his baseline so as to 'run clear of the tanks', the bund asserted itself.

The bund and baseline are parallels. Like the baseline, the bund is a leveller in an undulating terrain. If pickets, coffers, horizontal angles and mathematical equations levelled the seven-odd mile baseline, earth sloped by repose and faced with stone or vegetation levels the one-mile bund. The extremities of the baseline are held firm by the ground and observations of the stars while the trajectory between is a fleeting presence — it is physically there only when it is measured with the gravity of time and the weight of the earth. The ends of the bund, on the other hand, are fluid, operated by sluices, while the trajectory between is a firm presence weighed down by mud and stone and compressed by thoroughfare, deities and temporal occupations. Like the baseline, the bund is a beginning and, as such, an omni-presence in a territory of its own making. While the baseline begins a territory of entities and boundaries defined with mathematical clarity through a hierarchy of computed triangles, the bund initiates a surface of material flows. Rain water is the most desired part of this surface, the part for which engineers and historians say the bund was made in a land where rivers are scarce. On the basis of this flow, they define the surface behind the bund as a catchment. This surface, however, gathers more than water; it gathers settlement, flows which extend the surface generated by the bund beyond the physical limits of a catchment — roads, rails, pipes, airways, etc.

To prevent land from falling into enemy hands, people did not stop at contaminating the water behind a bund: this merely rendered the water unusable. Instead, they destroyed the bund and thus destroyed a whole surface of settlement. In this regard, the intersection of the Belandur bund and the Bangalore baseline in November 1800 was more than just a seasonal interference of a large tank; it was a call to heed a parallel line with a presence more latent and potentially extensive than immediately obvious.

Belandur Bund is an embankment of earth between two high grounds to which it is linked by sluices that facilitate overflows. These overflows, together with the underflow enabled by a plug in the low ground toward the middle of its length, modulates the wetness and dryness of the extended terrains on either side.

Much of this potential of the Belandur bund was unleashed in the decade following Lambton's measurement of the baseline when its surface, already encompassing the Bangalore pettah and a sprinkling of settlements inside and outside the Bound Hedge was extended with the introduction of Blakiston's Cantonment. If the GTS would separate with geodesic precision, Blakiston's cantonment and the pettah, marking each with its own property lines and land uses, the bund would blur their boundaries, uniting them in the ground and soil that it gathered. It is not surprising that when it was found necessary to re-measure the baseline in the 1860s, the bund had generated an infrastructure that was much more disruptive of the baseline than just 'the arm of a large tank' and a new level ground free of obstacles had to be found for the new baseline.

This hypothenule is computed, but may be measured during the dry season. From the exceslive rains that had fallen, the arm of a large tank had extended a confiderable way acrols the line; the angles for computing this distance, as well as those of the oblique directions, were the mean results of three different observations with the circular instrument; the bale at a level of the ground was computed.

Bund 1

Screen Print on paper, 22"x30" + Digital Plot

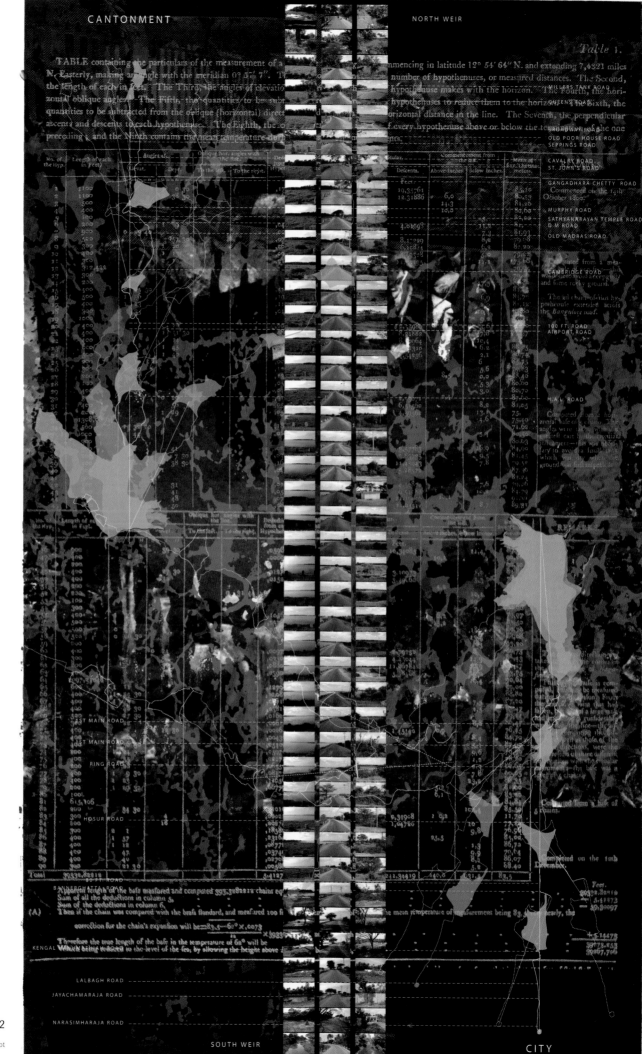

Bund 2

Screen Print on paper, 22"x30" + Digital Plot

DAY −3

DAY −2

DAY −1

DAY +1

DAY +2

DAY +3

DAY +4

DECCAN TRAVERSES

THE SURVEY
BASELINE
BUND
TANK
THOUSAND TANKS

95

TANK

The tanks of Bangalore were drawn by surveyors in 1791 with a clear delineation of bunds and collections of flows behind these lines that were inseparable or only tentatively separable from the lowlands of Bangalore's gently undulating terrain. Over the next century, surveyors developed a practice of representing tanks with definite boundaries rendered in blue.

Mrs. L.Bowring, wife of the chief commissioner of Mysore, on a carriage ride on the tableland in November 1868 soon after the rains — about the time of the year when Lambton's baseline was disrupted by the waters collected by the Belandur Bund — marvels at the sight of the many sheets of water: 'The sugar-cane and rice crops looked most flourishing in the low wet land under the great tanks, which have all the appearance of natural lakes. Many of these have been most skilfully constructed, giving proof that the natives knew something of engineering, long before English rule and public works were thought of'.[31] Her observations of what the locals call keres, echo those of Benjamin Heyne, the surgeon-naturalist who in 1800 took over the Sultan's garden known today as Lalbagh. 'Lakes, in the right sense of the word', he noted in his report to Colin Mackenzie, 'have nowhere been observed by me in this country but tanks or water reservoirs with artificial embankments are in great abundance'.[32]

Yet if tanks in their artificiality defy the idea of a lake, they confound the idea of a reservoir as well — 'a natural or artificial place where water is collected and stored for use'.[33] Tanks, however, collect earth: dry to wet to very wet earth. This earth is largely composed of clay running off the gneiss and granite surfaces of the tableland where it is formed by the hydrous alteration of rock. On the one hand, this clay is never without water. 'There are only two things in the universe', writes a contemporary naturalist, 'that require liquid water for their existence: organic life and clay'. On the other hand, he observes, water is never without clay. 'If you drop a particle of coarse sand in water, it will fall about four inches in one second. A particle of very fine clay, on the other hand, will take about 860 years to fall the same four inches'.[34] To see the dry bed of a tank is then not to see the absence of water but the presence of clay and silt, just as to see a full tank is perhaps not to see water alone but clay in suspension.

As collectors of earth in the lower reaches, tanks leave the soil in the higher reaches of the tableland more gravelly and sandy due to the washing away of the clay binder. In the vicinity of Bangalore, particularly toward the east, it also leaves the surface in the upper reaches lighter red as a result of the dissemination of ferric oxide. Captain Newbold, who crossed the peninsula at various latitudes in the 1840s making

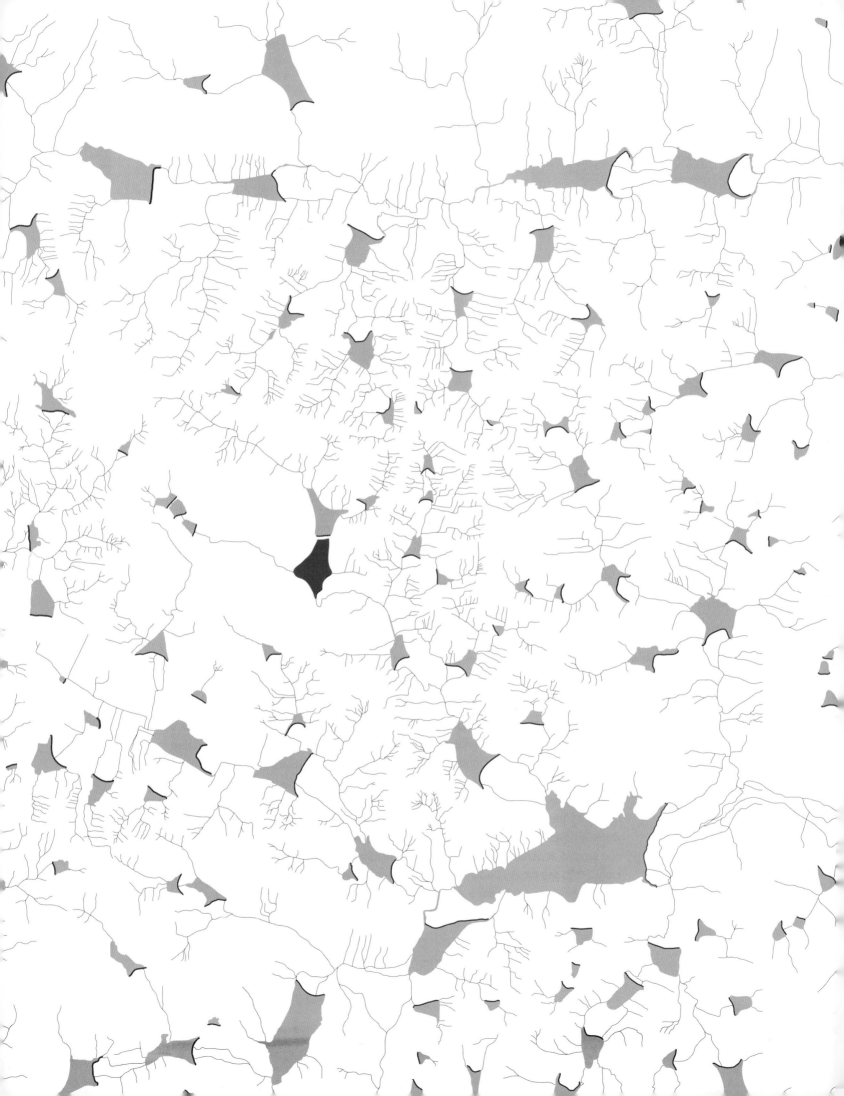

DECCAN TRAVERSES

THE SURVEY
BASELINE
BUND
TANK
THOUSAND TANKS

97

Lewis Rice, 'Bangalore'.

Mysore: A Gazetteer compiled for the Government of India,
(Westminster: Archibald Constable and Company, 1897)

The terrain of Bangalore from 1791 to the present reveals an infrastructure of tanks in a land where surface-runoffs are yet to form into rivers. Tanks as drawn in maps with lines that mark their edge and often rendered blue can be easily mistaken for lakes. This mode of representing tanks gives what are effectively impoundments of seasonal surface flows of material (water, silt, clay, etc.) a perennial presence of water.

observations on conditions of the ground and the underground, noticed the redness extending from Bangalore to the east. 'Covering the gneiss and granite', he writes, 'a reddish loam is usually found, varying from few inches to twenty feet in depth, containing beds of red clay, used in making tiles, bricks, &c.; the result evidently of the weathering of the granite gneiss, and hornblende rocks'. Red soil, geologists say today, is largely residual, the weathering of rock. But there is often in these parts an intermediate material with a high content of iron called laterite. Neither rock nor soil or perhaps both, laterite, they say, is the result of lateritisation, 'a disease from which no rock can escape, given the necessary climatic environment'. Triggered by 'an upper detrital layer of ferruginous debris', this disease or, as it is also described, decomposition, decay, even rotting, transforms crystalline rock into a porous and clay-like threshold to soil.[35]

The term laterite was coined by Francis Buchanan in 1801. He witnessed it 'in immense masses, without any appearance of stratification' on the west coast where it is 'placed over the granite that forms the basis of *Malayala*'. It is, he reports, 'full of cavities and pores, and contains a very large quantity of iron in the form of red and yellow ochres. In the mass, while excluded from air, it is so soft, that any iron instrument readily cuts it, and is dug up in square masses with a pick ax, and immediately cut into the shape wanted with a trowel, or large knife. It very soon after becomes as hard as brick, and resists the air and water much better than any bricks that I have seen in India'. It is, as if, quarrying laterite for building arrests the decay of the rock. Buchanan heard natives refer to it as brick-stone, its characteristic quality being that it is soft when beneath the ground and hardens on exposure, probably due to the drying out of its clay component though never completely. 'The most proper English name', for this material, he says, 'would be *Laterite* from *Lateritis*'. 'Later' is brick in Latin.[36]

On the eastern side of the Western Ghats, laterite is found in patches of high ground, caps formed and still forming with the 'in situ alteration' of the gneiss complex that comprises much of the Mysore Tableland. Laterite here is hardly used for building. Instead its clay component, washed into tanks in the lower reaches, is collected and moulded into shapes such as bricks, deities, pots, etc.

But if the tank is a source of much more than water, it is also a destination of much more than the clay coming off the higher reaches of the tableland. It takes in idols of Lord Ganesha on the tenth day of Ganesha Chaturthi, a festival which takes place at a time of the year when tanks 'have all the appearance of natural lakes'. The 'deity of the good harvest', moulded from clay, is immersed in the tank with a plea to return next year from a bigger tank. Before the next immersion, however, the waters must recede sufficiently to provide for the momentary consolidation of clay.

DECCAN TRAVERSES

THE SURVEY
BASELINE
BUND
TANK
THOUSAND TANKS

99

Rather than operating on a scale between full and empty, tanks operate between two ends of a clay economy — a bed that provides clay and a surface for a range of activities including bazaars, sports, games, fairs, etc. and a reservoir that provides water.

Bangalore's red earth in the low grounds — clay — comes largely from the laterisation of gneissic rock of the high grounds.

Tanks appear as lakes but only at a particular time of the year. However, tanks such as Ulsoor are often forced to maintain this appearance throughout the year. It was a tank when Cornwallis's army camped on its higher reaches in March 1791 and when Lt. Blakiston built the cantonment in the same area in 1807. It was a tank when Major Bevan witnessed the 'melancholy fate of three fine young officers who were drowned in the Ulsore tank'. Today it is held as a lake. This, however, does not stop the consolidation of its bed; it merely forces a massive dredging operation in place of a clay economy and an unsightly view in place of the seasonal use of a tank bed.

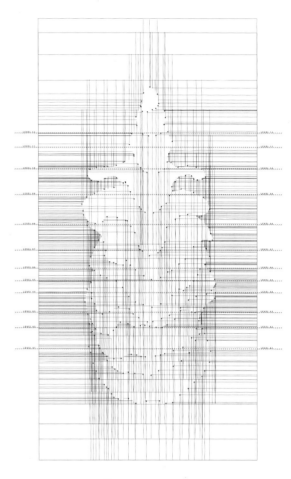

Horizontal sections through a Lord Ganesha idol made of the 'reddish indurated clay' eroded off the high grounds of the tableland, register the displacement of its form as it is eventually immersed in a tank.

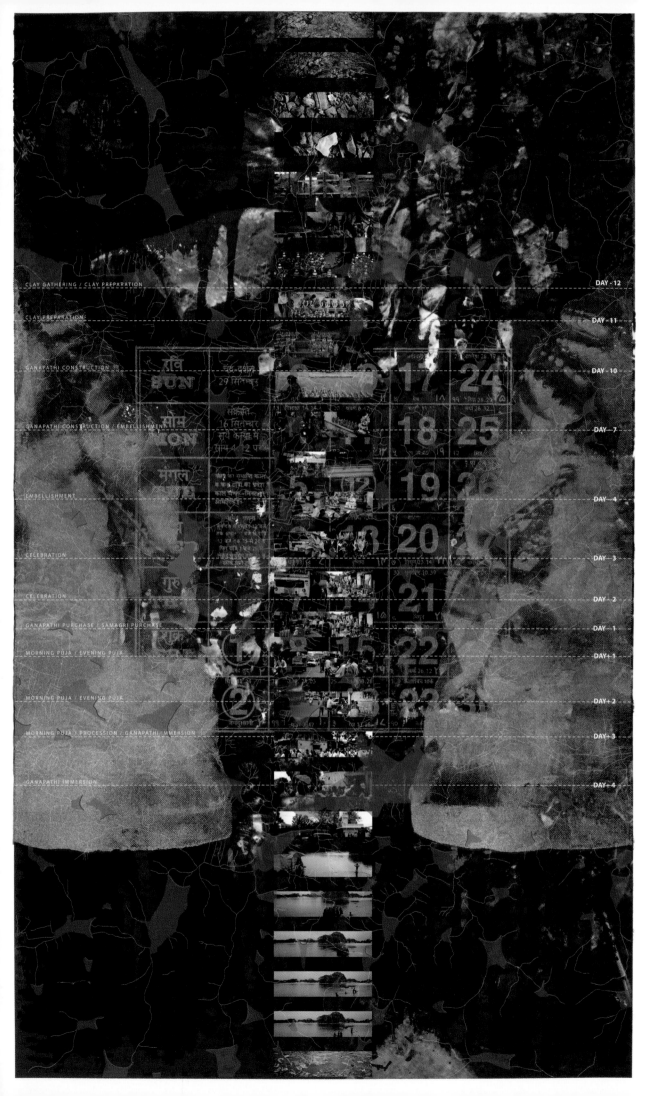

CLAY GATHERING / CLAY PREPARATION   DAY - 12

CLAY PREPARATION   DAY - 11

GANAPATHI CONSTRUCTION   DAY - 10

GANAPATHI CONSTRUCTION / EMBELLISHMENT   DAY - 7

EMBELLISHMENT   DAY - 4

CELEBRATION   DAY - 3

CELEBRATION   DAY - 2

GANAPATHI PURCHASE / SAMAGRI PURCHASE   DAY - 1

MORNING PUJA / EVENING PUJA   DAY+1

MORNING PUJA / EVENING PUJA   DAY+2

MORNING PUJA / PROCESSION / GANAPATHI IMMERSION   DAY+3

GANAPATHI IMMERSION   DAY+4

Tank 1

Screen Print on paper, 22"x30" + Digital Plot

Tank 2

Screen Print on paper, 22"x30" + Digital Plot

DECCAN TRAVERSES

THE SURVEY
BASELINE
BUND
TANK
THOUSAND TANKS

103

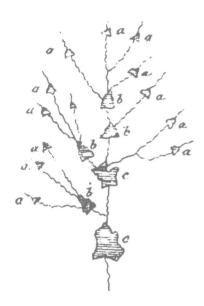

THOUSAND TANKS

Major Sankey, chief engineer of Mysore in the mid 1800s, saw tanks in a hierarchical system of flood control and water use. Major Sankey, 'Chief consideration in an Engineering point of view'.

Letter to the secretary to the commissioner for the Government of the Territories of His Highness the Rajah of Mysore, Dated 19 November 1866 [Karnataka State Archives, Bangalore]

Captain Newbold, in his traverses west to east through Bangalore in the early 1840s, suggested that the reddish loam containing beds of red clay used in making tiles, bricks, etc. that he saw in the vicinity of Bangalore was only a beginning. 'A similar formation', he observed, 'continues to Kolar'. It is another way of saying that to move east from Bangalore is to see streams increasingly suspended in favour of tanks and for much of the year water suspended in favour of earth. Indeed when Bangalore has looked for water it has turned west (and south) where the soil cover is thin and runoffs quickly turn into streams and rivers; for earth it turns east (and north). Here, the laterite caps in the higher reaches get more extensive while the tanks in the lower reaches become more abundant, culminating in a 'land of a thousand tanks' where a stream is an overflow rather than a flow and the tank is a way of life.

The land of a thousand tanks is largely the basin of the Palar, the flows of which, at least on the tableland, are as mysterious as its source. It is popularly believed to originate on Nandi Hill, thirty miles north of Bangalore. Here a stepped well marks its source. But the belief puzzled Lewis Rice as it would any geographer because the hill is separated from the Palar watershed by the South Pinakini into which the waters coming off the east side of the hill clearly flow. These are waters that empty into the Bay of Bengal fifty miles south of the mouth of the Palar. If Nandidroog 'be accepted as the source', Rice writes, 'it follows that the stream must at some point cross the S. Pinakini – a difficulty which the natives easily set aside by the hypothesis, for which there is no evidence, that it runs underground at that place'.[37] Perhaps the notion of underground is less suggestive of a link and more suggestive of a source spread across the earth of the Palar basin; an imminence best manifest in the unseen depth of a well on a sacred eminence.

But even as the underground explanation challenges the idea of an identifiable material source of the Palar, it also challenges the idea of an identifiable course often conceived in the case of rivers as a hierarchy of flows from tributaries to a main channel. Hierarchy of flows is how the British engineers perceived the Palar and consequently its thousand tanks. These catchments were seen as components in a hierarchical system

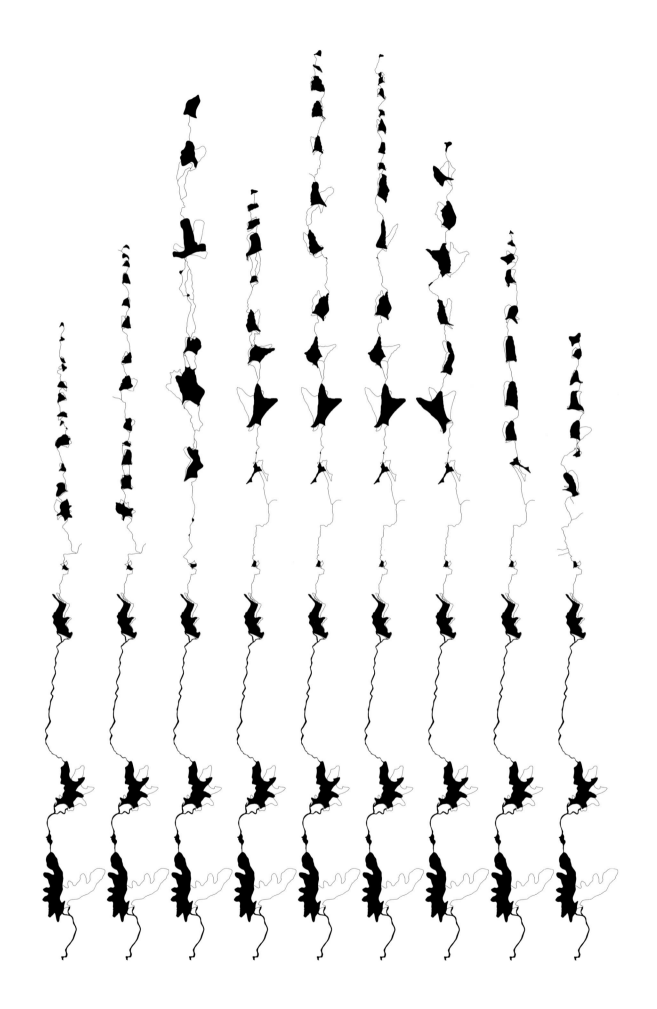

DECCAN TRAVERSES

THE SURVEY
BASELINE
BUND
TANK
THOUSAND TANKS

105

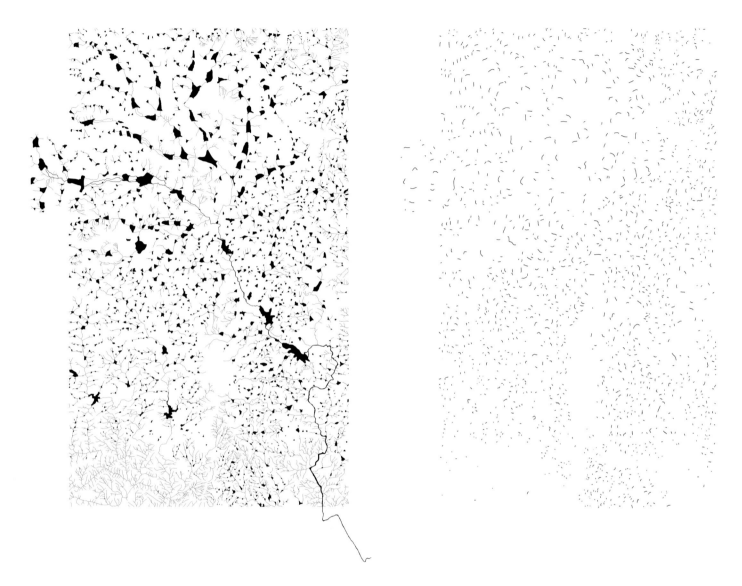

In the land of a Thousand Tanks, east of Bangalore, streams are overflows rather than flows and tanks are a way of life. Overflows point to a field of discrete lines that present bunds with sluices rather than to continuous flows from water body to water body.

Contrary to the engineer's view there is no dominant water course in the land of a thousand tanks. Instead there are many possible series reaching back from the 'thousandth tank' on the tableland via tenacious connections that are more political than physical, dependent on managed sluices more than natural sources. This thousandth tank is Ramsagar, the last recognised tank on the tableland before the waters of the Palar basin falls to the Carnatic, the land below the ghats.

of flood control and water use. Major Sankey, the chief engineer of Mysore, describes the system in general. 'Population taking possession of the high grounds, constructed the small tanks, *a*, *a*, *a*, *a*, and after these minor feeders had been thus brought under regulation, they then threw bunds up lower down forming other and larger tanks *b*, *b*, *b*, *b*, and eventually first class tanks *c*, *c*, further down still in the main stream'. If *c* had to survive a flood, it was important that the bund of *a* be maintained. When a flood did occur, Sankey observes, the natives got it wrong. They fixed the *c*'s as they were 'usually connected with large communities' while the *a*'s were left in the 'breached condition' maintaining the extra pressure on *c*. It was imperative to him that government care for the system.[38] But perhaps the underground link of the Palar with Nandi is here less suggestive of a main water course, and more a multiplicity of courses, each equal in its potential. This is particularly possible when one considers that water in this terrain moves as overflows rather than flows. Overflow points to bunds and their sluices rather than to water collection; to the complexities and multiplicities of human agency and interactions rather than to quantities of water; to negotiable flux rather than to controllable flood.

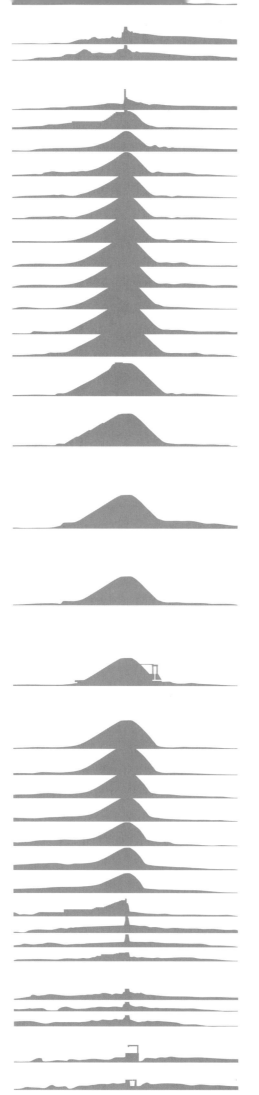

The Ramsagar bund is a mile-long line with two sluices and a plug. The tanks above it number 999; the tanks below it number 0. It makes the water and red soil that collect against its forty feet high embankment the Thousandth Tank.

The rock-sculpted Nagas, prevalent across the shifting surface of the land of thousand tanks, are both marks of firm ground and reminders of the source of red soil in the crystalline rocks of the 'higher reaches'.

DECCAN TRAVERSES

THE SURVEY
BASELINE
BUND
TANK
THOUSAND TANKS

107

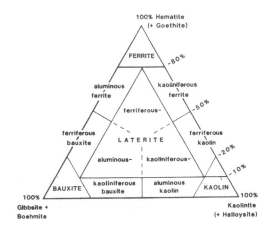

Red soil is largely residual rock. In this land, however, there is an intermediate material that is neither rock nor soil. It is the result of a transformation of crystalline rock into a material that Francis Buchanan in 1801 described as 'full of cavities and pores, and contains a very large quantity of iron in the form of red and yellow ochres.' This material is laterite.

In the land of a thousand tanks there is occasionally more than clay and silt in the water as Lt. John Warren discovered in 1802; there is gold. Drawing the eastern boundary of the Rajah's dominion for Mackenzie's *Mysore Survey*, Warren was told by a native that 'in the prosperous years when the gods favoured the Zillah of Cargoory with an ample harvest, grains of gold were now and then found in the ears of paddy, which grows under the tank lying north of that village'. He says that he treated it as a fabrication at the time but 'began to conceive that there might be more truth in the story than I at first imagined'. Prosperous years translated into abundant water, flooded fields in the lower reaches, and depositions on young plants, which 'carry up now and then a grain of gold in its growth'. Investigating the soil of water courses in the higher reaches and finding gold dust, Warren concluded that gold was coming off 'certain small hills, consisting of deep red clay, mostly flat at the top, and covered with a sort of conker stone, which formed, as it were a cover to the hill'. But even as the water courses were leading him to a tract of hills, he had found a group of people who mined for gold in the dry season when the earth was stable. They chose a place 'with a knowledge which they pretend to have of the promising appearance of the ground at the surface, and partly from the idea which they entertain, that the tract over which a peacock has been observed to fly and alight, is that of a vein of gold'. They then dug down and when they 'hit on a vein of ore' they would 'strike out galleries and follow it up until it is explored'. The ore itself was contained in 'a kind of quartz, decayed in many parts, and which . . . exhibits a variety of colours, from deep crimson to bright orange. These colours are (as I am assured by the miners) the marks which guide them in making a selection, as they pretend to have found from experience, that where the stone breaks without exhibiting any colour but its natural one, it contains little or no ore'.[39]

The decaying and eroding higher reaches, Warren surmised, was an 'impregnated tract I take to be about 45 miles, extending north to south'. Geologists would in time identify this ridge as the surfacing of a part of the Kolar Schist belt. It is an eighty-kilometre long 'patchwork of different terrane elements' within the vastness of the peninsula gneiss complex three-billion-year-old reworked terrane of granite and gneiss that dominates much of the tableland. In the land of a thousand tanks, maps reveal the presence of this island of welded materials, which averages six kilometres in width, by the absence of tanks. But a more contentious indicator today is the Kolar Gold Fields, an amalgam of corporate entities that grew into a settlement on this ridge beginning eight decades after Warren sent in his report to the East India Company directors. Where Warren saw pits thirty feet deep, these entities chased lodes, particularly the Champion Lode discovered by Captain Plummer in 1883 that

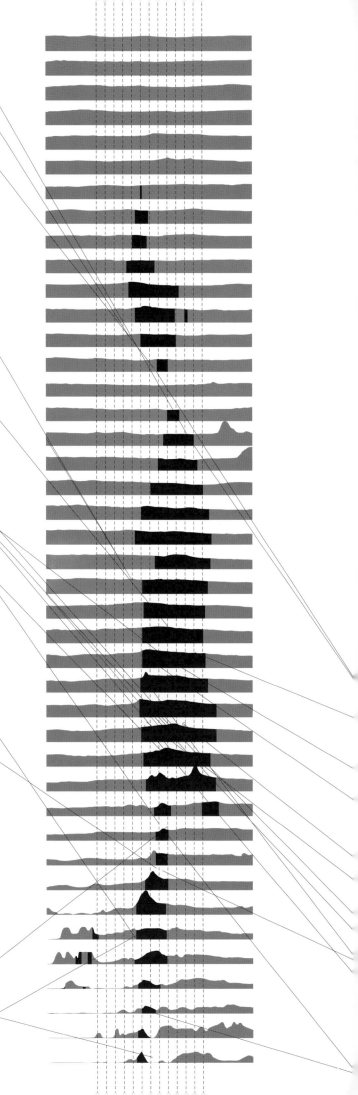

runs in widths as much as five feet, to a depth of three miles. It is one of the deepest penetrations into the earth. Evidently what lateritization exposed at the surface was the tip of a lode that Warren rightly conceived 'to branch out any where under the impregnated superior stratum'.[40]

The mines are closed today, largely flooded by the water that was kept out of active mines but allowed to collect in the abandoned shafts to supply the needs of the town and the processes of mining. It is as if in this terrain, which stands out conspicuously for its lack of tanks and a surface that is 'rocky and sterile, and unfavourable to the growth of trees',[41] the land of a thousand tanks turned down into the earth along the space left by the excavated gold lodes via a labyrinth of shafts.

DECCAN TRAVERSES

THE SURVEY
BASELINE
BUND
TANK
THOUSAND TANKS

109

Attempts to capitalise on the gold of KGF proved futile until Captain Plummer discovered the 'Champion lode' in 1883. This lode, shown in its longitudinal section, runs at an angle of 45° and in widths upto five feet, to a depth of more than three miles.
Geological Society of India, 'Kolar Gold Field, Longitudinal Section (Champion Lode System)', *Gold Mining Industry in India*, Memoir-1, 1963.

The Kolar Gold Fields is an amalgam of corporate entities as much as the schist belt beneath is a 'patchwork of different terrane elements' including gold lodes.
Lewis Rice, 'Plan of Kolar Gold Fields', Mysore: *A Gazetteer compiled for the Government of India*, vol. II, (Westminster: Archibald Constable and Company, 1897).

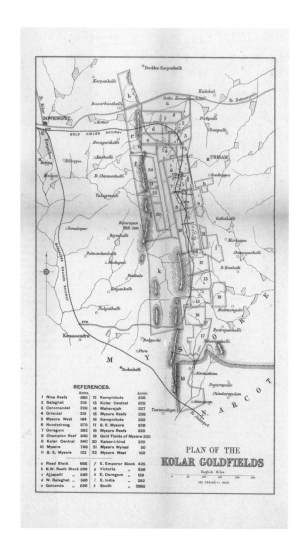

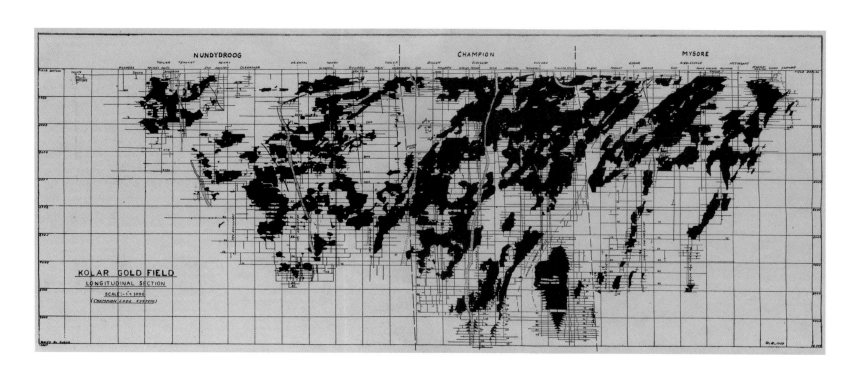

Thousand Tanks 1

Screen Print on paper, 22"x30" + Digital Plot

Thousand Tanks 2

Screen Print on paper, 22"x30" + Digital Plot

Earth 1

Screen Print on paper, 22"x30" + Digital Plot

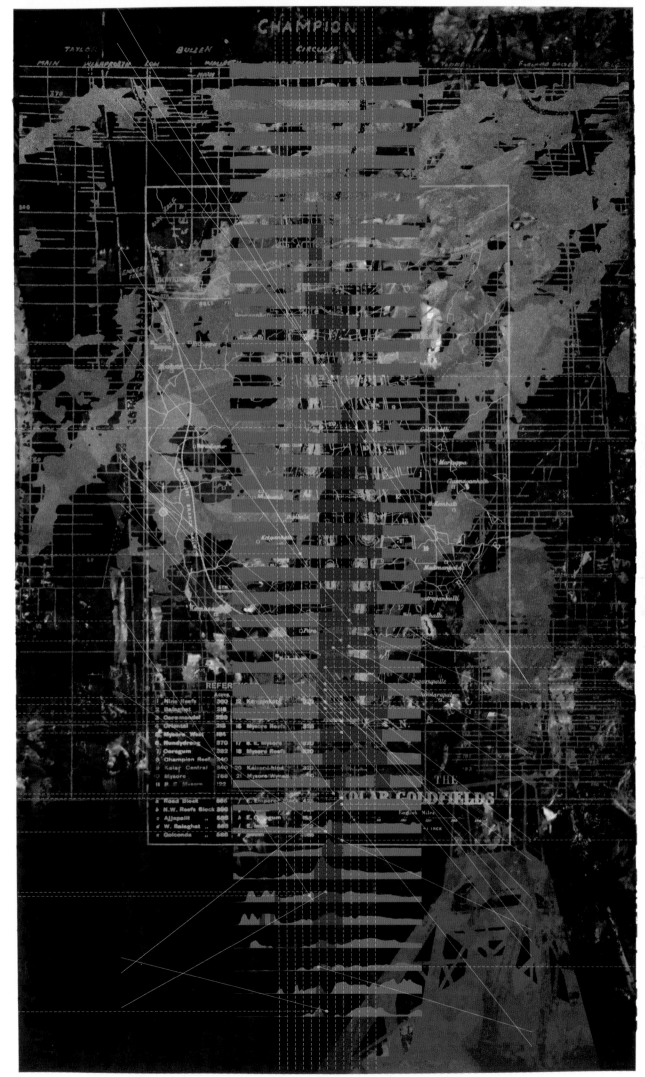

Earth 2

Screen Print on paper, 22"x30" + Digital Plot

THE PICTURE

HIGH GROUND

MANTAP

OUTCROP

FOURTH ISLAND

DECCAN TRAVERSES

THE PICTURE
HIGH GROUND
MANTAP
OUTCROP
FOURTH ISLAND

119

THE PICTURE

In 1799, Thomas Hope, an interior designer and avid collector of antiquities commissioned a painting by Thomas Daniell for the drawing room of his Duchess Street mansion in London. The mansion was furnished with his own designs and collections that sought 'a synthesis of all styles, of all religions'.[1] The drawing room, he writes in a text on the mansion, was 'principally fitted up for the reception of four large pictures, executed by Mr. Daniell, and representing buildings in India, of Moorish architecture'. Ultimately only three were hung. Two are believable places. The third, however, reveals not only the power of artists practising picturesque art to construct places, but also their ability — which has become so commonplace and taken for granted today — to isolate, extract and assemble objects with the eye alone. In the bottom right corner can be discerned two unique objects of the Gavi Gangadhareshwara temple complex in Bangalore: Shiva's monolithic granite trident and Vishnu's chakra. On the left is the towering gateway to Kailasanatha temple at Tiruchengodu on the South Pennar. Between the monoliths and the gateway are various objects including a Muslim grave, a temple tank, people going about their tasks, and a procession led by musicians and an adorned elephant. The scene leads down to a water's edge. Across the water, evidently the Yamuna, is the Taj Mahal set against a backdrop of hills containing some of the rock-cut temples of Ellora. The highest hill is crowned by a mantap, a four-columned structure commonly seen on the granite outcrops on the tableland, holding a statue of Nandi. To many at the time, particularly those who had never been to India, the composition presents a believable place, existing as depicted. To those who could construct a correspondence between Daniell's artwork and the Indian subcontinent, the painting was probably a travelogue, a journey already undertaken.

Thomas Daniell spent seven and a half years travelling the subcontinent accompanied by his nephew William Daniell. They landed in Calcutta in 1786 where for two years they painted scenes of the rising Company town to raise funds for a journey to the northwest. Following the defeat of Tipu Sultan in 1792 they came to Madras from where they embarked on a trip that began with an excursion onto the Mysore Tableland. They reached Bangalore on 30 April 1792, returning three days later to the Carnatic via Hosur, commenting on the nakedness and dangers of the country. Following a productive period in the Carnatic and then in Bombay

area where they were captivated by the rock cut temples of the region, they returned to England in 1793. Their collection of scenes as well as catalogue of objects and events (side-skips) which they maintained in parallel served them for many years, the assemblage in Hope's drawing room being one of many hundred paintings, aquatints, and sketches credited to them.[2] They published 144 aquatints including two scenes from the hill southward of Bangalore, in one of which can be detected the chakra and trident that feature in Hope's commission.

Daniell's *Large Composition of Architecture representing some of the most celebrated Hindoo and Moorish Buildings in India,* as his assemblage for Hope is called, provides a glimpse into the world of picturesque art. This art, a nascent practice in Europe, chose to represent landscape as a subject in itself. The idea embraced by the picturesque, according to Sidney Robinson, is that a work of art was not just a picture of what is real and therefore a representation; it is *like* a picture of what is real and therefore admits the possibility of misrepresentation.[3] The admission raises questions not just about an aesthetic and the artist's choices and freedoms, but also the disciplining of activities such as travel, architecture and landscape design and, indeed, what some say was at least for a while 'the English way of seeing'.[4] In the case of Thomas Daniell, however, his presence with other artists on the Mysore Tableland, a place largely unseen by people in Europe, raises questions not just about representation and misrepresentation but presentation.

In their brief time in Bangalore, which they found 'remarkable for the frequent appearance of the remains of ancient Hindoo architecture', the Daniells were drawn to a high ground south of the fort.[5] Here, writes William Daniell, they 'Spent the whole day at the Hills to the Sd. [southward] of Bangalore, where we collected several Scenes, among them a Distt. View of Severn Droog (or the Hill of Destruction) & one of the Fort of Bangalore'.[6] While the distant horizon mattered to them, the objects on the hill mattered more. The trident and chakra of the *Composition* were two of many objects that they recorded that day.

Thomas Daniell's *Large Composition of Architecture representing some of the most celebrated Hindoo and Moorish Buildings in India*, painted for Thomas Hope's drawing room. The painting assembles a number of scenes and artefacts that the Daniells captured on their travels through India. The trident of Shiva and chakra of Vishnu from their drawing of Gavi Gangadhareshwara temple in Bangalore, which the Daniells visited on 1 May 1792 are seen on the right.

[Private Collection, London]

DECCAN TRAVERSES

THE PICTURE
HIGH GROUND
MANTAP
OUTCROP
FOURTH ISLAND

121

Thomas Hope's illustration of the drawing room of his Duchess Street mansion in London. Although the room was fitted to receive four pictures of Thomas Daniell, the drawing shows three paintings by Daniell and a fourth (on the left wall) by Giovanni Panini of ruins in Rome. The *Composition,* with elements from Bangalore, is on the right wall.

Thomas Hope, *Household Furniture and Interior Decoration* (New York: Dover Publications)

TOP

Thomas and William Daniell 'Entrance to a Hindoo Temple, near Bangalore'. The painting presented the Gavi Gangadhareshwara temple in Bangalore to a wide audience in Europe through the publication of their work.

Oriental Scenery (London, 1799), Plate XVIII. [Yale Center for British Art, Paul Mellon Collection].

ABOVE

James Hunter, 'A Moorish Mosque at Bangalore'. His presentation of the Gavi Gangadhareshwara temple in Bangalore (which he or his publishers mistake for a mosque) appears less accurate in a world of art driven toward photographic representation.

Francis William Blagdon, *A Brief History of Ancient and Modern India* (London, 1802-05). [Yale Center for British Art, Paul Mellon Collection]

They were, as they still are, located at the entrance to the Gavi Gangadhareshwara temple which 'has a very striking effect from the size and singularity of the mythological sculpture wrought in stone, which appears in the court before the Temple. On the right is the trident of Maha-deva, and not far from it are two examples of the Chackra of Vishnoo, supported perpendicularly. Here are also pillars and altars for various religious purposes'. The temple itself, 'having now no establishment for religious duty, is accordingly deserted'. In fact, the whole hill with scattered objects besides the Gavi Gangadhareshwara temple, including another 'temple, but at present without an idol . . . the Chackra or Discus of Vishnoo placed horizontally, supported by a pillar, . . . a pavilion very neatly executed, . . . a stone pillar', presented an air of abandonment.[7] It was too soon after the end of the Third Mysore War, which began in earnest in what the English described as 'ravines' south of the fort with a skirmish between Colonel Fullarton's scouting troops and Tipu Sultan's men on 6 March 1791.[8] And it was perhaps too early to know if the abandonment would lead to ruin or re-occupation.

Ruins, however, were coveted subjects of picturesque art, or perhaps it was the act of ruining, returning to nature, roughening. Reverend William Gilpin, a contemporary of Thomas Daniell, asks artists to 'use the mallet instead of the chisel: we must beat down one half of it [a building], deface the other, and throw the mutilated members around in heaps'. In more general terms, roughness rather than smoothness which Edmund Burke used to characterise the idea of the beautiful distinguishes the picturesque landscape from beautiful landscape. To search for the picturesque was to look for the 'worn-out cart-horse, the cow, the goat, or the ass; whose harder lines, and rougher coats, exhibit more the graces of the pencil' instead of the horse with 'the elegance of his form; the stateliness of his tread; the spirit of all his motions; and the glossiness of his coat'. It was to reject the lawn for the 'piece of broken ground'. 'Plant rugged oaks', Gilpin said, 'instead of flowering shrubs: break the edges of the walk: give it the rudeness of a road; mark it with wheel-tracks; and scatter around a few stones, and brushwood; in a word instead of making the whole smooth, make it rough; and you make it also picturesque'.[9] The picturesque subject or scene characterised by 'irregularity', 'ruggedness', and 'variety' — was found in England; but it was more often contrived, giving the art a projective or critical edge rather than a representational cast; making it a practice that easily found its way into architecture and garden design. Contrivance was seen not just on aesthetic grounds but as an act of assisting nature, returning things to a natural, or at least more natural state. 'The picturesque eye', Gilpin noted, 'abhors art; and delights solely in nature: and . . .

art abounds with *regularity*, which is only another name for *smoothness*; and the images of nature with *irregularity*, which is only another name for *roughness*'.[10] Ultimately picturesque art situates the viewer between the artist's rendition of a place and the ideal picture leaving one to decide as Robinson puts it, 'whether one is being misled, entertained, or challenged'.[11] In other words, picturesque art was seen and judged within the limits of the picture frame.

However, with picturesque art on the Indian subcontinent, to which few from Europe had travelled, art escaped the frame; the artist's work here was understood back home as a presentation of what is seen rather than a representation of what should be seen. The principles of picturesque art, which by the turn of the eighteenth century had been 'communicated to every amateur like an infection through the agency of drawing masters, and instruction manuals',[12] was overwhelmed by the need to know what places actually looked like. This need was shared by artists themselves competing with one another for visual accuracy; those curious to know what places looked like in distant lands where the English were getting increasingly involved; those wanting to be reminded of places they had visited; and, most importantly, those communicating military intelligence and statistical information about a place. It was of course possible that the land was intrinsically picturesque. A land that was a source of wonder, fear and horror to European travellers in the past, with 'rampant vegetation demonstrating "disorder" and "irregularity"', with customs (like sati) that made little sense, and with 'much maligned monsters' in buildings and sculpture, could hardly have conformed to the smoothness that Gilpin described the picturesque as reacting against.[13] India, a commentator notes, 'unfolded before the artist's eye all of the elements that he formerly had to conjure up from imagination at home'.[14] In other words, the Indian subcontinent was not strange or different as much as rough in the extreme. One of the many handbooks emerging in the 1800s, encouraging travel to India, makes this evident. 'India abounds with objects of interest. It presents every imaginable variety of scenery. . . It is rich in historical associations, and there is scarce a hill which is not crowned with the picturesque ruins of some old fortress, little known or altogether unvisited by Europeans, but bound up in the native mind with many a strange tale and legend. In Europe the small remains of some ruined cloister, or the mouldering walls of a solitary castle are sought out with eager interest; but India is a land of ruined cities, and in one of these the antiquities of a whole European province might be collected'.[15]

The Daniells certainly placed themselves in the realm of the real in India, presenting real places rather than representing the ideal picture. The *Composition* was an exception in a body of work that they saw in a scientific rather than aesthetic context, fuelled as Thomas Daniell noted, 'by a race of students with no rapacity but for lettered relics: by naturalists, whose cruelty extends not to one human inhabitant; by philosophers extirpations of error, and the diffusion of truth. It remains for the artist to claim his part in these guiltless spoliations'.[16] The Daniells were constantly calling attention to a correspondence between artists' renderings and places that they visited. 'Compared [William] Hodges view of the fort with the original & which like all his others is exceedingly faulty' or 'could not find the view of one of the Gauts which Hodges has made an Aquatinta print of, there not being one of them like what he has represented'.[17] But Hodges, a pioneer among landscape artists who travelled to India in 1780, begged the comparison. He saw his own work as descriptive, 'closer to that of a historian than to a poet', his 'genius and fancy' submitted 'to the strictest veracity'.[18] In the preface to *Travels in India*, he describes his work as 'plain representations of what I observed on the spot, expressed in the simple garb of truth, without the smallest embellishment from fiction, or from fancy'. Like the Daniells who followed him, he saw himself filling a void in information.

The Daniells' own claim to accuracy lay to a large degree in their use of the *camera obscura*, the predecessor to the photographic camera. A reviewer of their work writes: 'The execution of these drawings is

DECCAN TRAVERSES

THE PICTURE
HIGH GROUND
MANTAP
OUTCROP
FOURTH ISLAND

123

On one hill south of the Bangalore Fort, the Daniells found a number of architectural curiosities which they 'captured' in several pencil sketches (and water colour washes) using a *camera obscura* on 1 May 1792. Three are shown here all titled 'Temple near Bangalore'.

British Library, IOR, WD 220, WD 223, WD 221 [By permission of the British Library]

indeed masterly. . . . Every thing is drawn with the most astonishing accuracy. The animals, trees, and plants, are studies for the naturalist'.[19] 'Their accuracy', Tillotson says, 'was something that came to be relied on and asserted even by those who were not in a position to compare their pictures with the actual scenes'.[20] But all the while the picturesque context of their work was noted. An anonymous reviewer in the *British Critic* in 1805 says, 'The plates are at once a profound study for the architect or antiquary and a source of delight to the lover of the picturesque'.[21] Accuracy continues to be a measure of the Daniells' work. Historians and enthusiasts journey in their footsteps verifying their work; finding that the scene of their pictures has changed or that the artists purposefully displaced the scene, or that the scene is just as they painted it.[22]

The scientific context and its measure of accuracy, however, take the picturesque work of art beyond the scene to the objects that comprise it. These objects, as much as the view, defined a place. Alternatively, objects were placed or displaced to make the scene. The Daniells maintained a catalogue of pictures of various objects with notes and measurements that they could insert at will into scenes. Increasingly, however, objects were being pictured as wholes in themselves, elements of 'the face of the country' and subjects of various empirical sciences that were staking their domain at the time. Plants, animals, rocks, buildings, clothing, people, etc., were being documented, conveying what a thing looked like while adding to a larger comprehension of place. Thus Charles Gold, for example, a captain in the Madras Army in Mysore in 1800, concentrated his efforts on portraying Indian costumes and objects of street life. Francis Buchanan and Colin Mackenzie employed artists in their survey of Tipu Sultan's former dominions. Surveyors were trained in the skills and principles of picturesque art as a way of documenting intelligence. A number of surveyors — Alexander Allen and Robert Colebrooke among others — published and marketed their work on the Mysore Tableland as picturesque art while a number of artists held their work up to scientific scrutiny.

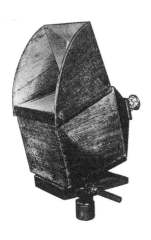

The Daniells claimed accuracy on the basis of their use of the *camera obscura*, the pin-hole camera and the predecessor to the photographic camera.

But even as the picture was conveying fact, comprehension and knowledge, it was communicating autonomy. The '"singularity" of objects was an important aspect of the picturesque', writes Mildred Archer in her work on the Daniells, the word singularity implying less an aesthetic uniqueness and more the ability to isolate, categorise, and, above all, transplant things.[23] It enabled the Daniells, drawn by the 'singularity of the mythological sculpture wrought in stone' on the hills southward of Bangalore, to place and displace things in Thomas Hope's commission. However, the things that they singled out did not just get assembled in surrealist fantasies such as the *Composition*; they were more seriously assembled in classification schemes, disciplines, myths, theories, systems, and practices by naturalists, historians, architects, archaeologists and indeed, ordinary people.

DECCAN TRAVERSES

THE PICTURE
HIGH GROUND
MANTAP
OUTCROP
FOURTH ISLAND

125

Distant View of SAVAN-DROOG *in Mysore*
from the last side

HIGH GROUND

The artist, in search of the picturesque, was encouraged to seek nature or 'return things to a natural state'. The droogs of the Mysore Tableland were curiosities that required little, if any, return. These 'natural' fortresses were subjects of war and of art in 1791-92 when Cornwallis's army, based in Bangalore, fought for possession of the Mysore Tableland. Colin Mackenzie, *Southeast View of Savandroog.*

British Library, IOR WD 573 [By permission of the British Library]

No sooner had they climbed upon the tableland on 22 April 1792, than the Daniells were drawn to the summits of its hills. 'We reached the Top of the Gaut in about three hours', writes William Daniell in his diary. 'On the Top of a hill to the left of the road near Naigengherry appeared something like buildings but so very singular that we walked up to examine them — they proved to be buildings but of a very uncommon form indeed — they were unlike any we had ever seen, built merely of large slabs of hard Granite — made several Sketches of them'.[24] Some of the hills of the tableland were accumulations of boulders; many were 'immense masses of naked stone'.[25] They were evidently an immediate attraction to most artists, whether they were professionals like the Daniells, route surveyors or ordinary soldiers. But as in the Daniells' case, this attraction did not begin with the hill as much as the architecture on them which ranged from simple four-columned structures crowned with sikaras called mantapams or mantaps, to forts that consumed whole hills making them 'droogs'. Robert Home, an artist who accompanied Cornwallis's army, describes a droog: 'This stupendous fortress', he says, 'enjoys such advantages from nature, as to need little assistance from art; though art seems to have neglected nothing to render it absolutely impregnable. It is a vast mountain of rock'.[26]

Architecture was in the nature of the droog, in the steep rock faces as much as in the steps, gates and (minimal) walls, in the stark juxtaposition of rock and the plains from which it sprung. That these droogs were first seen and drawn during the Third Mysore War when the whole hill appeared to resist and when their height and slope appeared more as obstacles than nature's grandeur, went a long way in projecting their artificiality. It is not surprising that route surveyors who painted them often described them by height and circumference at the base as if the latter was their line of detachment. Captain Newbold of the East India Company's Madras Army presents this objectivity in the 1840s. 'Every traveller, who has ascended the Ghauts, is struck by the singular appearance . . . of detached hills, and clusters of hills, starting up abruptly from the surface of the flat plains spread before him, with little or no tali, presenting a *coup d'œil* which has caused the not inapt comparison of a table with tea-cups here and there reversed on its surface. These hills are usually naked masses of gneiss or granite'.[27]

While the droog positioned the artist at a distance, presenting itself in its abruptness and entirety, and consuming his horizon, most other hills, like the one near Naigengherry, beckoned the artist to view their architectural curiosities against the distant horizon of a country that Benjamin Heyne said belied the idea of a tableland. 'The Mysore country, above the Ghauts', he says, 'is often called the Table Land, a denomination very little descriptive of its appearance; as it is by no means plain or flat, but in some parts mountainous, and everywhere undulating'.[28] Every once in a while, however, a collection of oddities, like the droog, were all consuming of the frame of the picture. This was the case with the hills 'southward of Bangalore'. Even though the Daniells 'collected several Scenes' here, it is their paintings of the collection of objects — the temples, chakras, mantaps, trident — seen against the hill itself that found a place in *Oriental Scenery*. One object, however, resisted the frame, 'the temple in which there is', William Daniel writes, 'the statue of a large Bull carved out of the Solid Rock which measures twelve feet from the top of his head to the bottom of the Chest'.[29] The sitting bull, worshipped as Nandi, the vehicle of Shiva, was the sculpted summit of one of the hills.

The Daniells sketched a glimpse of the Nandi as they saw it through the doorway of the temple, but drew no context in which to picture it. They could not position themselves (and their *camera obscura*) at a distance without losing the bull to the interior and darkness of the temple. They drew a part plan of the structure around the bull, the elevation of one of the many columns that surrounded the bull, and 'a Stone Pillar between thirty & forty ft. in height', in front of the temple all on one sheet of paper. It was more like a number of attempts to capture this object that emerged from the ground like a droog but refused to present itself in its entirety, than the 'accurate' and 'commanding' view they were used to presenting.

In the Bull Temple, the Daniells faced more than a scene; they faced a source. An inscription below the right fore leg of Nandi declares that the waters of the Vrishabhavati originate here. These waters join the Kaveri through the Arkavati. As a source, the presence of Nandi is acknowledged through the ritual of circumambulation rather than the distant view. The structure enveloping it ensures it is its own horizon.

The Nandi Bull emerges from a hill that is a rise on a ridge of a tableland that Heyne described as 'everywhere undulating'. This ridge begins at the foot of Nandidurg, a well-known droog fifty kilometres to the north. It runs via the Bull Temple and down to the east coast. It separates two watersheds — the Arkavati and the S. Pinakini.[30] Their waters flow into the Bay of Bengal through the Kaveri and the Ponnaiyar respectively. This ridge is, however, not a simple line of high points; it is a line of the highest origins of flows. These flows can be made to run one way or another with the subtlest modification of the surface. The ridge, in other words, is an ambiguous high ground. Kempegowda I chose to begin Bangalore on it in 1537, a mile north of the Bull Temple, as if to take command of its ambiguity.

DECCAN TRAVERSES

THE PICTURE
HIGH GROUND
MANTAP
OUTCROP
FOURTH ISLAND

127

HOOLIOOR-DROOG.

SAWEN-DROOG, from the N.

NORTH VIEW of SAVENDROOG from MAUGREE.

SOUTH EAST VIEW of OLIAM DROOG.

SOUTH WEST VIEW of GOTRADROOG.

DECCAN TRAVERSES

THE PICTURE
HIGH GROUND
MANTAP
OUTCROP
FOURTH ISLAND

129

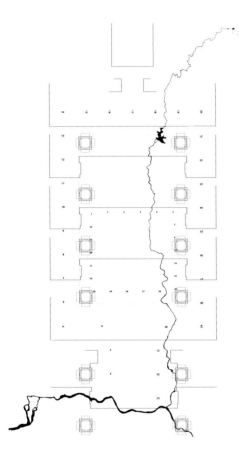

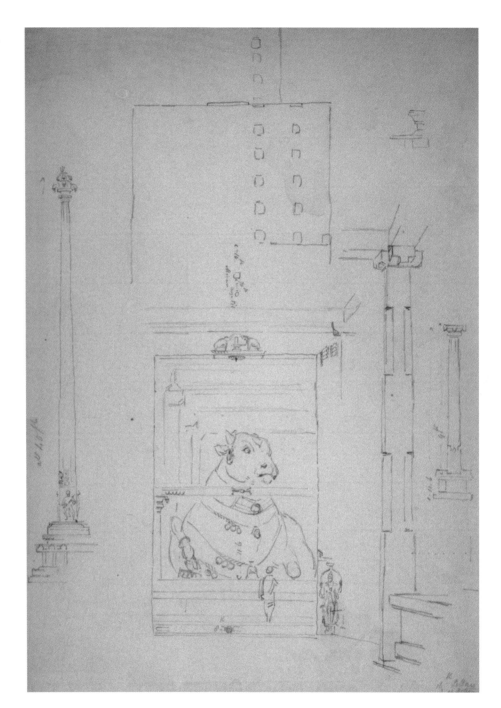

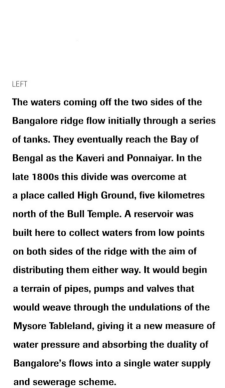

LEFT

The waters coming off the two sides of the
Bangalore ridge flow initially through a series
of tanks. They eventually reach the Bay of
Bengal as the Kaveri and Ponnaiyar. In the
late 1800s this divide was overcome at
a place called High Ground, five kilometres
north of the Bull Temple. A reservoir was
built here to collect waters from low points
on both sides of the ridge with the aim of
distributing them either way. It would begin
a terrain of pipes, pumps and valves that
would weave through the undulations of the
Mysore Tableland, giving it a new measure of
water pressure and absorbing the duality of
Bangalore's flows into a single water supply
and sewerage scheme.

The Nandi Bull is a celebration of the rock
outcrop, a sculpted summit enclosed
by a pavilion on eight columns and a
circumambulatory. This summit is part of
the surface west of the Bangalore ridge,
the rugged slopes of which drain into the
Vrishabhavati said to originate beneath
the Nandi. These waters join
the Arkavati, which connects with the
Kaveri at Sangam.

Thomas Daniell and William Daniell, *Sculpture of Nandi
in a temple near Bangalore (Mysore) and adjacent
monolithic pillar.* 1 May 1792. 'In one of the Temples on
the Hill', writes William Daniell on 1 May 1792, 'is the
statue of a large Bull carved out of the Solid Rock which
measures twelve feet from the top of his head to the
bottom of the Chest. Near to the Temple is a Stone Pillar
between thirty & forty ft. in height'.

British Library, IOR, WD 219 [By permission of the British Library]

High Ground 1

Screen Print on paper, 22"x30" + Digital Plot

High Ground 2

Screen Print on paper, 22"x30" + Digital Plot

DECCAN TRAVERSES

THE PICTURE
HIGH GROUND
MANTAP
OUTCROP
FOURTH ISLAND

133

MANTAP

In the nineteenth century travellers to Bangalore were told that to 'obtain some of the best glimpses . . . of the beautiful surroundings of Bangalore', they would need to seek the high grounds marked by 'lookouts'. Four of these lookouts are protected monuments. A plaque at each site reads: 'This is one of the four Watch Towers said to have been built by the famous Kempe Gowda of Magadi 1521-1569 and marks the limits to which it was predicted that the town of Bangalore would extend'.

In a land where the 'valleys are generally broad and open, the gradients of the rivers low, and the whole surface of the country presents the gently undulating aspect characteristic of an ancient land surface', even a low rise is a coveted place.[31] British surveyors in the early nineteenth century singled out these rises in maps of Bangalore with hachures, i.e., lines indicating relief. A few of them were marked with the name, 'lookout house'. A writer in 1895 describes these lookout houses as 'sentry-box shaped constructions of brick and mortar, on four pillars of grey granite on various hills, which were formerly Tippoo Sultan's military "lookouts". Wherever on the Mysore plateau Tippoo carried his ruthless warfare, he invariably built these coigns of vantage, and benefited exceedingly by them in all his daring exploits'. At the turn of the nineteenth century it meant that to 'obtain some of the best glimpses . . . of the beautiful surroundings of Bangalore, the visitor should first seek these lookouts'.[32]

Lewin Bowring, chief commissioner of Mysore in 1850-60s, presents these four-pillared structures differently, as limits rather than coigns of vantage. 'According to popular tradition', he says, 'the city is destined to still further expansion. On some of the eminences in the vicinity are picturesque little temples, called "Mantapams", which are assigned as the future limits of the place, two of them being far beyond the inhabited quarters'.[33] Lewis Rice, the director of Public Instruction, articulates the official position in the first state Gazetteer of 1877. He writes, 'At each of the cardinal points [of Bangalore] is an old watchtower, which marks, it is said, the limits to which it was predicted the town would extend. The prophecy has now been more than fulfilled'. Archaeologists would assert that these watchtowers were built, not by Tipu Sultan, but two centuries before him by Kempegowda II, the son of the founder of Bangalore.

But whether as lookouts or limits, the watchtowers are icons, drawing attention to something beyond themselves. As limits and cardinal points, they allude to an origin and centre largely supposed to be the two-square-kilometre walled entity or pettah drawn by surveyors in 1791-92 following the battle for Bangalore between Tipu Sultan and Cornwallis. The size of this envisioned entity, more than twenty

VIEW NEAR BANGALORE.

square kilometres in area is remarkable at a time when London was just breaking through 'the square mile'. But it was perhaps not all that unusual in the vicinity of Vijayanagar, the 'Queen of the Deccan' and capital of the kingdom of which Kempegowda I was a feudatory. Of that city, which was ruined in the 1560s, Domingo Paes says in the early 1520s: 'The size of this city I do not write here, because it cannot all be seen from any one spot, but I climbed a hill whence I could see a great part of it; I could not see it all because it lies between several ranges of hills. What I saw from thence seemed to me as large as Rome, and very beautiful to the sight'.[34] Today with the walls of the pettah gone, there is little to mark the origin or centre; instead the four watchtowers combine to suggest its presence.

The iconic nature of the towers was underscored by a number of artists during Cornwallis's campaign. They chose the high ground of these watchtowers, in particular the south tower, to draw the town of Bangalore, seemingly paying little or no attention to the structures themselves. In 1800 William Lambton used the site of the north watchtower on 'Muntapam Hill' as a third point of the 'first triangle' of his Great Trigonometrical Survey. The most popular enforcement of these watchtowers as icons, however, is by the traveller 'in search of the picturesque' who was told in 1895 that to 'obtain some of the best glimpses . . . of the beautiful surroundings of Bangalore, the visitor should first seek these lookouts'.

One tower, however, was not a lookout as much as looked at. It was chosen as a subject by a number of artists in the 1790s. The Daniells and Robert Home used it in the foreground to anchor their views of Bangalore and the extended surface of the Mysore Tableland with droogs in the distance. The Daniells

Thomas and William Daniell, 'View Near Bangalore'. The mantap in the foreground of the painting still stands today east of the Gavi Gangadhareshwara temple in Bangalore, identifiable by the distinct features of the rock on which it stands.
Oriental Scenery (London, 1799), Plate XVII. [Yale Center for British Art, Paul Mellon Collection]

DECCAN TRAVERSES

THE PICTURE
HIGH GROUND
MANTAP
OUTCROP
FOURTH ISLAND

135

DISTANT VIEW of SAVENDROOG.

SOUTH VIEW of BANGALORE, one Mile & a half distant on the Road to Seringapatam.

TOP

Mantaps such as this one at the summit of Savandroog are common features on the Mysore Tableland, often sheltering a sculpture of the Nandi Bull. In 1791, Major Dirom referred to them as 'swamey houses (Hindoo temples), on every eminence, even on the pinnacles of the Droog'.

MIDDLE

Thomas and William Daniell, *Temple Near Bangalore*. 1 May 1792. The Daniells drew the mantap many times on 1 May 1792. They describe it as 'a pavilion very neatly executed, which probably was the place for exhibiting to the multitude the idol belonging to the adjoining temple'.

British Library, IOR, WD 218 [By permission of the British Library]

BOTTOM

Robert Home, 'Distant View of Savendroog' and 'South View of Bangalore, one mile & half distant on the Road to Seringapatam'. For Home, the mantap provided an attractive anchor for views that extended across the tableland.

Select Views in Mysore, The Country of Tipoo Sultan from Drawings taken on the spot with Historical Descriptions (London: Bowyer, 1794).

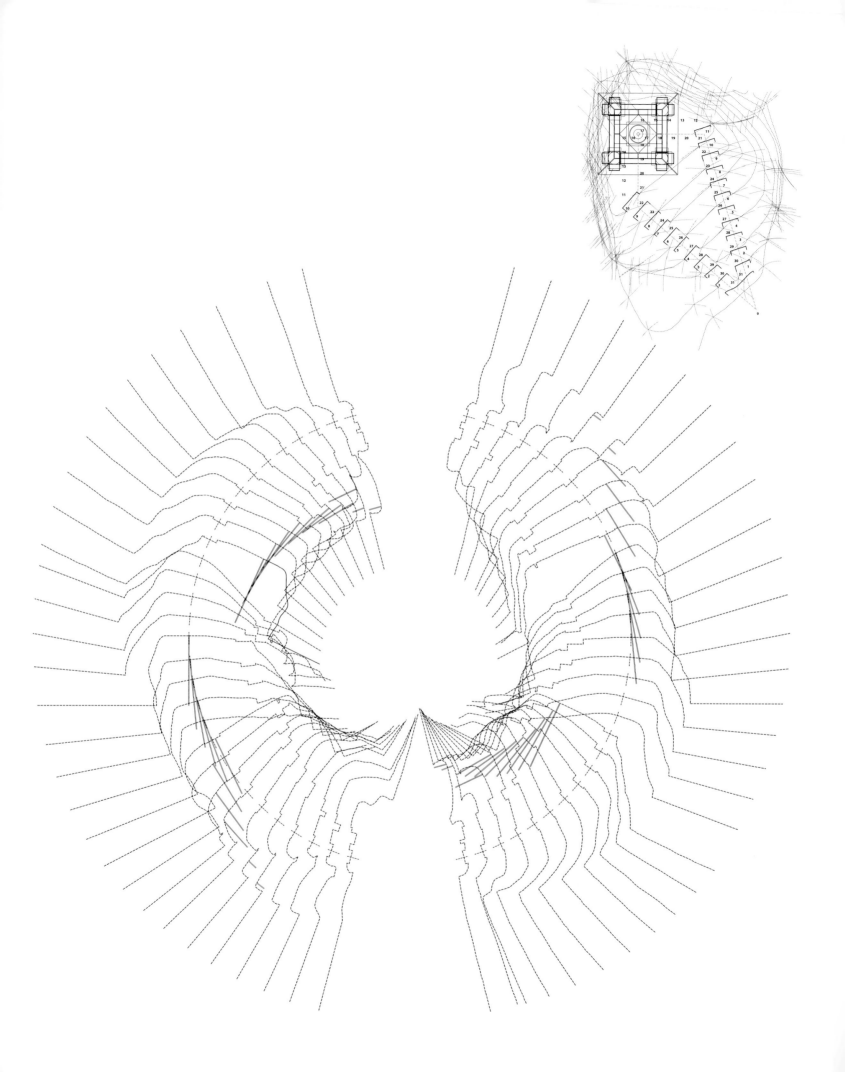

DECCAN TRAVERSES

THE PICTURE
HIGH GROUND
MANTAP
OUTCROP
FOURTH ISLAND

137

describe it as 'a pavilion very neatly executed, which probably was the place for exhibiting to the multitude the idol belonging to the adjoining temple'.[35]

Yet this mantap has eluded the myth of limits projected by archaeologists perhaps because it does not command the highest point in its immediate vicinity as do the four Kempegowda watchtowers. It does, however, command the rise upon which it stands — a twelve-foot high rock hewn with steps, making the rock part of the artefact rather than its base. This 'Fifth Mantap' confounds the architectural limits of the archaeologist's watchtower as a 'construction of brick and mortar on four pillars of grey granite'.

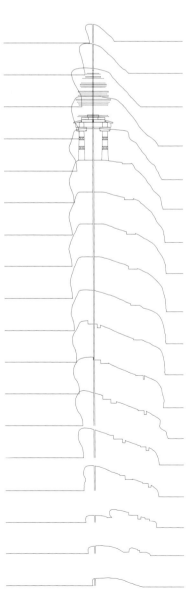

LEFT

The two flights of steps hewn in the rock invite a movement that includes the mantap in a circu-mambulatory.

Cracks are powerful levellers on the tableland. They initiate a break up of high grounds into the soil of the lowlands. The high ground of the mantap is, however, held fast. This structure strides a crack through the rock that artists in the 1790s drew into their scene. These men were perhaps drawn as much by the strange-ness of the 'object' as by the roughness of the rock.

Mantap 1

Screen Print on paper, 22"x30" + Digital Plot

CAMERA OBSCURA, an optical apparatus consisting of a darkened chamber (for which its name is the Latin rendering) at the top of which is placed a box or lantern containing a convex lens and sloping mirror, or a prism combining the lens and mirror. If we hold a common reading lens (a magnifying lens) in front of a lamp or some other bright object and at some distance from it, and if we hold a sheet of paper vertically at a suitable distance behind the lens, we see depicted on the paper an image of the lamp. This image is inverted and perverted. If now we place a plane mirror (each as a piece of glass) behind the lens inclined at an angle of 45° to the horizon so as to reflect the rays of light vertically downwards, we can produce on a horizontal sheet of paper an unperverted image of the bright object (fig. 1) and the image has the same appearance as the object and is not inverted as when the reflection of a printed page is viewed in a mirror. This is the principle of the camera. In copying any object, whether drawing from nature, or to secure a picture of a drawing, it is necessary to bear in mind that the image should appear at the place of the drawing. The image formed at the image is traced by a pencil and it will be noticed that this image is real—not virtual as in the case of the glass.

Generally the mirror and lens are combined in a single piece of worked glass represented in section in fig. 2. Rays from external objects are first refracted at the convex surface *a b*, then totally reflected at the plane surface *a c*, and finally reflected at the concave surface *b c* (fig. 2), so as to form an image on the sheet of paper. The concave surface may take the place of the plane surface performs the functions of a mirror. The prism *a b c* is placed at the top of a small tent furnished with opaque curtains so as to prevent the diffused daylight from overpowering the image on the paper, and in the darkened tent the images of external objects are seen very distinctly.

FIG. 1.

Object   Mirror   Image without Mirror
Lens

Image with Mirror

FIG. 2.

Mantap 2

Screen Print on paper, 22"x30" + Digital Plot

DECCAN TRAVERSES

THE PICTURE
HIGH GROUND
MANTAP
OUTCROP
FOURTH ISLAND

141

OUTCROP

**The Lalbagh Rock, one of the many 'prodi-
gious outbursts' of the 'nether-formed
rocks' of the Mysore Tableland was declared
a national monument in 1975.**

Captain Newbold, who apparently crossed the southern peninsula not once but a number
of times in the late 1830s and early 1840s, adds a depth to the Mysore Tableland when he
writes of a surface 'broken by prodigious outbursts of plutonic and trappean rocks'. The
'bare extensive surfaces of the granitic, trappean, and hypogene rocks, afford, on a grand
scale, exposés, not to be surpassed in any other portion of the globe . . . 'and the geological
anatomist of the earth's skeleton may, in the peninsula of India advantageously study a
huge and disjointed mass of the nether-formed rocks which constitute the framework of
our planet'.[36]

In 1975 this dimension of the tableland – the nether-formed rocks – was declared a national monument.
The Geological Survey of India chose the site of the south Kempegowda Tower as a manifestation of this
monumentality, a 'prodigious outburst' commonly known as the Lalbagh Rock. A plaque at the foot of it
reads: 'This monument is over a typical exposure of Peninsula Gneiss . . . among the oldest rocks of the
earth dating back to 3000 million years. The antiquity of these rocks has attracted geologists all over
the world and has given rise to erudite scientific papers on the evolution of the earth by the pioneers of
the Mysore Geological Department, Geological Survey of India and scholars from the Academy. Stone
quarrying of this gneiss still continues to be an endless source of material for research in the various
branches of earth science'. The rock was named Peninsula Gneiss by geologist William F. Smeeth in
1916. He ended the rock's brief reign as 'Fundamental Gneiss', a name given to it by his predecessor
in the Mysore Geological Department, Robert Bruce Foote, who considered it the foundation material
of geological activity on the tableland. Foote's single source theory proved unconvincing in the light of
the discovery of events that did not just rework and metamorphose the mixtures of granitic rocks of
which the gneiss is composed, but introduced new material from the earth's mantle. Geologists today
prefer to call it Gneiss Complex, signifying a material that has undergone 'several plutonic, volcanic
and sedimentary cycles which have telescoped together more than once through deformation and
metamorphism'.[37]

One gets a glimpse of this hyperactivity on the surface of the Lalbagh Rock. A maze of contorted foliations
– flows of rock material under high stress – reveal the many times this rock reached temperatures
and pressures high enough for the re-crystallising and reordering of its mineral matter along lines of

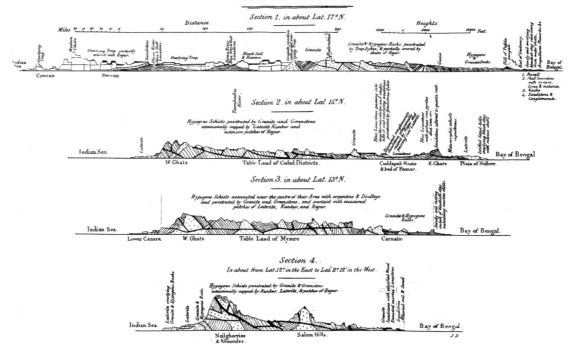

FOUR SECTIONS ACROSS THE PENINSULA OF INDIA.

Section 1. in about Lat. 17°N.

Distance.   Heights.

Section 2. in about Lat. 15°N.

Section 3. in about Lat. 13°N.

Section 4.
In about from Lat. 12° in the East to Lat. 11°12' in the West.

EAST VIEW of BANGALORE.

DECCAN TRAVERSES

THE PICTURE
HIGH GROUND
MANTAP
OUTCROP
FOURTH ISLAND

143

Detail of drawing of the Lalbagh Rock surface by the Geological Survey of India. Flows, islands, and fields on the surface reveal the dynamism of the rock before it attained 'geological stability' three billion years ago. But this stability is relative given the widely accepted view today that the Indian subcontinent rafted up on the lithosphere following the break-up of the super-continent, Gondwanaland, more than a 100 million years ago. It is also relative, given the on-going processes of weathering, such as exfoliation, that steps the surface.

stress but not high enough for a melt down that would return it to magma. Added to foliations, the surface features islands of gneiss, flows of pink and porphyritic granite, and fields of pegmatite. It is a complexity that is multiplied at the scale of the tableland where geologists see a maze of enclaves, belts, sutures, basins, fissures, fractures and dykes, but also a larger dynamism that derives from mobilisations and collisions of continental plates, intrusions of magma from the mantle below the thirty-five-kilometre thick crust, and cycles of volcanism and sedimentation. The dating of Peninsula Gneiss by geologists at three billion years is said to mark the end of its metamorphism, when it is supposed to have attained 'geological stability'. But this is a relative notion given the widely accepted view today that the Indian subcontinent drifted up from the present Antarctic region following the break-up of the super-continent, Gondwanaland, 100-odd million years ago. By this view, the Lalbagh Rock was in place on the tableland as it rafted on the lithosphere across the earth, an outcrop that only in the most recent instant of its long geological life became the site of a visionary's watchtower, a cardinal point of Bangalore, and a popular coign of vantage.[38]

While Lalbagh, a public garden, is an appropriate site to declare the monumentality of the Gneiss Complex to the public, it is the Lalbagh quarries (now discontinued) and stone quarries elsewhere that 'have contributed in a large way to . . . researches and have inspired several teachers and students of universities and research organizations. These quarries still continue to be an endless source material for research in all the various branches of Earth Sciences'.[39] Here the language is not one of views and limits, but burning, pegging, hammering, chiselling, dynamiting, levering, loading, transporting. It is the instability of the rock that is exploited here rather than its stability. Its metamorphosis is made to continue. There is little time to study foliations; here they are the planes along which rocks split by heat on the surface. When the heat source is the sun, this splitting is referred to as exfoliation. 'The exfoliation of whole mountain masses, on the grand scale, by such natural causes, produces some of the most picturesque features of an Indian landscape', says Captain Newbold.[40] When heat is applied by burning eucalyptus leaves or, in Newbold's time, 'Acacias common to the surrounding plains, viz., those of the Babul and Kirkar' it is called stone quarrying.[41] This stone is used in pavements, drains, compound walls, columns and roofs; the size-stones of foundations and walls; the jelly under rail tracks and in concrete and asphalt. It is ubiquitous, the ordinary stone of Bangalore.

The monumentality of Peninsula Gneiss adds to the stability of the Kempegowda Watchtower at the summit of Lalbagh Rock and the people who gather there everyday in the footsteps of the picturesque artist to enjoy the scene. From here, Robert Colebrooke, Claude Martin, James Hunter and Robert Home, recorded the Sultan's cypress garden, the pettah beyond, and the droogs in the distance. But the Gneiss Complex, with its life events so telescoped into one another, its materials so interwoven, is far from stable. Extracted, shaped, transported, and placed, it continues to reconstitute the surface of the Mysore Tableland.

TOP LEFT

Captain Newbold, 'Four Sections Across the Peninsula of India', *Journal of the Royal Asiatic Society,* **vol. 8, 1846. 'Section 3 in about Lat. 13° N' cuts the Mysore Tableland, through Nandidroog fifty kilometres north of Bangalore.**

BOTTOM LEFT

Robert H. Colebrooke, 'East View of Bangalore'. The Lalbagh Rock was a coign of vantage for artists like Colebrooke in 1791. From here he recorded the scene of Bangalore Fort and Pettah in the distance with the Sultan's garden or the Cypress Garden in the middle ground.

Twelve Views of Places in the Kingdom of Mysore (London, 1794). [Yale Center for British Art, Paul Mellon Collection]

Compound walls made of slabs of gneiss called chaptis are a common sight in Bangalore. The 'gneissose rock is everywhere abundant', writes Lewis Rice in the first state Gazetteer of 1877, 'and is extensively quarried for building purposes. Large slabs, of from 3 inches to 2 feet in thickness, are readily obtained by the simple application of heat to the surface. Then by pooling small holes in the required direction and wedging, the stone can be separated with great precision into pieces of almost any dimensions. Pillars thus prepared and 25 feet in length have been extensively employed as telegraph posts while in the High School at Bangalore single stones 35 feet high and not more than 15 inches square have been used to support the roof'.

LEFT

Foliations are flows of rock material under high stress. In a quarry, they are planes along which gneiss is split by the heat of burning leaves, accelerating what happens to this rock under the sun.

RIGHT

Quarrying for 'ordinary stone' begins by burning leaves on the rock surface causing it to expand and crack along a plane of weakness. The detached surface is marked, pegged and split into chaptis, chiselled into size stone, broken into jelly, or ground to dust.

DECCAN TRAVERSES

THE PICTURE
HIGH GROUND
MANTAP
OUTCROP
FOURTH ISLAND

145

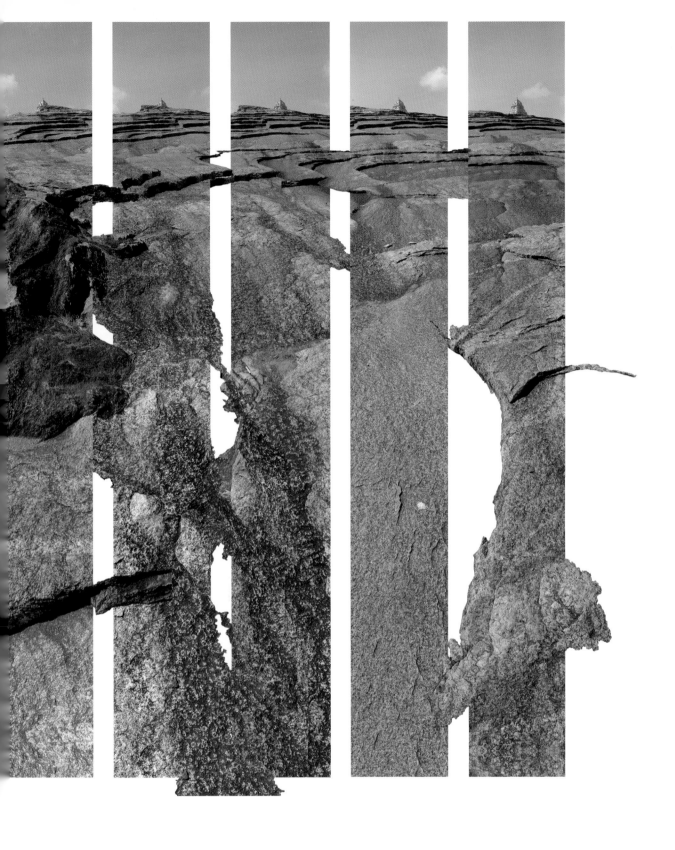

The marks on the Lalbagh Rock — the foliations, the islands of black granite, the flows of pink and porphyritic granite, the fields of pegmatite, the water stains, the 'steps' left by exfoliations caused by sun or by quarrying, and the smoothening of the surface by daily users – provide a glimpse of the hyperactivity through which this rock was formed and continues to transform today.

Outcrop 1

Screen Print on paper, 22"x30" + Digital Plot

Outcrop 2

Screen Print on paper, 22"x30" + Digital Plot

E - EROSION MALINGE

PATALESWARA

TALAKAD   D - DEPOSITION

purvavahini (east flowing)

ARKESWARA

SKETCH MAP
of
TALKAD

PATALESWARA

VAIDEYESWARA

ARKESWARA

MARALESWARA

MALLIKARJUNA

TALAKAD

MALINGE

HEMMIGE

paschimavahini (west flowing)

DECCAN TRAVERSES

THE PICTURE
HIGH GROUND
MANTAP
OUTCROP
FOURTH ISLAND

151

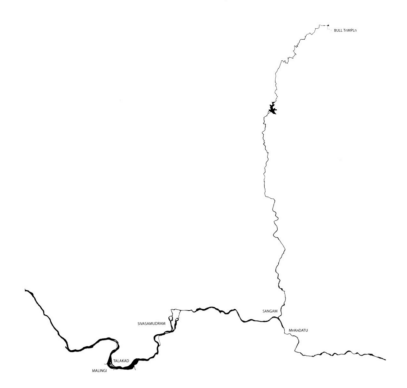

BULL TnMPLn

SANGAM

SIVASAMUDRAM

MnKnDATU

TALAKAD

MALINGI

FOURTH ISLAND

The Kaveri, which collects the waters of the Vrishabhavati, believed to originate in the Bull Temple in Bangalore, pivots on the island of Sivasamudram. It transitions at this point from a meandering stream on the surface of a plateau at Talakad to a torrential river within the gorges of Mekedatu.

Geologists speak of a gradual increase in metamorphism from north to south of the Mysore Tableland. The rock to the south was apparently subject to higher temperatures and pressures and dehydrating fluids, which increased the presence of less hydrous minerals such as pyroxene. At some point, however, the gradation becomes a transition and the grey-white peninsula gneiss so visible in the Lalbagh Rock gives way to a 'darker', 'more coarsely granular', 'greasy-looking' rock called Charnockite or pyroxene granulite.[42] But before it was given these names, this rock was called mountain gneiss. It presents granulite in terms of another transition — the shift from the Mysore Tableland where gneiss is a dominant presence to the hilly tract of the Biligirirangan and Mahadeswara ranges and, beyond them, the Nilgiris where Charnockite takes over the land in massifs.

The transition from gneiss to granulite occurs over a thirty to sixty kilometre zone. For a small stretch in the middle of the peninsula, this zone is crossed by the Kaveri. Flowing from west to east at this point, this sacred and contentious river constructs its own shift. It falls dramatically on either side of the island of Sivasamudram and in that fall changes from a meandering stream on a plateau to a rapid one within gorges. It is a transition from a river of sand to a river of rock. Geomorphologists see it as a recovery of youth.

Moments, however, before it turns young at Sivasamudram, an aging Kaveri is celebrated at Talakad. Here, a quiet, meandering river displays remarkable power. It cuts the outer bank of a bend while depositing sand on the inner bank, changing course like a moving snake. At Talakad, however, the sand collected on the inner bank developed into dunes that have buried the once famous capital of the Gangas, a dynasty believed to have ruled the region in the first millennium.

People withdrew in the face of this phenomenon, which curiously began only in the seventeenth century, until archaeologists in the nineteenth century sought to recover the city from beneath the sands. 'Without the directions of Government', Lewis Rice observed, 'the people would do nothing, professing to look upon the phenomenon as the result of the curse . . . and deeming it useless to fight against fate'. The curse, Rice explains, is of Rangamma the consort of the Vijayanagar governor of Seringapatam, Tirumala

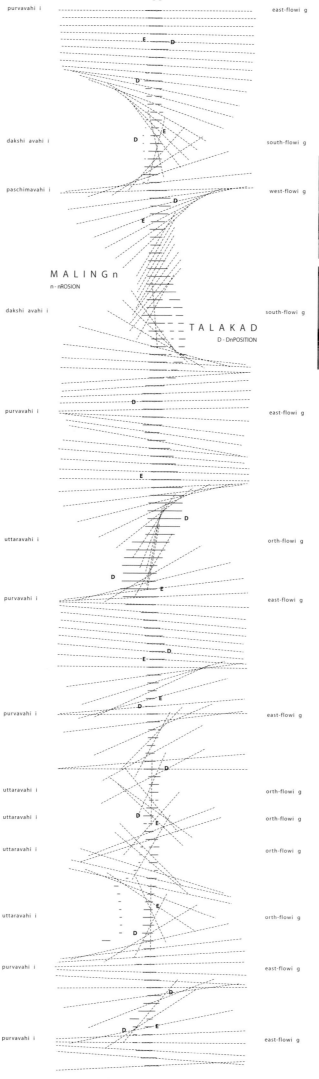

A

purvavahi i   east-flowi g

E   D

D

dakshi avahi i   E   south-flowi g

D

paschimavahi i   west-flowi g

D

E

MALINGn

n - nROSION

dakshi avahi i   south-flowi g

TALAKAD

D - DnPOSITION

purvavahi i   D   east-flowi g

E

D

uttaravahi i   orth-flowi g

D

purvavahi i   E   east-flowi g

D

E

purvavahi i   E   east-flowi g

D

D

uttaravahi i   orth-flowi g

uttaravahi i   D   E   orth-flowi g

uttaravahi i   orth-flowi g

uttaravahi i   E   orth-flowi g

D

purvavahi i   east-flowi g

D

purvavahi i   D   E   east-flowi g

B

Vaidyeswara Temple that adjoins this tank (BOTTOM LEFT) **is the centre of the** *Panchal-inga darsana.* **It was spared by the Kaveri. Between this 'celebrated temple dedicated to Iswara and the present channel of the river', writes Francis Buchanan in 1800, 'were formerly situated a large fort and a great number of temples'. Four of the latter – Arkeswara, Pataleswara, Maraleswara, and Mallikarjuna temples** (ABOVE) **– have become part of the darsana, a ritual that acknowledges the meander.**

LEFT

Between its emergence from the Western Ghats and the island of Sivasamudram, the Kaveri is a meandering river, the meander being a mode of flow of a river across a relatively flat alluvial terrain. Through the meander, the river deposits on an inner bend (a point bar) and erodes the outer bend (a cut bank), thereby gradually changing course. In this stretch, however, one bend in the Kaveri is majestic. It has eroded away the town of Malingi on its outer side and buried Talakad on its inner side. This bend acknowledges all four cardinal directions – north, south, east, west – in a magnificent sweep.

DECCAN TRAVERSES

153

THE PICTURE
HIGH GROUND
MANTAP
OUTCROP
FOURTH ISLAND

Sand dunes surround the Kirtinarayan temple, one of the many structures unearthed in Talakad but not included in the *Panchalinga darsana*.

Raja. Betrayed by Raja Wodeyar of Mysore, in whose care she had left the reigns of government while she attended her husband convalescing at Talakad, she threw herself into the Kaveri, damning the place: 'Let Talakad become sand; let Malingi become a whirlpool; let the Mysore Rajas fail to beget heirs'.[43] The new administrators sought a verifiable cause, explaining the phenomenon as a unique combination of a bend in a river, a drop in water levels with the construction of a weir two kilometres upstream in the seventeenth century, and strong southwest monsoon winds. For thousands of people, however, the phenomenon lies in the power of the Kaveri invoked by Rangamma. Even as archaeologists uncovered temples, they have situated these temples in a pilgrimage that follows, perhaps appeases, the meander of the Kaveri at Talakad. At a time determined by celestial alignments they gather at Talakad. Beginning in Vaidyeswara Temple — the only temple to escape burial — and the adjacent tank, they visit four temples, each associated with a cardinal direction of the flow of the Kaveri as it winds around Talakad. It is a ritual — the *Panchalinga darsana* — that imbibes the power of a meander.

The pilgrimage at Talakad occurs a short time before the operator of the quiet meander 'precipitates its waters over a perpendicular rock' on either side of the island of Siva-samudram in, what Francis Buchanan describes as, a 'cloud of vapour which is formed by its violence', 'thundering noise', and 'awful whirlings of its tumultuous abyss'. The sight, he says, was too much for words. 'I have never seen any cataract that for grandeur could be compared with this. . . The pencil of an artist might be well employed in imitating its

The Kaveri below Sivasamudram is at times a river of just rock.

magnificent scenery, and would convey a better idea of its grandeur than my power of description can venture to attempt'.[44] Many artists beginning with Thomas Fraser, a surveyor on Colin Mackenzie's team for the Mysore Survey, would describe the picturesque island of Sivasamudram through the 'celebrated falls of the river Kaveri, unrivalled in all India for romantic beauty'.[45]

In 1791, however, it was enclosure rather than scene that drew people to Sivasamudram. They were seeking protection from Cornwallis's army. 'Every human being on the route', writes Mark Wilks, 'was so completely removed beyond the reach of the English army, that they appeared to be traversing a country of which the population had been utterly destroyed by some recent convulsion of nature; . . . in fact they were all collected with their cattle and movables on the island of Sheven Sumooder, the place afterwards so frequently visited by English travellers, on account of the magnificent falls of the Caveri'.[46]

Protection situates Sivasamudram in a more extended trajectory, between the islands of Seringapatam, a few kilometres upstream, and Srirangam below the passes in the Carnatic. Called Adiranga, Madhyaranga and Antyaranga (beginning, middle and end), these islands are dedicated to Ranganatha, the protector reclining on a five-headed serpent whose coils are said to indicate the cycles of time. Each island is more than just 'a tract of land completely surrounded by water, and not large enough to be called a continent', which is how islands are often defined. Each divides and unites the mighty Kaveri, doubling the land touched by a river that is venerated by millions as a 'Goddess' who 'fulfils wishes abundantly — regardless of who you are; with a massive rush she gushes at one spot; at another place she flows with perfect gracefulness. . .'.[47]

The promise of the Kaveri has long encouraged the making of islands, of doubling the touch of a sacred river. Already in 1890 the Kaveri, before it reached Sivasamudram, was divided by twelve anicuts (sill-like structures or weirs), from each of which water was

DECCAN TRAVERSES

THE PICTURE
HIGH GROUND
MANTAP
OUTCROP
FOURTH ISLAND

155

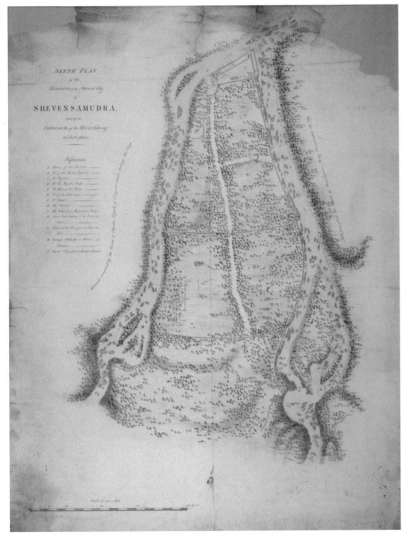

Anon., *Plan of the remains of the ancient city of Sivasamudram and the Cauvery Falls (Mysore).*

British Library, IOR, WD 2631 [By permission of the British Library]

led off for irrigation. 'The dreams which revealed to favoured mortals the plans of these ingenious works', Wilks found in the early 1800s, 'have each their appropriate legend which is related with reverence, and received with implicit belief'.[48] Sometimes the divide wrought by the anicut had more purpose as when the waters of the Kaveri were sought for Mysore City in the early 1800s with a channel that was at times over 100 feet deep, cut through 'solid granite', and carried over other rivers. The rejoining of these waters is not clear except in the case of the most recent and grandest effort. It begins in an anicut at the head of Sivasamudram built in the early 1900s to channel water through the first hydroelectric plant in Asia. Its proposal was made by the Mysore government in 1900 'to develop and utilize the natural power of the Kauveri Falls at Sivasamudram, which is now running to waste'.[49] In the 1970s the channel from the Sivasamudram anicut was extended to Bangalore via a pipeline and three pumping stations to raise water the required 300 metres over the 100-odd kilometre distance. The return of these waters is via a drainage network, the Vrishabhavati and the Arkavati rivers to a reunion at Sangam.

Lewin Bowring regretted the Company's choice of Bangalore as a cantonment and headquarters of their army when Seringapatam, the first island (Adiranga) in three chosen for protection in the Kaveri, was deemed unhealthy in the early 1800s. 'It has many advantages in regard to climate and situation', he says of Bangalore, 'but there is a great deficiency of water... a plateau where nothing will vegetate'.[50] Others have regretted a capital leaving the Kaveri, 'south India's greatest river', the coveted site of kings. 'By locating their capitals and dynastic temples on the river and its branches, these kings acknowledged the Kaveri as a source of divine power'.[51] Planners in the twentieth century would heed the call of the Kaveri. But instead of bringing the capital to the Kaveri, they took the Kaveri to Bangalore, creating, inadvertently perhaps, a contentious fourth island.

BHIMnSHWARI

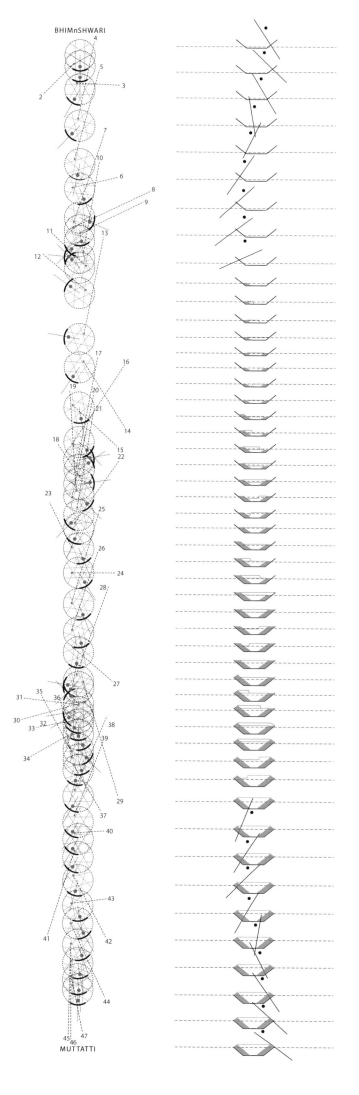

MUTTATTI

DECCAN TRAVERSES

157

THE PICTURE
HIGH GROUND
MANTAP
OUTCROP
FOURTH ISLAND

FAR LEFT

The Sivasamudram Falls is the beginning of a Kaveri, the crossing of which requires either a 'goat's leap' as at Mekedatu or vessels called koracles. Domingo Paes, a Portuguese traveller to India in the early 1500s, described these vessels in 1520 as 'round like baskets; inside they are made of cane, and outside are covered with leather; . . . Men row them with a sort of paddle, and the boats are always turning round, as they cannot go straight like others'.

LEFT AND ABOVE

The Kaveri gathers waters; but it also gathers particles of crystalline rock eroded off the tableland. In standing water this sand settles quickly; in a flowing Kaveri, however, it could be held in suspension as far as its delta where it extends and deepens the coastal plain. Much of the sand though settles midstream in braids between Talakad and Sivasamudram from where it is mined by men in circular iron vessels, ten feet in diameter, and trucked to places like Bangalore for the construction industry.

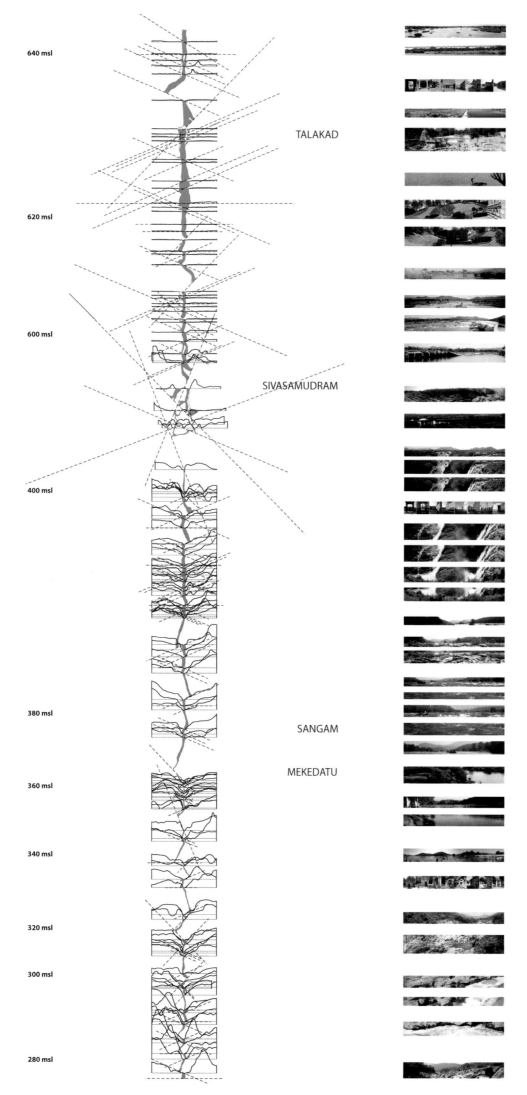

640 msl

TALAKAD

620 msl

600 msl

SIVASAMUDRAM

400 msl

380 msl

SANGAM

MEKEDATU

360 msl

340 msl

320 msl

300 msl

280 msl

Between Talakad and Mekedatu the Kaveri falls over 300 metres in a transition from the flatness and sand of the Mysore Plateau to the gorges and rocks of the Biligirirangan Hills.

THE PICTURE
HIGH GROUND
MANTAP
OUTCROP
FOURTH ISLAND

159

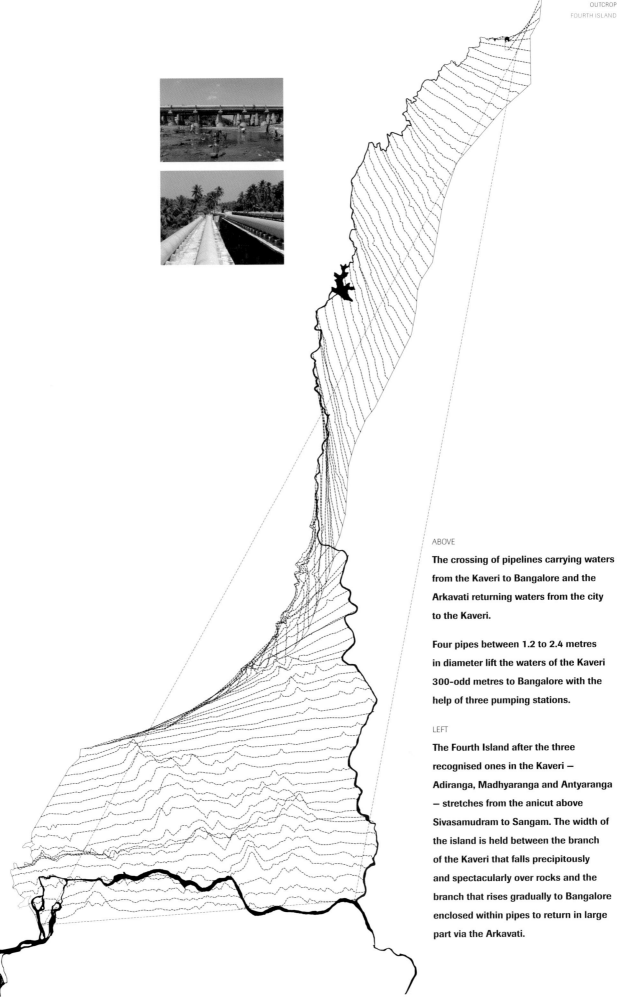

ABOVE

The crossing of pipelines carrying waters from the Kaveri to Bangalore and the Arkavati returning waters from the city to the Kaveri.

Four pipes between 1.2 to 2.4 metres in diameter lift the waters of the Kaveri 300-odd metres to Bangalore with the help of three pumping stations.

LEFT

The Fourth Island after the three recognised ones in the Kaveri — Adiranga, Madhyaranga and Antyaranga — stretches from the anicut above Sivasamudram to Sangam. The width of the island is held between the branch of the Kaveri that falls precipitously and spectacularly over rocks and the branch that rises gradually to Bangalore enclosed within pipes to return in large part via the Arkavati.

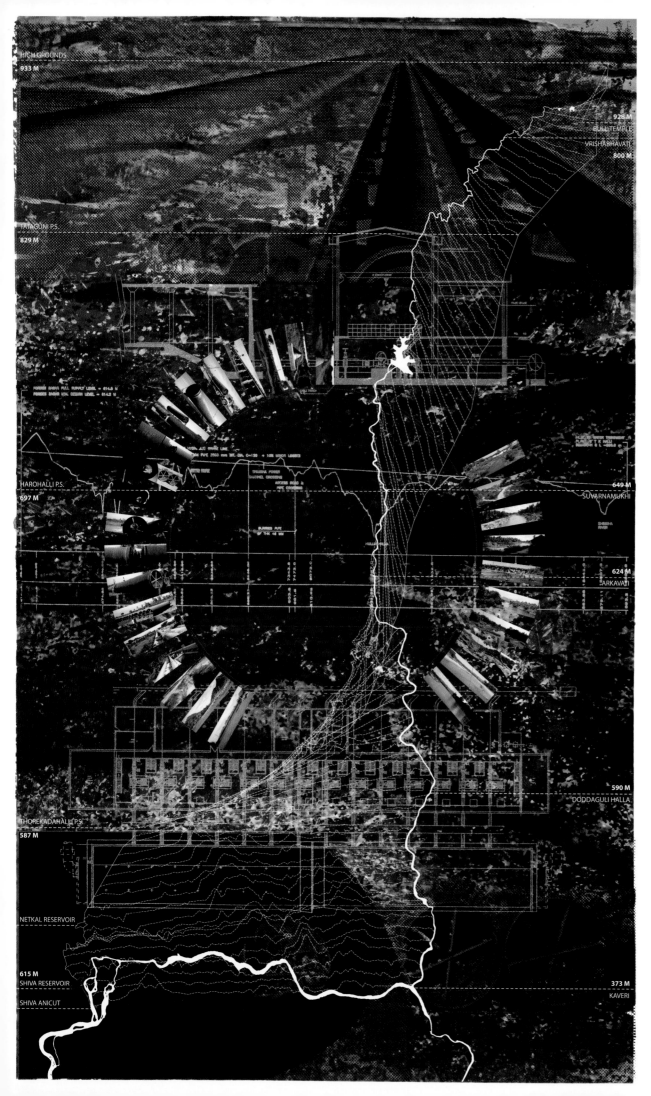

HIGH GROUNDS
933 M

928 M
BULL TEMPLE
VRISHABHAVATI
800 M

TATAGUNI P.S.
829 M

HAROHALLI P.S.
697 M

649 M
SUVARNAMUKHI

624 M
ARKAVATI

590 M
DODDAGULI HALLA

THOREKADAHALLI P.S.
587 M

NETKAL RESERVOIR

615 M
SHIVA RESERVOIR

373 M
KAVERI

SHIVA ANICUT

Fourth Island 1

Screen Print on paper, 22"x30" + Digital Plot

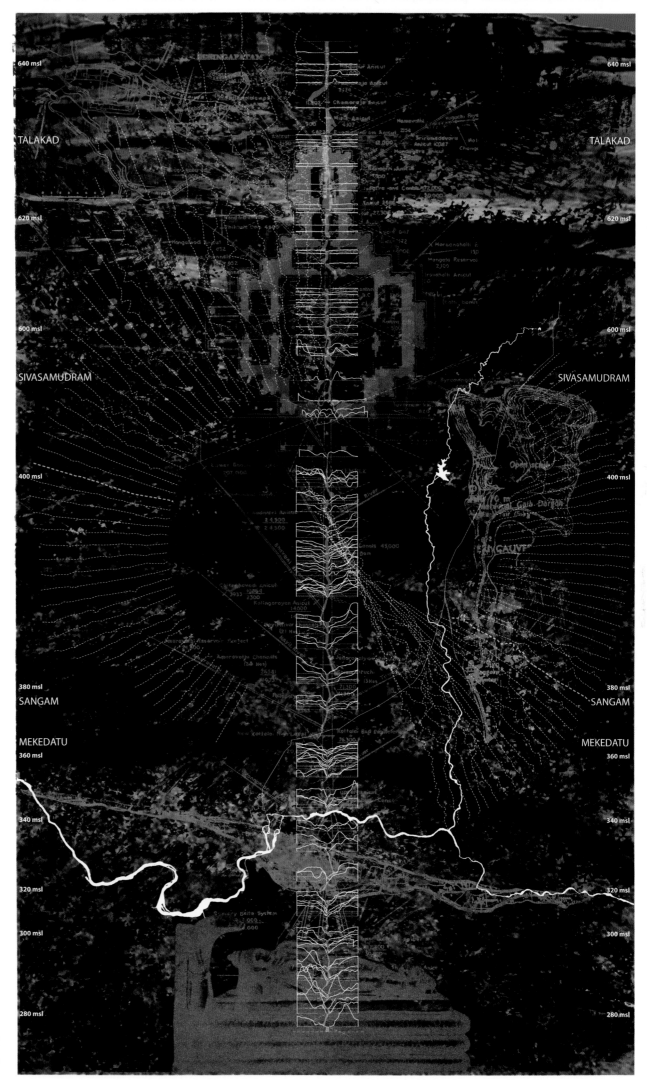

Fourth Island 2

Screen Print on paper, 22"x30" + Digital Plot

Water 1

Screen Print on paper, 22"x30" + Digital Plot

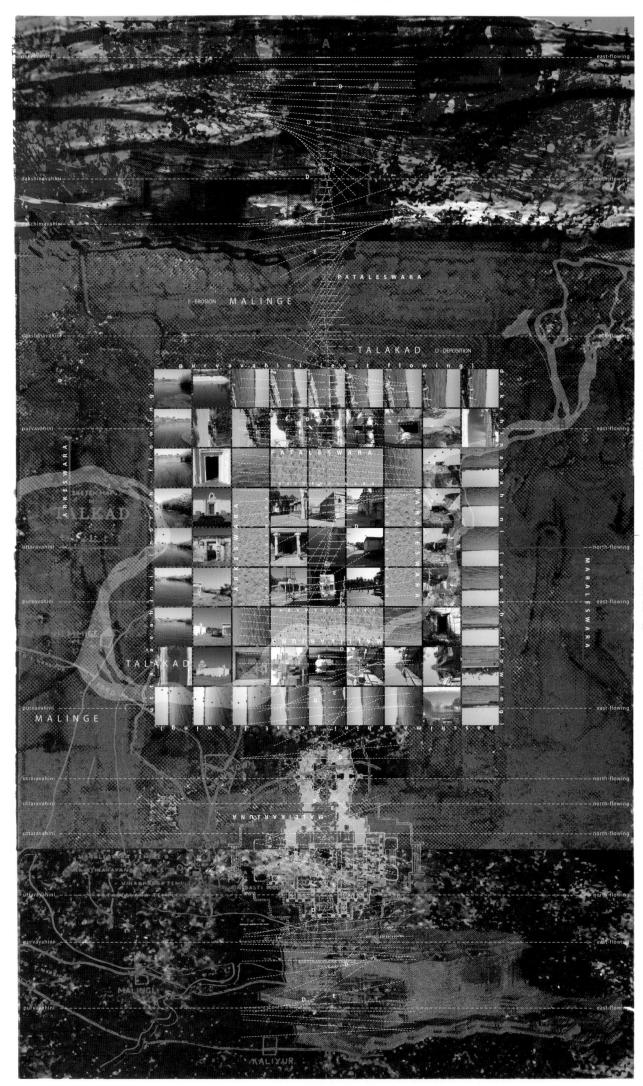

Water 3

Screen Print on paper, 22"x30" + Digital Plot

THE GARDEN

GARDEN CITY

TOTA

GLASS HOUSE

HILL STATION

VIEW OF BANGALORE, WITH THE CYPRESS GARDEN, FROM A

THE GARDEN

In 1819, Major Gilbert Waugh, an officer of the Madras European Regiment and Paymaster of Mysore, offered his garden in Bangalore to the East India Company. Nathaniel Wallich, superintendent of the Botanical Garden at Calcutta, was asked by Governor-General Warren Hastings to review the offer. Expressing knowledge of the garden, Wallich recommended its acceptance as an intermediate garden in the acclimatising of European plants given that his own endeavours in Calcutta were frustrated by 'the excessive heat and profuse wetness' of Bengal. For 'Europe fruit trees to bear the vicissitudes of this country', Wallich writes, 'intermediate depots or auxiliary nurseries become very desirable, and for such a purpose the Garden of Major Waugh seems to be in every point of view highly calculated. Its peculiarly fine situation and most flourishing condition, its containing a vast variety already of those very trees which it is so material to introduce into Bengal, the existing opportunity of appropriating it as a branch of this Garden not only with a view to the good of this country but as eminently suited for promoting the reciprocal communication of useful and ornamental plants from and to England'. The garden, he concludes, would 'prove highly advantageous to the successful pursuit of horticulture in India'.[1]

According to Alexander Cole, Resident of Mysore, Waugh had made an extraordinary effort. He had, Cole writes, 'devoted a considerable portion of his time, attention and fortune to the liberal and useful pursuit of enriching this country with the most valuable productions of Europe and China . . . brought to perfection in the congenial climate and soil of Bangaloor'. To him, the 'country is indebted for a considerable variety of valuable exotics'.[2] The governor general was convinced. But four months after accepting Waugh's garden 'as an intermediate nursery for introducing and acclimatizing in India the trees and plants of Europe and of China' he withdrew saying that 'the estimated value of the garden is so considerable that the acceptance of it on the part of Government would be a serious injury to Major Waugh'.[3]

It is possible that the Company had found another garden to fulfil the role of intermediary. In 1816 the Farhatbaksh gardens at Saharanpur in the foothills of the Sivaliks had been proposed to assume the same role. At 1,000 feet, its proponent writes, Saharanpur was appropriate for 'the naturalization of many of the valuable vegetable productions of colder climates' while also being a place where 'the more tender inhabitants of the south might be gradually inured to a colder atmosphere'. It could be made into a 'garden stocked with the familiar fruits of Europe, the cinchona of South America, and all those vegetables and medicinal plants which persistently defied Calcutta's skills to grow them'.[4] Hastings approved the garden at Saharanpur in the same year that he declined Waugh's garden at Bangalore.

The Company was evidently looking for ways to introduce, acclimatise and disseminate plants on the Indian subcontinent that they now administered in almost its entirety, and the botanical garden was a leading player in this enterprise. It served as a node in a web of plant movements between lands witnessing the introduction of new plant material and vocabularies even as they were entering a global commercial and increasingly colonial network.

This web of movement was many decades, perhaps centuries, in the making. But in the last quarter of the eighteenth century it was given a direction and purpose. This was a time when botanical enquiry and horticulture were consumed by economic

Ships, carrying plants across many latitudes, longitudes and for many months were the quintessential botanical gardens of the late eighteenth century. *Endeavour*, the ship that carried Captain Cook around the world between 1769 and 1771, was also a prominent vehicle in the field of economic botany. On it, Joseph Banks, future president of the Royal Society and architect of plant movement across the world, collected 3,600 dried plant specimens besides seeds, animals, and artefacts.

botany, a field driven by the idea of progress, or what Richard Drayton calls the 'cult of improvement'. Improvement, he says, 'once a slogan for the local activity of the [European] gentry, became a criterion for responsible authority, and a mission towards which government might legitimately expand its powers'.[5] Col. Robert Kyd voiced the essence of this idea when he made his proposal for a botanical garden at Calcutta to the Company in 1786. 'I take this opportunity of suggesting to the Board the propriety of establishing a Botanical Garden not for the purpose of collecting rare plants (although they also have their use) as things of mere curiosity or furnishing articles for the gratification of luxury, but for establishing a stock for disseminating such articles as may prove beneficial to the inhabitants, as well as the natives of Great Britain, and which ultimately may tend to the extension of the national commerce and riches'.[6]

On the terrain of economic botany one garden stood out more than others: the Royal Gardens at Kew, 'the great botanical exchange house for the empire, the entrepôt through which plants moved east to west, and south to north'.[7] Located upriver from London, this garden received an impetus from the association of Sir Joseph Banks and King George III. Banks, president of the Royal Society from 1778 to 1820, had sailed around the world with Captain Cook on the *Endeavour* in 1769-71 collecting 3,600 dried plant specimens (1,400 of them 'new' to science) in addition to seeds, bottled animals, artefacts, and drawings by artists who accompanied him. But, as interested as he was in dried specimens, his interest in the movement of living plants was greater. Name and taxonomy ultimately mattered less to him than the use of plants and the knowledge of their cultivation and he saw in the king's garden at Kew an opportunity for his enterprise. This garden was at the time a combination of two royal enclosures: one steeped in the English landscape movement with its defiance of classical geometry, the other a physic garden, a tradition of cultivating plants with healing

DECCAN TRAVERSES

THE GARDEN
GARDEN CITY
TOTA
GLASS HOUSE
HILL STATION

171

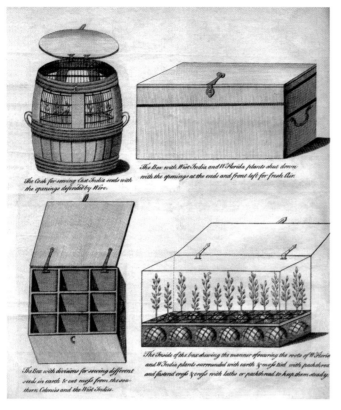

The Cask for sowing East India seeds with the openings defended by Wire.

The Box with West India and W. Florida plants shut down with the openings at the ends and front left for fresh Air.

The Box with divisions for sowing different seeds in earth & cut moss from the southern Colonies and the West Indies.

The Inside of the box shewing the manner of securing the roots of W. Florida and W. India plants surrounded with earth & moss tied with packthread and fastened cross & cross with lathe or packthread to keep them steady.

John Ellis, 'Boxes for conveying Plants by Sea'.

Directions for Captains of Ships, Sea Surgeons, and other curious Persons, who collect Seeds and Plants in distant Countries, in what Manner to preserve them fit for Vegetation (London 1770).

properties. Physic gardens leaned toward the exotic but also toward scientific organisation, expansion, curiosity and experimentation.[8]

With encouragement from the King, Banks took over this garden at Kew, extending its collection from plants of medicinal value to all plants with any possible value, from a concern for the improvement of individuals to the improvement of humanity. He made it a critical node in the global transfer of plants and global experimentation in their cultivation, but always also a place of collection and nomenclature. From the 1780s onwards, Drayton writes, Kew 'became a de facto national collection, to which seeds and bulbs were sent from every part of the world. More strikingly, Kew became a source of plants, and of gardeners, sent outwards to Britain's overseas dominions'.[9]

In the mid-1700s, however, it was not gardeners radiating from Kew but 'collectors' sent on voyages by Banks. The plant material returning to him though, came from a wider network of men who 'botanised' in their spare time — surveyors, missionaries, surgeons and missionary-surgeons. There were other important hubs in this network of amateurs, including Carl Linnaeus who devised a system of classifying plants and encouraged the introduction and acclimatisation of those that promised to be beneficial to his country of Sweden. To these men, the botanical garden was more than a collection of dried specimens in folders of cotton paper named and housed in herbariums or a collection of live specimens 'brought to flower'; it was 'the promotion of public utility & science', an agenda that interested the English East India Company, more so because it was shifting its status from trader to knowledgeable administrator. It certainly blurred the line between profit and social benefit, knowledge and altruism. Perhaps this was the reason why a number of men already botanising on the subcontinent joined the Company as surgeon-naturalists and garden superintendents.

This was the route of Benjamin Heyne, Gilbert Waugh's predecessor as keeper of the botanical garden in Bangalore. In 1799 he was ordered by Lord Wellesley to take charge of what was then the Sultan's garden. It was part of the agenda of the Topographical Survey of Mysore led by Colin Mackenzie, on whose team Heyne was appointed naturalist and medical officer. In a special order Wellesley instructs Heyne to appropriate 'the Sultan's garden at Bangalore . . . as a botanical garden' and develop it 'as a depository for useful plants sent from different parts of the country. . . . A decided superiority must be given to useful plants, over those which are merely recommended by their rarity or their beauty, and it will be Dr. Heyne's primary care to attend to such as may furnish any facility in the supply of food or forage; . . . to collect with care all that is connected with the arts and manufactures of this country, or that promises to be useful in our own; to give due attention to the timber employed in the various provinces as are deficient in that necessary produce, and to collect with particular diligence the valuable plants connected with his own immediate profession'.[10]

Heyne was in a line of missionary surgeon-naturalists led by Johann Koenig, a student of Linnaeus. These men came to the Danish trading post of Tranquebar near Tanjore, the site of one of the earliest Protestant (Moravian) missions in India (begun in 1706). They were distinguished by their unusual interest in botany. These men, called the Tranquebar Botanists, 'exchanged specimens, formed a herbarium, named plants which until experience gave them confidence they did collectively, applying the word "nobis" (named by all of us) to their plant labels'.[11] Heyne, however, like Koenig three decades before him, was drawn beyond taxonomy, to the web of economic botany. He sought the patronage of the English East India Company, which was employing medical men in the role of surgeon-naturalists. Heyne's opportunity came when he was recommended by William Roxburgh to be his successor in charge of the botanical garden at Samalkot (200 miles north of Madras). Roxburgh, a surgeon with the Company and author of *Flora Indica* or *Description of Indian Plants* (1820), was posted to the area in the 1780s and had begun the garden as an experimental plantation, growing coffee, pepper, breadfruit, cinnamon, indigo, opuntia, etc. on the promise of economic betterment.

In less than a decade the garden at Samalkot was declared a failure and when the defeat of Tipu opened the Mysore Tableland, Robert Clive, governor of Madras, urged that the garden be moved onto the tableland. 'I think it proper in this place', he writes to the directors of the Company, 'to state my intention of taking the necessary measures for establishing a botanical Garden in some part of the Mysore Country where I understand the climate is favourable to institutions of this nature'.[12] Indeed from the time of the Third Mysore War, it was known that a number of places on the tableland were conducive to English plants, horticultural experimentation working quietly behind the scene of battles in the one-year that Cornwallis took to subdue Tipu Sultan. Roderick Mackenzie had singled out Bangalore for special mention in this regard, the troops having a chance here to try longer experiments. 'Situated nearly in the centre of the peninsula, and abounding with reservoirs of water, the lands benefit by the monsoons of either coast, without being deluged by the weight of their fall; the soil is fruitful, and produces the necessaries of life in great plenty; cabbages, lettuce, and other European culinary wares, planted by British officers, throve in the gardens all around without any extraordinary attention; and cypress, plantain, guava, with trees and shrubberies of various description, rising in clumps in all directions, afforded abundance of shade'.[13]

Heyne, made available for Mackenzie's Mysore Survey by the failure of the Samalkot garden and the promise of a 'salubrious' territory, was asked by Clive to look for a suitable replacement not just for this garden but also 'The Honourable Company's Nopalry' at Marmelon begun in 1788 by physician-general of Madras, James Anderson. A nopalry was a plantation of prickly pear (*Opuntia* species brought to India by the Portuguese) grown to feed insects of the *Dactylopius* species from Central America, Mexico and Peru. When dried and powdered the insects provided cochineal, a scarlet dye used in fabrics. Besides cochineal, which he promoted with particular zeal, Anderson sought to advance the silk, cotton, sugarcane, and coffee industries, all the while also collecting plant species from various parts of the world for the possibility of introducing, even inventing, an industry.

It suited Heyne to select the same garden that he was asked by the governor-general to make into a plant depot to meet Clive's request. In May 1800, he reports to the governor: The 'Sultan's Garden was given up to me which since my return from Seringapatam I have endeavored to find in a condition that answers the purposes. . . . The trees and plants brought with me from Madras as Oaks, Pines, Nutmegs, Cinnamon, etc., I have to report as promising very well, and upward of 250 different seeds have been sown of which I will give a list in the accounts ordered quarterly. The extent of the Garden is according to actual measurement 41 English acres, 4 Pales and 174 square feet or 31 Cawnies of ground

DECCAN TRAVERSES

THE GARDEN
GARDEN CITY
TOTA
GLASS HOUSE
HILL STATION

173

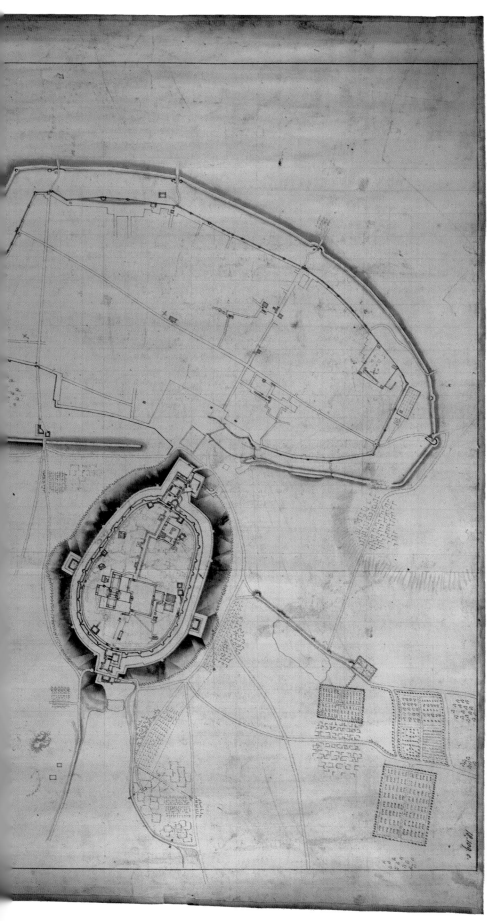

Plan of the Fortress of Bangalore, 1791. The Sultan's gardens, within the enclosure of Lalbagh today, is to the southeast of the fort.

British Library, Add 18109-c [By permission of the British Library]

The Royal Gardens at Kew was made by Joseph Banks and King George III ('Farmer George') into a centre of economic botany, a field of plants and transplants for social benefit and economic profit.

1443 square feet. At present are employed in it 20 gardeners, 2 Maistries, and 1 Daroga, paid by the Circar and understanding from the Residency at Seringapatam that this Establishment is conceived to be separate from the Survey'.[14] Two years later he explains his choice: 'The cause of my recommending Bangalore formerly were chiefly the favourableness of its climate which is more moderate than any on the coast, the relative goodness of its soil, the favourable situation of the spot with regard to its watering as well as the vicinity of one of the greatest towns on the peninsula, its centrical situation, and ultimately the advanced state of a well laid out Garden'.[15] Francis Buchanan who visited Bangalore in the days after Heyne took charge was quick to endorse his choice. 'In this climate', he said, 'the cypress and vine grow luxuriantly, and the apple and peach both produce fruit . . . I think there can be little doubt that in this country all the valuable plants of the *Levant* would succeed'. [16]

Serving two masters was difficult for Heyne. He was constantly reminded of his duty to the Mysore Survey and the governor-general's task — 'You will

M. *Bangalore dis.t ab.t 3 Miles.*
A. *a Rock Hill on which there is*   SOUTHERLY VIEW of BANGALORE, *by* COL.L CLAUDE MARTIN.   T. *The Pettah of Bangalore.*
R. *a Pagoda.* R. *Cyprus Garden of Tipoo.*   I. *Shevaganga Hill.*
Pub.d May 1.st 1792 by I. Sewell   N. *Saren Droog.*

only occupy such portion of the Garden at Bangalore as may be sufficient for the purpose of a Temporary depot . . . [B]ut you are most especially to observe that this temporary establishment at Bangalore is in no respect whatever to interfere with the primary object of your statistical enquiries with Colin Mackenzie'.[17] In 1802, citing ill health, he asked to be relieved from the Survey. He was made 'Botanist and Naturalist to superintend the Gardens at Bangalore'. However, Lord Valentia, who met him here in 1804, writes of his continued engagement with the object of the survey. 'Mr. Heyne, the Surgeon at this station waited upon me . . . He presented me with the seeds of several plants, and drawings of them, possessing great merit by a native. His knowledge of botany, and his indefatigable exertions, will render the collection he is forming of the plants of the tableland of Mysore valuable and interesting'.[18]

The first published view of the Sultan's Gardens by Colonel Claude Martin (1792), aide to Lord Cornwallis in the Third Mysore War. The gardens were economic as much as aesthetic ventures by Hyder Ali and Tipu Sultan with plants from Mauritius, Persia, China and elsewhere. Claude Martin, *Southerly View of Bangalore*.
Published by J. Sewell, 1792. British Library, IOR P 256
[By permission of the British Library]

For the five years that Heyne was superintendent, the Company's Garden at Bangalore, like the ones at Samalkot and Marmelon, was in constant danger of failing the Company's ambitions for economic returns. These were turbulent years in the assessment of the garden's success: its role viewed at times as providing food for the regimental messes, at other times as demonstrating to the natives the cultivation of European vegetables (potato, turnip, etc.), and at yet other times contributing to the Company's edge in a competitive world market. Its botanical side was hardly considered. In 1806 Heyne reports that 'The first object when allowed to reside at Bangalore in order to superintend the Garden was the introduction of potatoes, turnips and other useful vegetables. . . . I am confident that the confirmation of my first ideas of being able in a few years to supply the Madras Market is not far distant'. In the same report he speaks of encouraging native gardeners to undertake the cultivating of these vegetables. 'I beg leave to observe that hitherto I have been more solicitous to distribute Potatoes among the Gardeners and encouraging them by purchasing the product that to plant them in the Company's Garden

DECCAN TRAVERSES

THE GARDEN
GARDEN CITY
TOTA
GLASS HOUSE
HILL STATION

175

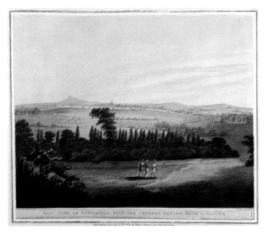

A number of artists drew the gardens of Hyder Ali and Tipu Sultan which they often referred to as the 'Cypress Gardens' after its most conspicuous tree. The Daniells, who came by on 2 May 1792, however, were an exception. '[W]e rode to the Cypress Garden', writes William Daniell in his diary, 'but found nothing there to employ us. The Cypress Trees were large but the building Paltry'.

Robert Home, 'East View of Bangalore with the Cypress Garden'.
Select Views in Mysore, The Country of Tipoo Sultan from Drawings taken on the spot with Historical Descriptions (London: Bowyer, 1794).

James Hunter, 'East View of Bangalore with the Cypress Gardens from a Pagoda'. Francis William Blagdon, *A Brief History of Ancient and Modern India* (London, 1802-05). [Yale Center for British Art, Paul Mellon Collection]

next season, however (in May) I will plant about 4 acres to shew them that the cultivation of this useful root on a large scale is possible'.[19]

Heyne was working to a plan that he put forth in 1800. The Company's garden was to comprise three departments: botanical, practical, and economical. Each had its own reservoir fed by the large tank that existed to the south. The botanical department was divided for annuals and biennials on either side of the 'principal walk' and further subdivided for water and swamp plants, plants growing in stony and sandy soil, and plants from other parts of the world 'chiefly intended for exhibiting the characteristics of the vegetable kingdom in the parts of the globe they are to represent'. The practical department, which was to occupy the middle of the Garden, 'is to contain in different divisions all plants used in medicines and in the different arts for example dyeing and manufacturing cloth, joinery, tanning'. The economical department 'comprehends in different divisions whatever is used for food, an orchard with all culinary vegetables of this country and other produce of nurseries for useful plants to be distributed for general introduction as of coffee, vines, spices, and fruit trees'. This department, he says, would be the first as 'it will serve as a depository and nursery for all plants until the other parts of the Garden are regularly laid out'. The principal divisions were to be 'distinguished by the breadth of the walks and a row of handsome trees as the Cypresses on both sides', and subdivisions were to be 'enclosed by evergreen hedges not so high as to prevent the circulation of the air, the walks between them to be only half as broad as the principal ones'.[20]

Lt. John Blakiston, the architect of Bangalore's cantonment, writes in his memoirs of Heyne's achievement: 'Here was a large botanical garden supported by government. The plants, fruits, and vegetables, of most climates grow here, and many of them in perfection. Potatoes and cabbage, which, when I first arrived in India, were considered rare articles (the former being procured from Bengal, and no larger than a walnut) had, after the establishment of the cantonment, been produced in great abundance, and of excellent quality; and before I quitted the country [1812], the potato of Mysore had become an article of trade to most parts of India'.[21]

In 1807 Heyne asked to be transferred to Cuddapah and it was recommended that the Company's garden at Bangalore be given either to the Mysore government or the commandant of the newly-established Bangalore cantonment, 'either of whom will probably preserve the Apple, Peach and Loquat trees for the fruit which they produce. Potatoes, vegetables in the neighbourhood of a great Military Cantonment will be cultivated by individuals and in proportion to the demand and value in the market'.[22] The Resident of Mysore, Lt. Col.

Malcolm, was approached to put the matter to the Mysore government. Citing the lack of rains and fear that the garden would go to ruin, Malcolm proposed instead that the garden be put 'in charge of an industrious and skilful person who under certain conditions which shall include the preservations of the fruit trees and the extension of the cultivation of potatoes will be allowed to dispose of the produce'.[23] This person was evidently Gilbert Waugh. His tenure as the keeper of the garden extended well beyond the six-months intended by the Resident, long enough for him to take possession of it, so much so that in 1819 he, rather than the Mysore Rajah, was placing the garden 'unconditionally at the disposal of Government with a view to its becoming a source of supply to British India for many of the fruits etc. of England, China & other Countries, together with most of the varieties of Asia which have been introduced with much care and unlimited expense'.[24] Waugh was re-issuing the garden's promise in the net of economic botany now considerably wider than twenty years previously when Heyne took over the Sultan's garden.

Drawing identifying characteristics of plants was a defining activity of a botanical garden and the training of natives to draw was a legacy of surgeon-naturalists of the East India Company like Benjamin Heyne. However, none of the plant drawings done under Heyne by a native, which Lord Valentia in 1804 found 'possessing great merit', and which the Court of Directors of the Company in 1806 say that they 'received and deposited in our library' appear to have survived. A century later, however, artists such as K. Cheluviah Raju would be prolific in their renderings of plants cultivated in Lalbagh, as Heyne's 'Company Garden' came to be called in the 1820s.

[Lalbagh Library, Bangalore]

The 'Rain Tree' (Samanea saman), a popular avenue tree closely associated with the image of Bangalore today, was one of many plants that
would be introduced through the Sultan's garden as it evolved through
the eighteenth century along a trajectory set by Benjamin Heyne and
Gilbert Waugh.

15° 00'

14° 45'

14° 30'

14° 15'

14° 00'

13° 45'

13° 30'

13° 15'

13° 00'

KEW   50° N

MALTA   40° N

SAHARANPUR   30° N

CALCUTTA   20° N

JAMAICA

LATITUDE

BANGALORE   12° 57' N
OOTACAMUND   10° N

PERADENIYA

SINGAPORE   0°

10° S

MAURITIUS   20° S

DECCAN TRAVERSES

THE GARDEN
GARDEN CITY
TOTA
GLASS HOUSE
HILL STATION

179

GARDEN CITY

Waugh's garden was taken by the Mysore Rajah's government after Hasting's rejection of it in 1819. It was given the name 'Laulbagh', a name largely believed to have been taken from Tipu Sultan's palace garden at Seringapatam which was destroyed in 1799 when the Company army used its trees as timber in the siege of that island's fort. Lalbagh, though, was a common name for what Issac Burkill calls 'gardens of ease' built under Persian influence in North India and carried, he says, to South India by rulers like Tipu Sultan.[25] Applied to Waugh's garden in Bangalore in the 1820s, however, Lalbagh had less to do with either the Sultan's memory or with Persian influence. It had more to do with the English garden. It would be described by a garden superintendent in 1874 as follows: 'The Lal Bagh is a name which is not familiar to Englishmen; it is derived from the Hindustani language, and signifies red-as-ruby garden. The word Bagh in India means the same as the word garden in England. . . English fruits and vegetables do well; and we have all the ordinary ornaments of an English garden, such as Violets, Pansies, . . .'[26] This English garden had much to do with pleasure. 'In the public garden of Lalbagh', notes Lewin Bowring, chief commissioner of Mysore (1857-62), 'the visitor might at first imagine himself transported to a purely European pleasure-ground, till advancing he sees the gorgeous creepers, the wide-spreading mango and the graceful betel-nut trees which characterize the East. The garden is a beautiful retreat . . .'[27] Within the parameters of a retreat, the garden carried out the three steps of economic botany, viz., introduction, acclimatisation and dissemination. The public came to be transported to a European pleasure ground, but also to take seeds, seedlings, plants, and lessons in cultivation.

The turn to a public garden began in earnest in 1836 when the Agricultural and Horticultural Society of India, a popular movement, was given charge of Lalbagh by Mark Cubbon, the chief commissioner of Mysore under the Madras government that was administering the state in place of the Rajah who had been stripped of his powers in 1831. 'Great public benefit may be expected to arise from this institution', he said, 'not only in objects merely Horticultural and the extension of Botanical knowledge, but in the promotion of the agricultural interests of the country by the introduction of new and valuable

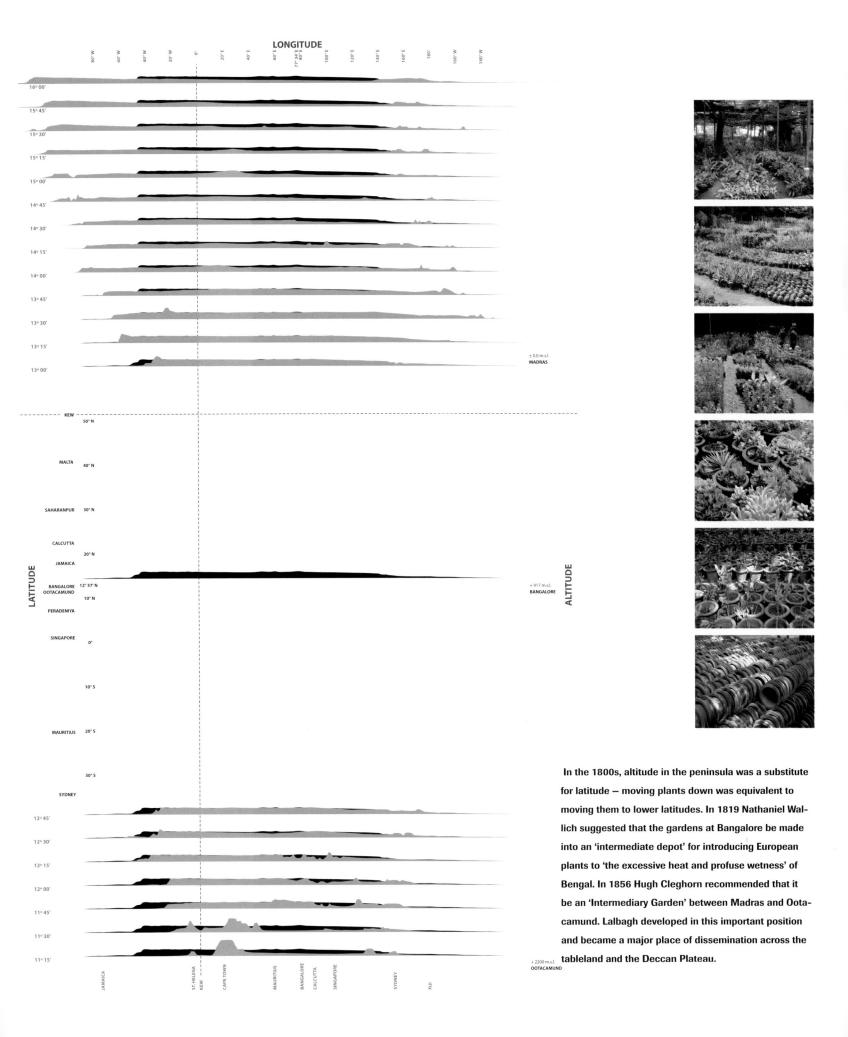

LONGITUDE

LATITUDE

ALTITUDE

± 0.0 m.s.l.
MADRAS

+ 917 m.s.l.
BANGALORE

+ 2200 m.s.l.
OOTACAMUND

In the 1800s, altitude in the peninsula was a substitute for latitude — moving plants down was equivalent to moving them to lower latitudes. In 1819 Nathaniel Wallich suggested that the gardens at Bangalore be made into an 'intermediate depot' for introducing European plants to 'the excessive heat and profuse wetness' of Bengal. In 1856 Hugh Cleghorn recommended that it be an 'Intermediary Garden' between Madras and Ootacamund. Lalbagh developed in this important position and became a major place of dissemination across the tableland and the Deccan Plateau.

DECCAN TRAVERSES

THE GARDEN
GARDEN CITY
TOTA
GLASS HOUSE
HILL STATION

181

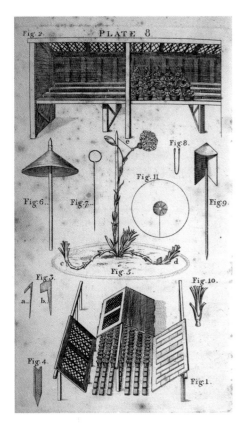

In his report of 1838, William Munro, secretary of the Mysore Agri-Horticultural Society, writes of how the Society had effected 'considerable improvement . . . in the flower pots which after some trouble are now regularly made after the English shape and size, and are kept in the gardens, sized and marked to agree with books on English gardening'.

William Curtis, *The Botanical Magazine or Flower-Garden Displayed. . . . A Work intended for the Use of such Ladies and Gentlemen, and Gardeners, as wish to become scientifically acquainted with Plants they cultivate,* vol. 1, Plate 8 (London: Stephen Couchman, 1793). [Annenberg Rare Book and Manuscript Library, University of Pennsylvania]

LEFT

Nurseries in and around Bangalore carry out Lalbagh's experimental and demonstrative agendas.

productions suited to the climate amongst which may be enumerated varieties of sugarcane and tobacco far superior to any, now produced in Mysore and by affording the people the means of obtaining gratuitous instruction in improved modes of cultivation'.[28]

The Society was founded by William Carey in 1820 in Calcutta, gathering members there and in branches elsewhere on the subcontinent. Like Joseph Banks, they were ardent advocates for the advancement of horticulture and agriculture. The Company welcomed their energy and even patronised the society with grants and land for experiments in cultivation. In a number of places, including Bombay (1830), Madras (1835), Ootacamund (1848), and Lahore (1851), botanical gardens began as a result of this movement by amateurs. In the case of Bangalore, Lalbagh was available.

The Society ran the garden through a committee subscriptions from members. The need for funds and membership encouraged public-oriented activities such as flower shows which brought people to the garden as viewers and as participants. They experimented with manures, plantings, and ploughs. The Society introduced useful crops, sought more productive ones, and, above all, made every effort to expose local people to the benefits of new introductions and technologies, giving tickets of admission to influential people to pass on to 'any native who might wish to go into the garden for the purpose of seeing, gaining information or receiving seeds'.[29] The results went beyond plants and crops to 'rendering the inhabitants yearly more and more alive and expert at the application of skill and adaptation of scientific invention'.[30] This aim would continue to remain with Lalbagh.

The Society dissolved in 1842, the fluctuating nature of a military station cited as the reason. Their contribution was recognised by the Madras government which notes its successes a decade later: 'Most of the approved European vegetables were brought into general cultivation, and several exotic fruit trees were successfully introduced, and the finer varieties propagated. Gardening among the Mysoreans received a considerable impulse, as shown in the increased quantity and improved quality of European fruits and vegetables procurable in the bazaars'.[31] More importantly, however, they cultivated the 'Garden City' — a population cultured through the garden to appreciate the benefits of economic botany. It is not surprising that a decade after the Society's closure, it took some work to single Lalbagh out in a land where it was once conspicuous. When Hugh Cleghorn, botanical advisor to the Madras government, was asked in 1856 to identify a place for a garden in Bangalore that would serve as an intermediary between Madras and Ootacamund in acclimatising plants to the subcontinent, Lalbagh was not the obvious choice. 'Several localities were examined; and it was ultimately agreed that the Lal Bagh (formerly selected by Hyder for a garden) was, on the whole, the most eligible spot for the purpose'.[32]

Cleghorn was acting on a recommendation he had made when asked by the government to initiate a more coordinated system of plant introductions in the Madras Presidency:[33] 'The difference of temperature between the Neilgherry Hills and the Carnatic plains is so great that I fear many valuable plants acclimatized in the former, would not succeed if at once transplanted into the latter, and I would therefore suggest that Government should propose to the Commissioner of Mysore, the establishment of a Garden under skilled Superintendence at Bangalore'.[34] Cleghorn left Bangalore in October 1856 convinced that it 'is much better suited for agricultural and horticultural experiments than either Ootacamund or Madras; and, from its central position and intermediate elevation, the finer kinds of vegetables and better sorts of graft trees may be disseminated with great success'.[35]

Thus in 1856 the Sultan's Garden, which had fallen into disrepair, was revived yet again. Cleghorn's recommendation led to a string of superintendents from Kew who resuscitated the garden, rekindling its place on the world-wide web of economic botany. These professionals were what the Agri-Horticultural Society had called for, viz., scientific and practical men who took the Mysore Tableland as their field of work while maintaining Lalbagh as the exemplar public garden that combined leisure with learning through information and demonstration. In 1874 Edward Lear calls it 'the Kew of India. Never saw a more beautiful place, terraces, trellises, etc., not to speak of some wild beasts. Flowers exquisite'.[36] But beyond its aesthetic value, Lalbagh became under these professionals, a powerful instrument of industry, economic development and material improvement.

Under them, Lalbagh was clearly permeating the tableland, most obviously in the 'charbaghs' that characterise the many city parks and institutional gardens of the state and the 'nurseries' that experimented with hybrids and new introductions, but also in agricultural fields, forests, farms, railway corridors and stations, avenues, plantations, hill stations, vineyards and traffic islands. It was contributing to both sides of what was becoming an increasingly engrained divide — town and country or urban and rural. 'Finer skills and more developed ideals', writes Gustav Krumbiegal who took over Lalbagh and the other gardens of the state from Cameron in 1908, set horticulture apart from agriculture but it also takes it beyond use and commerce toward the refined art of 'Landscape Gardening', from where it is a 'natural step to Town planning. The laying out of Open Spaces, avenues, and Boulevards are but natural adjuncts to Landscape Gardening'.[37] The distinction, which would not have occurred to either Joseph Banks or Benjamin Heyne a century before, endowed towns and cities with the finer arts of 'gardening' and 'town planning', implicitly attributing to villages and the country rougher utilitarian and

Month	Scientific name	Common name
	Amherstia nobilis	
		silk cotton
	Tabebuia argentea	
		Tabebuia spectabilis
JAN	Saraca asoca (ashoka)	
	Magnifera indica	
	Salmalia malabarica	
	Magnolia grandiflora	
	Tabebuia spectabilis	
	Jacaranda mimosiflora	
		ashoka
FEB	Butea monoperma	
		mango
	Alstonia scholaris	
	Pterospermum acerifolium	
		k. champa
		tree of gold
	Grevillea robusta	
		jacaranda
		flame of the forest
	Delonix regia	
MAR		
		temple tree
	Enterolobium saman	
		silver oak
	Terminalia arjuna	
	Michelia champaca	
	Syzygium cumini	kadamba
APR	Azadirachta indica	queen's flower
		pink cassia
		rain tree
		magnolia
		arjuna
		jamun
MAY		neem / margosa
	Lagerstroemia speciosa	
	Cassia nodosa	
		red cassia
		copper pod
		gulmohar
JUN	Anthocephalus cadamba	
	Cassia marginata	
JUL		
		sampige
AUG		
		coral wood
		Tabebuia avellanedae
		purple bauhinia
		Cassia spectabilis
		african tulip
SEP	Peltophorum pterocarpum	amherstia
	Plumeria rubra	
OCT	Parkia biglandulosa	
	Adenanthera pavonina	
		devil's tree
	Cassia spectabilis	
	Millingtonia hortensis	
NOV		
	Tabebuia avellanedae	
	Bauhinia purpurea	
		cork tree
	Spathodea campanulata	
DEC		Parkia biglandulosa

DECCAN TRAVERSES

THE GARDEN
GARDEN CITY
TOTA
GLASS HOUSE
HILL STATION

183

informal practices. In Bangalore, Krumbiegal initiated a public movement in the vein of the short-lived Agri-Horticultural Society; but as would be expected of its now urbane membership, agriculture was dropped from its name and its interest. It is called the Mysore Horticultural Society.

In time, town planning as an instrument of horticulture would enforce the separation of urban from rural by enclosing the former, conceptually at first, but from the 1960s, physically, with a green belt. Enclosure put into effect one of the most distinctive characteristics of the garden. According to *The Dictionary of Art*, 'The etymology of words for garden confirms their essential characteristic of enclosure. The enclosed area is visibly different from the surrounding land by virtue of the extent, scope and variety of its elaboration and decoration'.[38] Enclosure allowed Bangalore to be portrayed as a protected and privileged entity — a 'pensioner's paradise', 'haven', 'retreat'. Lalbagh, Bangalore's first garden, had cultivated the Garden City.

LEFT

Gustav Krumbiegel, superintendent of Lalbagh in the 1910s and 1920s, believed that town planning was a 'natural step' from 'landscape gardening'. He is said to have undertaken a number of design initiatives including parks and the planting of roads so that at least one tree was in bloom at any time of the year, a phenomenon called serial blossoming. One visitor during his tenure writes, 'the cleanliness and the picturesque layouts of the parks in the city cannot fail to impress and delight the visitor even under the condition of drought and the wealth of colour in the gold mohar and cassia trees now in full bloom, in some measures provide relief'.

ABOVE

Charbaghs in neighbourhood parks, institutional gardens, and even homes reflect the formal vocabulary introduced through Lalbagh. The centre of these Charbaghs is less the source of four rivers that it is believed to be in the Persian ancestor of the same name and more an intersection of two paths marked by a water fountain, flower pot, statue or some other signifying object.

The Garden City title for Bangalore comes as much from the gardens, avenues, parks, traffic islands, etc. within the city, as from the city itself being an entity that contrasts with its rural surroundings.

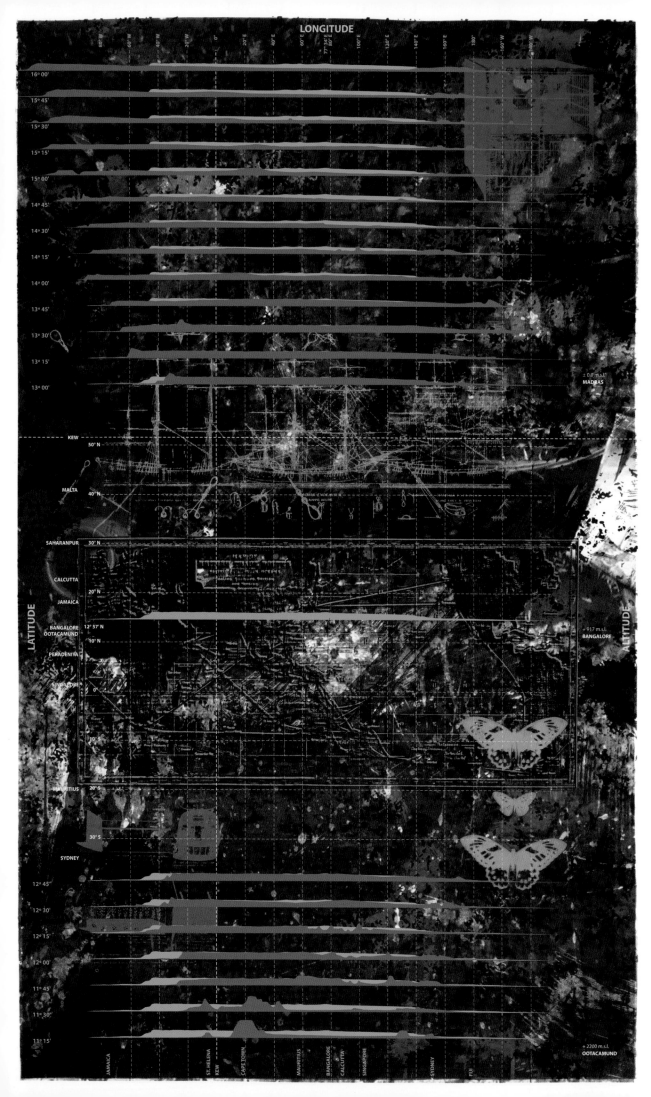

LONGITUDE

LATITUDE

ALTITUDE

Garden City 1

Screen Print on paper, 22"x30" + Digital Plot

Garden City 2

Screen Print on paper, 22"x30" + Digital Plot

BUYING

TYING

7

1

SELLING

WEIGHING

...DAY MARKET

7

6

...LESWARAM MARKET

GANES...

SIFTING

...SHMINARAYANASWAMI TEMPLE

THREADING

...A MANDIR

INDIRANAGAR...

SOMESHWARA T...

5

6

NEW

...Y MARKET

...YANAGAR MARKET

AUSTIN TOWN M...

...AJI TEMPLE

WEIGHING

5

4

...IGANGADESHWARA TEMPLE

WILSON GARDENS M...

...L TEMPLE

JAYANAGAR SHOPPING COM...

4

THREADING

3

THURSDAY M...

...ASHAKARI TEMPLE

MEASURING

DECCAN TRAVERSES

THE GARDEN
GARDEN CITY
TOTA
GLASS HOUSE
HILL STATION

187

TOTA

A yellay tota with the betel-leaf vine growing around the betel nut palm. Folklore has it that Lalbagh was once a yellay tota. Translated as garden, tota differs from the pleasure garden in that it produces goods for a market rather than being a place for leisure.

In 1800 Francis Buchanan, a naturalist under the orders of Governor-General Richard Wellesley, set out to investigate 'the state of agriculture, arts, and commerce; the religion, manners, and customs; the history natural and civil, and antiquities' of the former dominions of Tipu Sultan. He identified three cultivated 'grounds' on the tableland: the *tota*, the wet land, and the dry field. The wet land and dry field, he describes as 'open' and planted with crops and grains. The first was irrigated with water collected in tanks, the second was dependent on rains alone. The tota, a Kannada word which he translates as garden, was by contrast 'enclosed' and of four kinds: the kitchen garden (*tarkari tota*) for growing vegetables, the coconut garden (*tayngana tota*) which included other fruit trees, the betel-leaf garden (*yellay tota*) producing the leaf chewed in *supari*, and the flower garden (*huvina tota*) cultivated by those who made garlands. The tota was further distinguished from the open cultivations by a social hierarchy. 'A gardener is here a separate profession from a farmer, and is considered as inferior in rank'. In common with the wet lands and the dry fields, however, totas were places that produced goods for the market.[39]

At Bangalore, in the second week of May 1800, Buchanan records a visit to the 'gardens made by the late Mussulman princes, Hyder and Tipoo'. Though he refers to them as gardens, they do not appear to fit any of his categories of the tota. Their form appeared to him to be in the 'Mussulman fashion', making them evidently extraordinary elements in a journey underwritten by the ordinariness of the tota, the wet land and the dry field. The gardens, Buchanan notes, 'are extensive, and divided into square plots separated by walks, the sides of which are ornamented with fine cypress trees. The plots are filled with fruit trees, and pot-herbs. The Mussulman fashion is to have a separate piece of ground allotted for each kind of plant. Thus one plot is entirely filled with rose trees, another with pomegranates, and so forth'. He observes, however, an experimental aspect to the garden. Tipu Sultan, he found, used the garden to introduce mulberry (from China via Bengal) for making silk, an industry that thrived in the pettah. '*Tippoo* had commenced a trial, but his arbitrary measures were little calculated to ensure success. Some mulberry trees, however, that remain in his gardens, show how well the plant agrees with this climate'.[40] There were custard apples, apples, peaches, varieties of rice, wheat, sorghum, beans, roses, and so on.

Two huvina totas, one planted with jasmine and the other with marigold. Both flowers are extensively used in making garlands.

In the city market flowers are sold by the kilogramme

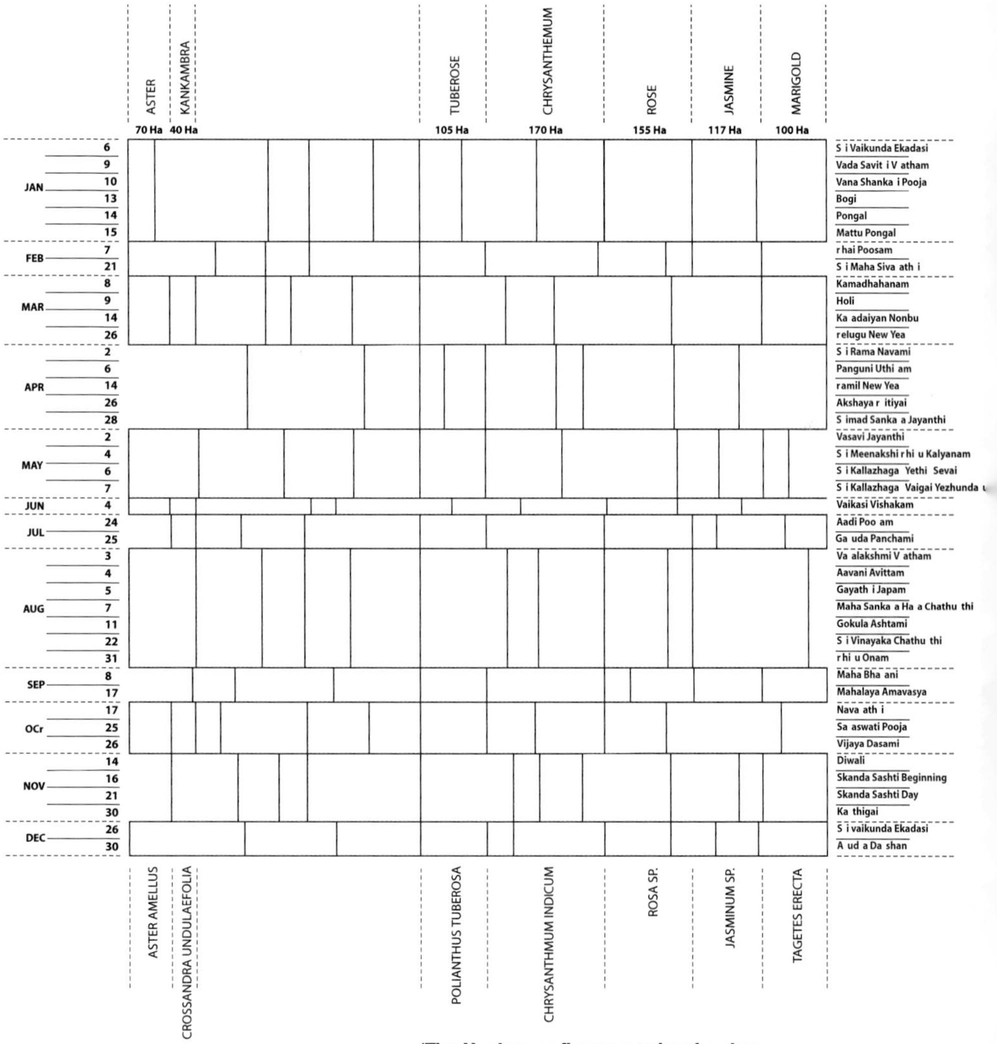

Chart — flower crops (column headers with area):

ASTER 70 Ha | KANKAMBRA 40 Ha | TUBEROSE 105 Ha | CHRYSANTHEMUM 170 Ha | ROSE 155 Ha | JASMINE 117 Ha | MARIGOLD 100 Ha

Botanical names (below): ASTER AMELLUS · CROSSANDRA UNDULAEFOLIA · POLIANTHUS TUBEROSA · CHRYSANTHMUM INDICUM · ROSA SP. · JASMINUM SP. · TAGETES ERECTA

Calendar (months, dates) and festivals:

JAN	6	S i Vaikunda Ekadasi
	9	Vada Savit i V atham
	10	Vana Shanka i Pooja
	13	Bogi
	14	Pongal
	15	Mattu Pongal
FEB	7	r hai Poosam
	21	S i Maha Siva ath i
MAR	8	Kamadhahanam
	9	Holi
	14	Ka adaiyan Nonbu
	26	relugu New Yea
APR	2	S i Rama Navami
	6	Panguni Uthi am
	14	ramil New Yea
	26	Akshaya r itiyai
	28	S imad Sanka a Jayanthi
MAY	2	Vasavi Jayanthi
	4	S i Meenakshi r hi u Kalyanam
	6	S i Kallazhaga Yethi Sevai
	7	S i Kallazhaga Vaigai Yezhunda
JUN	4	Vaikasi Vishakam
JUL	24	Aadi Poo am
	25	Ga uda Panchami
AUG	3	Va alakshmi V atham
	4	Aavani Avittam
	5	Gayath i Japam
	7	Maha Sanka a Ha a Chathu thi
	11	Gokula Ashtami
	22	S i Vinayaka Chathu thi
	31	r hi u Onam
SEP	8	Maha Bha ani
	17	Mahalaya Amavasya
OCr	17	Nava ath i
	25	Sa aswati Pooja
	26	Vijaya Dasami
NOV	14	Diwali
	16	Skanda Sashti Beginning
	21	Skanda Sashti Day
	30	Ka thigai
DEC	26	S i vaikunda Ekadasi
	30	A ud a Da shan

In the gardens of the Mussulman princes, part of Lalbagh today, Buchanan had discovered that the Mysore Tableland was already on a global terrain of economic botany. These gardens cut across his categories of cultivated grounds. This was a tota of totas but also a dry field of dry fields and a wet land of wet lands. Other 'royal gardens' at Malavalli, Seringapatam, Sira, Bednore, and elsewhere in Mysore were similar points of generation and connection.

'The Huvina, or flower gardens', writes Francis Buchanan in 1800, 'are cultivated near towns and populous places which afford a market for their produce'. Produced by the hectare and sold by the kilogramme, the flowers of the huvina tota are less about being seen and appreciated and more about being used for occasions, felicitations and rituals.

DECCAN TRAVERSES

THE GARDEN
GARDEN CITY
TOTA
GLASS HOUSE
HILL STATION

189

The jasmine or mallige, a popular fragrant flower that adorns women's hair and deities appeared in William Curtis's *The Botanical Magazine* **as a flower native to India.**

The Botanical Magazine or Flower-Garden Displayed. . . . A Work intended for the Use of such Ladies and Gentlemen, and Gardeners, as wish to become scientifically acquainted with Plants they cultivate, vol. 1, (London: Stephen Couchman, 1793) [Annenberg Rare Book and Manuscript Library, University of Pennsylvania]

However, while the generative garden like Lalbagh remains a place to connect materially with the totas, the dry fields, and the wet lands of the Mysore Table-land, and indeed with the fluid terrain of economic botany, a more common threshold is the market. Here exchange and movement occur in a manner not unlike the world of Joseph Banks and Francis Buchanan. The material involved, however, is neither dried specimens heading to herbariums nor plants travelling between botanical and horticultural enterprises; it is the pro-duce of Buchanan's 'cultivated grounds'. This material draws attention to merchants and merchandise. It is the other end of economic botany, which many see as the starting point of the field — the world of consumers, profit, bargains, and social benefits. Indeed it was the basis of the partnership that Joseph Banks struck with the East India Company, often declaring that particular discoveries and cultivations would be 'essentially advantageous not only to science, but to the investment of the Company'.[41]

The hub of this economic world is a kilometre east of the gardens of the Mussulman princes, just outside the walls of the pettah, the City Market or the Krishnarajendra Market. Produce comes here from cultivated grounds at distances modulated by concerns for its freshness as much as by tariffs, borders, seasons, mishaps and disasters. Today, this distance extends across the tableland and to the land below the ghats. It is this terrain of movement that John Cameron sought to intersect in the late nineteenth century with a new vegetable that he had introduced into Lalbagh from the global fabric of plant movement: chow-chow. He writes of going on horseback to the tollgate early on a 'market day' to hand the vegetable to gardeners who had come there to sell their produce, seeking to interest them in cultivating it. The vineyard-looking chow-chow crop is today a common sight across the tableland. Later, superintendents preferred to intersect the market more formally through 'progeny orchards, nursery centres and places of demonstration of new crops and new technology to the farmers'.[42]

While much of the produce of cultivated grounds disperses from City Market to other markets and homes, one particular material suspends consumption long enough to generate a second life in the city, viz., flowers. This produce of the huvina tota, Buchanan said, was grown by those who make garlands. The garlands are actually made by vendors in the market, threaded into strings of jasmine (mallige), tuberoses, marigolds, asters, roses and their combinations. He would certainly find the paths in this flower market slovenly if not disordered as he did the Sultan's gardens at Bangalore, saying at the time, 'The walks are not gravelled and the cultivation of the whole is rather slovenly. . . The taste of Haider accorded more with the English than that of his son. His walks are wider, his cypress-trees are not so much crowded'.[43] Walks in the flower market are dictated less by order and more by the immediacies and adjacencies of daily settlement. They respond to the contingencies of a terrain that is subject, on the one hand, to a fragile infrastructure of road and rail and, on the other hand, to events on diverse and emergent calendars. Flowers here are sold by weight rather than admired as individual specimens. Strings of flowers from here find their way to other markets, homes and temples, but they also move around the city in women's hair and on deities in vehicles. They are everyday adornments as well as marks of auspicious occasions and felicitations. In contrast to the fixity and sequential rhythms of the blossoms of gardens, these flowers are a fleeting presence, embellishing diverse and multiple rituals, events and individuals.

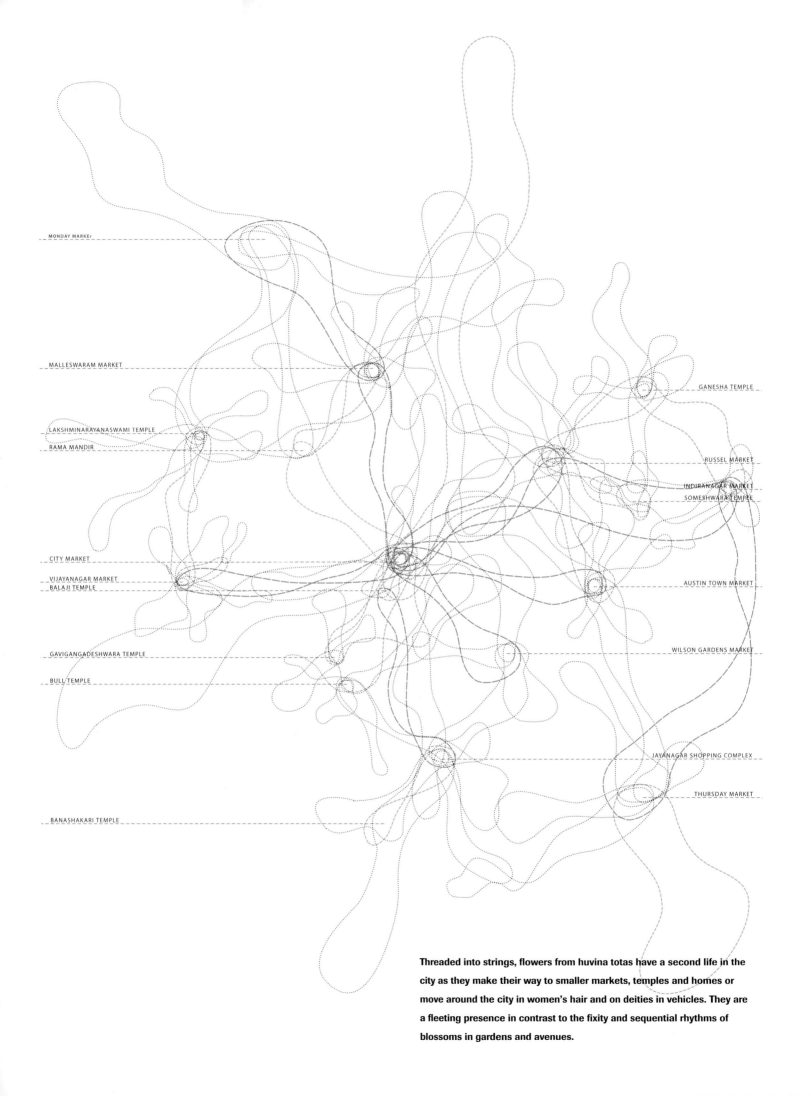

MONDAY MARKET

MALLESWARAM MARKET

GANESHA TEMPLE

LAKSHMINARAYANASWAMI TEMPLE
RAMA MANDIR

RUSSEL MARKET

INDIRANAGAR MARKET
SOMESHWARA TEMPLE

CITY MARKET

VIJAYANAGAR MARKET
BALAJI TEMPLE

AUSTIN TOWN MARKET

GAVIGANGADESHWARA TEMPLE

WILSON GARDENS MARKET

BULL TEMPLE

JAYANAGAR SHOPPING COMPLEX

THURSDAY MARKET

BANASHAKARI TEMPLE

Threaded into strings, flowers from huvina totas have a second life in the city as they make their way to smaller markets, temples and homes or move around the city in women's hair and on deities in vehicles. They are a fleeting presence in contrast to the fixity and sequential rhythms of blossoms in gardens and avenues.

DECCAN TRAVERSES

THE GARDEN
GARDEN CITY
TOTA
GLASS HOUSE
HILL STATION

191

City Market or Krishna Rajendra Market provides a view into the huvina tota, the fields
of flowers. Here flowers are sorted, weighed, threaded and sold by the arm-length.
Vendors' piles are constantly reconfigured. Buyer's walks are dictated less by designed
orders as in the English garden and more by the immediacies and adjacencies of daily
settlement of vendors, prices and negotiations.

Tota 1

Screen Print on paper, 22"x30" + Digital Plot

Tota 2

Screen Print on paper, 22"x30" + Digital Plot

DEDICATED TO H.R.H. PRINCE ALBERT, K.G., ETC. ETC. ETC.

TALLIS'S

HISTORY AND DESCRIPTION

OF THE

CRYSTAL PALACE

Exhibition of the World's Industry in 1851,

ILLUSTRATED BY

BEAUTIFUL STEEL ENGRAVINGS,

FROM ORIGINAL DRAWINGS AND DAGUERREOTYPES

BY BEARD, MAYALL, ETC. ETC.

VOL. III

DECCAN TRAVERSES

THE GARDEN
GARDEN CITY
TOTA
GLASS HOUSE
HILL STATION

195

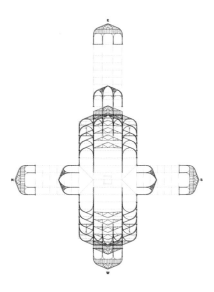

GLASS HOUSE

Four decades after the Great Exhibition in London, a crystal of a kind was assembled in Lalbagh. It was many times smaller than Paxton's creation, but it uses a key innovation of his design — web-like cantilevers inspired by the stem of the giant water lily of Brazil which supports two-metre-diameter-leaves, the buoyancy of which can hold upto seventy pounds. It helped him maximise the surface of glass and minimise the iron work, leading one commentator to remark that in the Crystal Palace 'all materiality merges into atmosphere'.

During his tenure as chief commissioner of Mysore in the 1850-60s, Lewin Bowring observed that 'at the monthly shows, held in the neat market place in the cantonment, a stranger will be surprised to see the interest taken by the native gardeners in the improvement of their stock, and the intelligent competition to which these periodical exhibitions have given rise'.[44] If demonstration set the tone of the European pleasure ground in Bangalore in his time, it appears that exhibition set the tone of the market. A decade before Bowring took over the administration of Mysore, Prince Albert had offered a glimpse into this market on a global scale. 'Whilst formerly . . . knowledge was confined to the few, now . . . knowledge acquired becomes at once the property of the community at large; for, whilst formerly discovery was wrapped in secrecy, the publicity of the present day causes that no sooner is a discovery or invention made than it is already improved upon and surpassed by competing efforts'. The consort of Queen Victoria was drumming up support for the Great Exhibition of the Works of Industry of All Nations in London. The exhibition was to be 'a true test and a living picture of the point of development at which the whole of mankind has arrived . . . and a new starting-point from which all nations will be able to direct their further exertions'.[45]

The Great Exhibition ran from 1 May to 11 October in Hyde Park, London, featuring more than one hundred thousand exhibits. 'Every possible invention and appliance for the service of man found a place within its embracing limits; every realization of human genius, every effort of human industry might be contemplated therein, from the most consummate elaboration of the profoundest intellect, to the simplest contrivance of uneducated thought'.[46] Little remains in memory of the exhibits. The building, however, that housed the exhibition is not easily forgotten. This 'House of Glass', John Tallis wrote at the time, 'will exist in the annals of history, long after the vaunted pyramids of Egypt, of which the builders and the object are already alike unknown, shall have crumbled to dust'.[47] This eighteen-acre enclosure (1,851 feet long, 450 feet wide) was the work of a gardener, Joseph Paxton.

The flower shows began in 1836 when Lalbagh was in the hands of the Agri-Horticultural Society of India. The object of the shows then was to raise money and interest in horticulture, demonstrate new plants and technologies to local inhabitants, and encourage 'intelligent competition'.

DECCAN TRAVERSES

THE GARDEN
GARDEN CITY
TOTA
GLASS HOUSE
HILL STATION

197

John Tallis, 'The Transept of the Great Exhibition'. The Crystal Palace covered close to eighteen acres of Hyde Park. With a height of 108 feet to the top of the barrel vault that defined its transept, it took in some of the elm trees of the park, always reminding visitors of its roots in the botanical conservatory.

History and Description of the Crystal Palace, and the Exhibition of the World's Industry in 1851 (London: John Tallis & Co.)

Paxton's model was the plant conservatory – a greenhouse that provided a tropical environment in a temperate land. As head gardener of the Duke of Devonshire's estate, Paxton had experimented with the construction of conservatories, seeking to increase the proportion of glass to support structure. It was a need for light (and warmth) well understood by a gardener who was the first to bring the giant Brazilian water lily, *Victoria amazonica* (*Victoria regia* at the time), to flower in Europe. His success at maximising light is recognised in the name that the building in Hyde Park acquired: Crystal Palace. 'As in a crystal', one commentator notes, 'there is no longer any true interior or exterior. The barrier erected between us and the landscape is almost ethereal. . . We find ourselves within a cut-out segment of atmosphere'.[48] Programmatically too this was an open place. 'This glass-covered vacuum will suit anything one wishes to bring into it', observes Gottfried Semper; it is 'to a certain extent the embodiment of the tendency toward which our age seems to be moving'.[49] The Crystal Palace was dismantled and moved to Sydenham Hill in Kent, south of London, where, doubled in size, it lived up to Semper's image, housing everything from concerts to horticultural shows, games to photographic exhibitions, demonstrations to science fairs.

In 1889, a 'glass-covered vacuum' like the Crystal Palace, though many times smaller than Paxton's creation, came to Lalbagh from England. When its kit of parts first arrived and the Prince of Wales laid the foundation stone in November of that year, it was considered a place for horticultural shows. Since then, however, its record of events is comparable to the complex on Sydenham Hill. And although it is often referred to as a conservatory, the term is less an acknowledgment of its greenhouse effect and more an admission of an enclosure. One author refers to this structure as the sanctum sanctorum of Lalbagh, while the former president of India, R. Venkataraman called it the diamond in the pendant in the necklace of Bangalore's parks. But even more than enclosure, it is the ability to stimulate competition and invention through exhibition that the Glass House draws comparisons with Paxton's creation.

The competitive side of the Crystal Palace is revealed in force in Bangalore on the occasions of horticultural shows, a tradition that began with the Agri-Horticultural Society in the 1830s to gain membership, support and to 'educate the natives'. Today, people attend the shows in thousands. At these times the Glass House becomes a startling contrast even to the gardens that surround it, but more importantly it becomes a space invested in by competitors. They are there to exhibit their goods; but they are also there to touch the spirit of the Crystal Palace – the 'stimulus for invention' and the 'improvement of stock'. A former superintendent of Lalbagh provides an extensive list of plants introduced and popularised through exhibits in the Glass House, some of them becoming commercial crops in the region, others reaching home gardens.[50] But these occasions are not just about plants leaving the Crystal Palace; they are also about the Crystal Palace leaving Lalbagh as people put their gardens on show and in competition organised by the Mysore Horticultural Society. Ultimately Lalbagh itself leaves Bangalore. Writing about how William New, the first superintendent in the post-1856 era, inspired him with the idea of development through the Lalbagh shows, M.H. Marigowda, superintendent in the 1950s and 1960s writes, 'it occurred to me that if the East India Company could make use of Lalbagh to develop Great Britain, why should we not make use of Lalbagh to develop every family in every village in the state? Literally, "I let go Lalbagh to every village in Karnataka"'.[51]

Glass House 1

Screen Print on paper, 22"x30" + Digital Plot

Glass House 2

Screen Print on paper, 22"x30" + Digital Plot

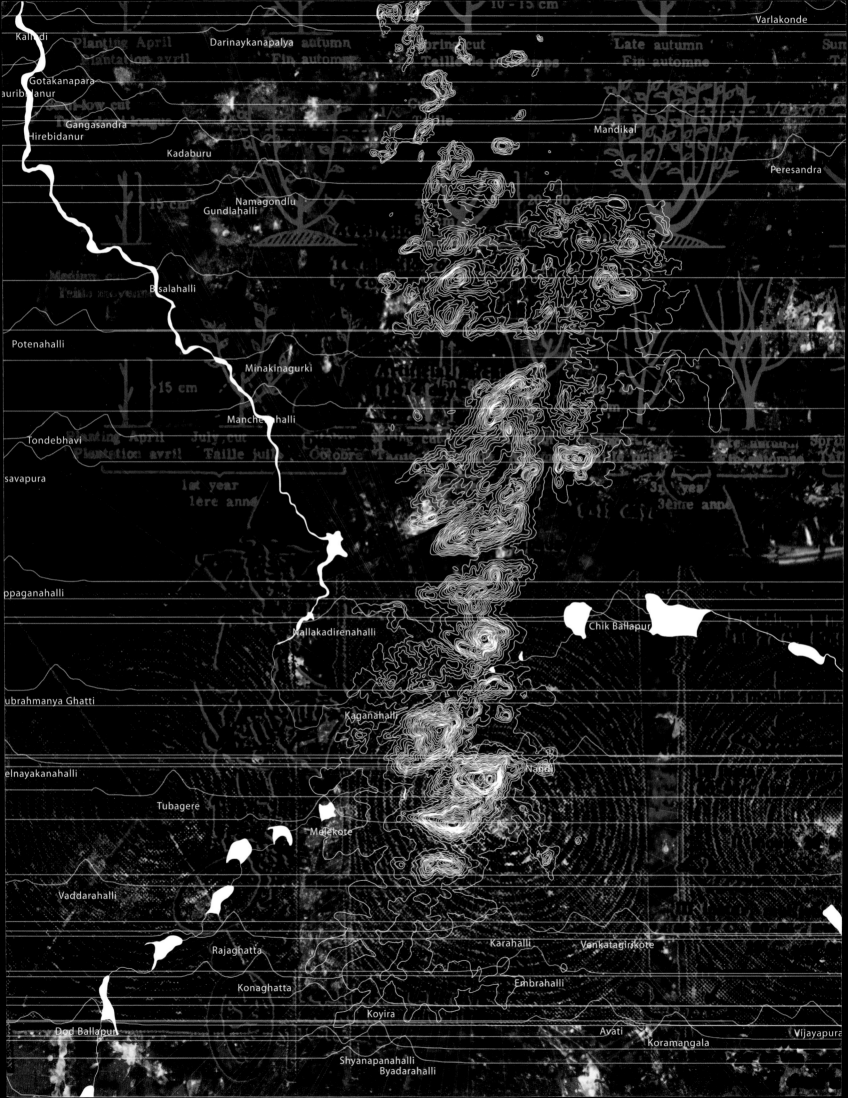

DECCAN TRAVERSES

THE GARDEN
GARDEN CITY
TOTA
GLASS HOUSE
HILL STATION

201

HILL STATION

Robert H Colebrooke, 'North West View of
Nandydroog'. The droog, bare of trees in
1791 would become a popular and verdant
hill station, its popularity beginning with
soldiers posted there. To be 'stationed at
Nandidroog pleased us all as it was a retired,
quiet and cool station', writes Major H.
Bevan. It was different for the natives. 'The
servants', writes Mrs Bowring, 'object to the
durg entirely, owing to the cold, so there was
a general distribution of blankets and coats'.

Twelve Views of Places in the Kingdom of Mysore
(London, 1794). [Yale Center for British Art, Paul
Mellon Collection]

The line of the Bangalore ridge, which divides the waters of the Arkavati on the west from
the South Pinakini on the east, extends north to culminate in an intersection with a similar
line running east-west fifty kilometres north of Bangalore. It is a T-Junction of ridges. The
east-west ridge, geologists say, is a further up-warping of a surface that had already gone
through a plateau uplift, an event which raised the land in dome-like fashion as the Indian
plate passed over a 'hot spot' on its migration north well before it collided with the Eurasian
plate to raise the Himalayas. Centred near the present west coast, the dome fractured down
its middle. The west half 'down-faulted' and drifted away to make room for the Arabian
Sea and expose the formidable Western Ghats that once kept travellers from the interior;
the east half, which slopes distinctly from the Western Ghats toward the east, drains the
entire Mysore Tableland into the Bay of Bengal. The east-west line, between the thirteenth
and fourteenth parallels, divides this slope into a north and south surface. The Arkavati
and South Pinakini gather two of the many folds of the latter.

As if to celebrate the point at which these two cardinal ridges intersect is one of the
highest grounds on the tableland, Nandi Hill. Its situation was somehow obvious to
surveyor Robert Colebrooke who drew it in 1791 during Cornwallis's campaign. Calling
Nandi a 'fortified mountain', he writes, 'The plain on which it stands, is supposed to be the
highest in the Peninsula of India, and the summit of the hill the most elevated point'.[52] This mountain
is the culmination of a string of granite hills that increase in height as they come from the north to
meet the intersection. Apparently moulded in a pocket below the surface as intrusive rock, these hills
– batholiths to the geomorphologist – were eventually exposed with the erosion of the gneiss terrane
around them. Their southern culmination in Nandi is dramatic. To Mrs Bowring, coming from the south,
it was a 'great rock mountain rising in a precipitous manner, and its gigantic sides looking ready to fall
and crush you'.[53] Eight decades earlier this was a very real fear. In the 1791 battle for the mountain, writes
Roderick Mackenzie, 'stones of immense weight . . . rolling down from the works at the summit of the
hill, with astonishing velocity, were . . . more formidable to our troops than all the other defences'.[54]

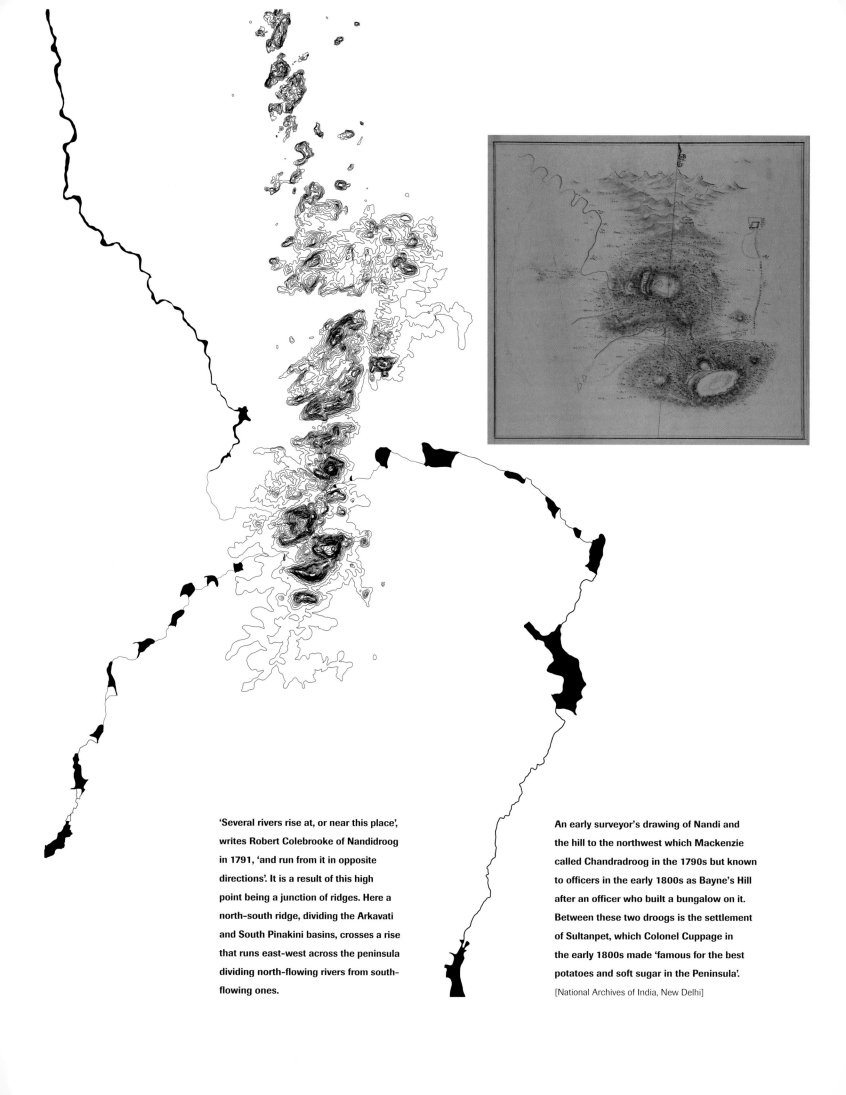

'Several rivers rise at, or near this place', writes Robert Colebrooke of Nandidroog in 1791, 'and run from it in opposite directions'. It is a result of this high point being a junction of ridges. Here a north-south ridge, dividing the Arkavati and South Pinakini basins, crosses a rise that runs east-west across the peninsula dividing north-flowing rivers from south-flowing ones.

An early surveyor's drawing of Nandi and the hill to the northwest which Mackenzie called Chandradroog in the 1790s but known to officers in the early 1800s as Bayne's Hill after an officer who built a bungalow on it. Between these two droogs is the settlement of Sultanpet, which Colonel Cuppage in the early 1800s made 'famous for the best potatoes and soft sugar in the Peninsula'.

[National Archives of India, New Delhi]

DECCAN TRAVERSES

THE GARDEN
GARDEN CITY
TOTA
GLASS HOUSE
HILL STATION

203

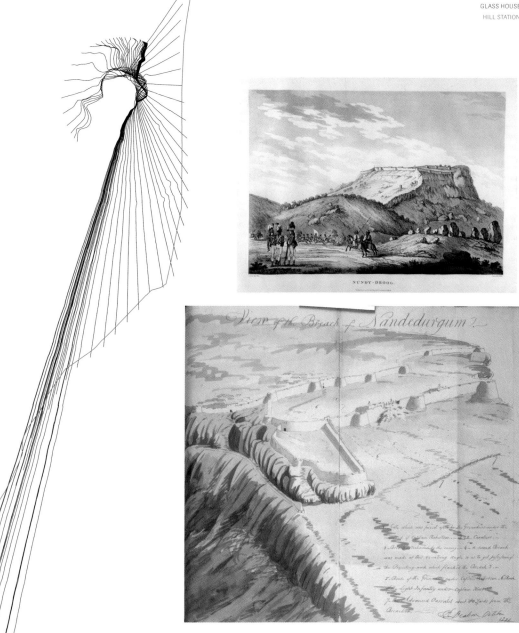

In 1791 the English were convinced that 'Nundydroog was fixed on as the pillar to which the Sultaun's chain for supporting his ambitious projects against the north, must have been fastened'. A century later the hill would be made a key station in the growing enterprise of economic botany begun from Lalbagh and spreading across the tableland.

Alexander Allan, 'Nundy-Droog'.

Views of the Mysore Country (London, 1794) [Yale Center for British Art, Paul Mellon Collection]

Major Alexander Beatson's survey of the summit of Nandidroog.

Geographical observations on the Peninsula of India, vol. 1. British Library, Mss. Eur. D48 18 [By permission of the British Library]

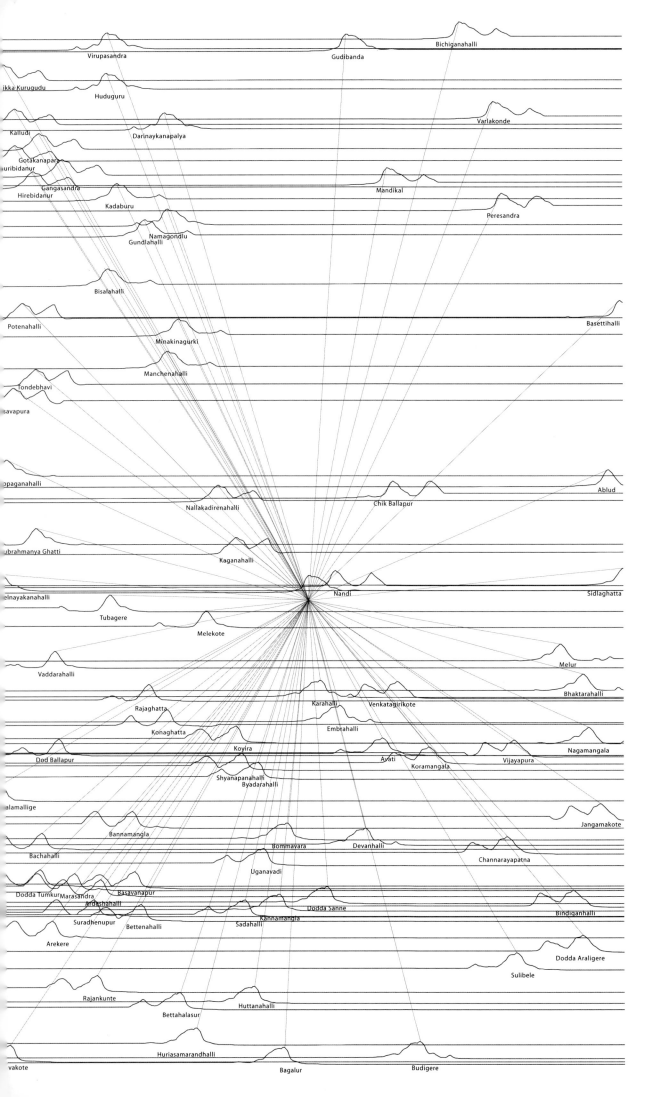

Nandi Hills has long been
a sacred source of water,
which disperses from it
in all directions. It makes
this range an omnipres-
ence on the tableland, one
that is reinforced visually
on the level surface that
extends from it.

DECCAN TRAVERSES

THE GARDEN
GARDEN CITY
TOTA
GLASS HOUSE
HILL STATION

205

The British at the time were convinced that this droog 'was fixed on as the pillar to which the Sultaun's chain for supporting his ambitious projects against the north must have been fastened'.[55] It was by all accounts one of Tipu Sultan's favourites and with Savandroog one of the most 'impregnable'. But this highpoint of intersecting ridges would achieve even more fame as a 'beautiful spot' nearly two thousand feet above the 'plains'.[56] A primary agency in this transition from droog to spot was economic botany, its cultivation of a plateau of rich soil water sources on the summit. Most significantly, however, it was the climate at the summit. If ascending the passes from the Carnatic was to approach the eastern shores of the Mediterranean (the Levant) from the tropics, ascending Nandi was to continue further into the temperate latitudes. 'The climate upon this hill during the day is truly European', writes Colonel Welsh who took command of this 'enormous mountain' in 1809. It made the plateau an experimental ground for plant introductions for men like Colonel Cuppage who had already made the foot of the hill 'famous for the best potatoes and soft sugar in the Peninsula' and gardens which 'abound in almost every fruit and vegetable of Europe and Asia combined'. Here he left behind what Welsh found to be 'a beautiful garden . . . the trees of which, still standing, are watered with dew and misty clouds, which are continually passing over the hill. Amongst them we found an enormous peach, a few plum, and several flourishing Seville orange trees; all three being rarities in the East Indies'.[57] By the 1890s this mountain was admired more for its lush vegetation than its rock surface. Portrayed by a number of artists in 1791 as largely bare, a century later it was teeming with 'luxuriant vegetation' and a 'greater variety of species. And in the warm season, when vegetation is nearly dormant on the plains, this little sanitarium is verdant and refreshing'.[58]

Cocoon mats and fields of mulberry reveal a sericulture industry that cultivates the plains around Nandi today.

The climb to the summit was, meanwhile, becoming less a formidable ascent and more a welcome transportation from one climate to another. Some saw it as an escape from the heat of the plains – 'the thermometer was 62° this morning indoors, while in Bangalore it was 87°', notes Mrs Bowring. Others saw it as a sanatorium, a place to recover from 'the fatigues of a long spell of work'.[59] Sir Mark Cubbon built a summer bungalow on the highest point of the plateau in the 1850s formalising Nandi as a summer retreat. The idea of a summer retreat has become so self-evident that historians suggest Tipu Sultan coveted the place for the same reasons. It was twice removed from his capital at Seringapatam, his 'Summer Palace' in Bangalore being the first step toward a cooler climate.

To John Cameron, superintendent of Government Gardens, however, the extremes of foot and summit mattered less than the slope in between. Asked to propose 'an experimental garden at Nundydroog', in 1890, he suggested a 'gradation system working from top to bottom, the selection of sites at intervals of varying elevation is exactly what would be required. Plants from cooler climates would thus be gradually inured to the uniform heat of the surrounding plains'.[60] As an acclimatising gradient, this hill could do in one place what a number of gardens at varying altitudes did together in a fine-tuning of the acclimatising process.

The descent of European plants parallels the waters coming off this hill, which locals have long seen – along with the other hills of this range – as a source of a number of sacred streams. Many of these are seasonal but they are located with precision, their sources marked by wells or tanks. Mackenzie describes the source of the Arkavati, which he visited in April 1792. The 'stream issues from a metal head, formerly it was said to be of silver; the stream is said to be highly reverenced by the Gentoos; it was cool, and flowed in abundance'.[61] The number of venerated origins in these hills is a cause of wonder, but so are the many destinations of the waters coming off them. These destinations range across many hundred miles along the east coast, from the mouth of the North Pennar to the mouth of the Kaveri. They present a land surface that extends inland from the coast in discrete folds that keep dividing and multiplying as they disperse into higher ground. But as divergent as these folds are, they mysteriously gather in this small range of hills that is often called after its southern-most celebrity, the Nandi Hills.

The surface of the tableland with its juxtaposition of sudden elevations and extended plains, is celebrated at Nandi between the Yoganandisvara and Bhoganandisvara temples. The former, which is on the summit, points toward the other side of a material source, the detachment aspired to by the ascetic. The latter, in the plains northeast of the hill, celebrates the fulfilment of the material source in the harvest each year. Between detachment and enjoyment is an acclimatising gradient that represents the potential of economic botany on the tableland.

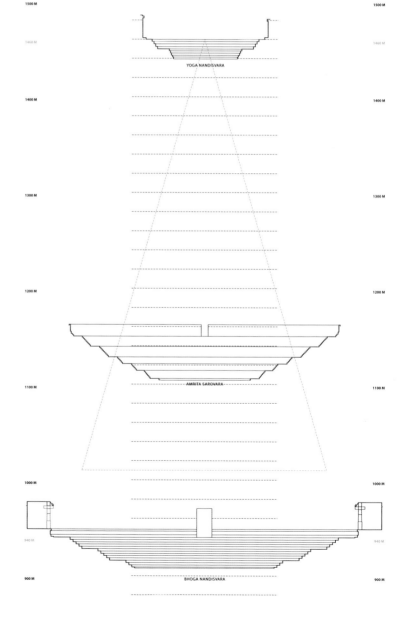

DECCAN TRAVERSES

THE GARDEN
GARDEN CITY
TOTA
GLASS HOUSE
HILL STATION

207

**The tanks of Bhoganandisvara
Temple at the foot of Nandi Hill
and Yoganandisvara Temple
on its summit.**

**Looking out from the summit
of Nandi.**

Air 1

Screen Print on paper, 22"x30" + Digital Plot

Wet Crops.

| Oryza sativa, *Linn.* | ... | Rice | ... | ... | Bhatta, nellu. |
| Saccharum officinarum, *Linn.* | ... | Sugar-cane | ... | ... | Kabbu. |

Garden Crops.

Allium cepa, *Linn.*		Onion		Nirulli.
„ sativum, *Linn.*		Garlic		Bellulli.
Arachis hypogæa, *Linn.*		Ground-nut		Kallélayi, nela kadale.
Capsicum annuum, *Linn.*		Chilly		Mensina káyi.
Carum copticum, *Benth.*		weed		Oma.
Carthamus tinctorius, *Linn.*		Safflower		Kusumba.
Coriandrum sativum, *Linn.*		Coriander		Kottambari.
Cuminum cyminum, *Linn.*		Cummin seed		Jirige.
Curcuma longa, *Roxb.*		Turmeric		Arisina.
Trigonella fœnum græcum, *Linn.*		Fenugreek		Mentya.
Zingiber officinale, *Rosc.*		Ginger		Sunti.

Miscellaneous

Areca catechu, *Linn.*		Areca-nut		Adike.
Cocos nucifera, *Linn.*		Cocoa-nut		Tengina kayi.
Coffea arabica, *Linn.*		Coffee		Húndu, kápi.
Elettaria cardamomum, *Maton*		Cardamom		Yelakki.
Morus indica, *Linn.*		Mulberry		Uppu nerle, kambali gida.
Musa sapientum, *Linn.*		Plantain		Bále.
Piper betle, *Linn.*		Betel vine		Víled-ele.
„ nigrum, *Linn.*		Black pepper		Menasu.
Triticum sativum, *Linn.*		Wheat		Gódhi.

Dry Crops.

Eleusine coracana				Rági.
Panicum frumentaceum				Sáme.
Panicum italicum, *Linn.*		Italian millet		Na...
„ semiverticulatum				Háraka.
Pennisetum typhoideum		millet		Sajje.
Sorghum vulgare				Jola.
Cajanus indicus				Tógari, tovari.
Cicer arietinum, *Linn.*		chick-pea		Kadale.
Dolichos biflorus				...lu.
„ labiab, *Linn.*				
Lens esculenta				Kadale...
Phaseolus mungo, *Linn.*		Green gram		...tu.
Vigna catiang				Alasandi, taduvani.
Guizotia abyssinica				Huchchellu, rámtil.
Ricinus communis, *Linn.*		Castor oil		Háralu.
Sesamum ind...				Ellu, achellu.

Miscellaneous

Brassica nigra, *Koch.*		Mustard		
Crotalaria juncea, *Linn.*		Indian hemp		
Gossypium herbaceum		Cotton		Arale.
Hibiscus cannabinus, *Linn.*		Deccan hemp		
Nicotiana tabacum, *Linn.*		Tobacco		Hoge soppu.

1500 M
1460 M
1400 M
1300 M
1200 M
1100 M
1000 M
940 M
900 M

YOGA NANDISVARA

AMRITA SAROVARA

SRINIVAS SAGAR
NORTH PENNAR / NORTH PINAKINI

KHANDVARA KERE
SOUTH PENNAR / SOUTH PINAKINI

BHOGA NANDISVARA

Air 2

Screen Print on paper, 22"x30" + Digital Plot

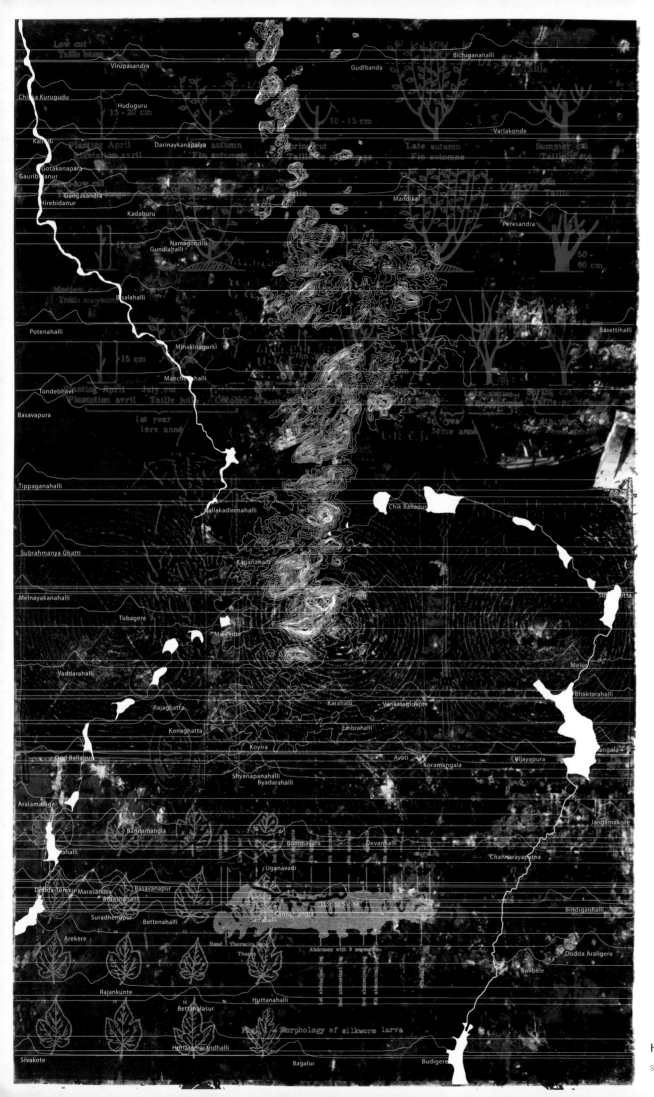

Hill Station 1

Screen Print on paper, 22"x30" + Digital Plot

APR · APR

MAY · MAY

JUN · JUN

JUL · JUL

AUG · AUG

SEP · SEP

OCT · OCT

NOV · NOV

APR · APR

DEC · DEC

MAY · MAY

EPILOGUE

Traversing Again

Bangalore is a place of remarkable beginnings. The war of 1791-92, Lambton's trigono-metrical survey, Heyne's botanical garden, and picturesque art initiated material changes and vocabularies that have played a significant role in cultivating both the Garden City and the 'eye' through which it is seen. The open horizons that amazed 'outsiders' two centuries ago when they described this land as a 'naked country' were quickly consumed by trees from across the world, gardens encoded with 'horticultural taste', parks, and other endeavours of economic botany. Less obvious but equally transformative is the drawing of boundaries, land-uses and entities by surveyors which were formalised in maps commonly used to navigate and administer the land today, even serving as the ground upon which plans for Bangalore and the larger region are conceived, read (by an increasingly involved public) and implemented. Besides physical cultivations and formal demarcations, these open horizons were also consumed by a photographic way of seeing that was introduced through the picturesque artist's promise of truthful depictions of places, things and events. It cultivated an appreciation for the 'scene' but also for visually articulated 'facts' and 'visions' that are not merely restricted to academic and professional discourse but form a critical part of everyday communication between ordinary people. Even as these enterprises were extending from their alien beginnings into the everyday life of people on the Mysore Tableland, they were giving Bangalore a prominence not only in the Indian subcontinent and the nascent British Empire, but also in the scientific and artistic inquiries triggered by the European Enlightenment.

These initiatives, though, were not alone in their extraordinary act of transgression and cultivation. In fact, they derive a certain particularity from their intersections with proc-esses of transformation generated earlier on the Mysore Tableland — the establishment of Kempegowda's pettah, numerous mantaps, bunds, tanks, and totas. These are not necessarily 'local', 'insider' or 'indigenous' elements as provincial interests may like to see them; they are signs of earlier initiatives to gather, familiarise, and settle — perhaps colonise — a land. These efforts cultivated their own landscape and their own eye. Their difference with the enterprises of the turn of the eighteenth century, however, is more profound than can be granted by simple reason, given that the call of the Enlightenment was to see a *terra incognita* that promised not merely a new view of things but also new things to view. The difference demands leaps of imagination that few are willing to risk or to humour. But without a speculative leap, things are too easily reduced to the entities singled out by British surveyors. Tanks, for example, despite being attributed to the ingenuity of a people who predated the era of European colonisation are still represented in the mode of the surveyor — by a peripheral line and coloured blue in maps. This clear and distinct articulation has made tanks amenable to control as reservoirs, scenic lakes, perennial wetlands, or prime properties easily bypassed by drains and made available for development. However, as temporal gatherings of water, clay, activities and settlement, tanks call for a leap beyond the surveyor's mode of representation to one that accommodates its open and shifting nature, a mode that may perhaps encourage negotiation rather than control. Similarly, Kempegowda's pettah is not necessarily the spatial entity drawn by the men who were facilitating its capture in 1791. If folklore is taken seriously, the challenge is to imagine and communicate this venture as an emergent and unfolding event. By extension, the four Kempegowda watchtowers may not be the 'limits' of a vision of the future city as represented by surveyors with an eye for boundaries and bounded entities, but the beginnings of landscapes and cultivations yet to be fathomed.

In short, then, there are landscapes that do not just predate the enterprises of the European Enlightenment as much as cross them and continue on their way. Along with the ventures of the 1800s, they are dynamic living trajectories, each a way of seeing as much as making a land. We call these trajectories *traverses*. Traverse, a word that found common usage among naturalists of the nineteenth century who recorded their observations as they crossed a land, refers as much to an act of transgression that stems from the imposition of a new imagination as it does to the transformative power exercised by the land on the traversor, compelling a constant negotiation in the pursuit of a shifting horizon. It invokes landscape as a phenomenon that is always in the making — both, in the eye and in the land. On this dynamic terrain Bangalore is not a demarcated entity but an intensity of coexistent traverses begun in the 1800s and in the centuries before. It is here that Lambton's measurement of the earth's curvature, which marked a land with property lines, crossed an enterprise that worked a land of flows and overflows using tanks and bunds. This is also where the route surveyor's plotting of distance and time that gave rise to the language of maps intersected Kempegowda's perception of a field of initiations marked by events. Bangalore is where the Daniells' articulation of a country of objects and scenes in pictures encountered a world of embodied seeing expressed in practices like circumambulation. And, finally, it is here that the economic botanist's pursuit of a world of plants through gardens networked by latitudes and altitude intersected a trajectory of festivals and rituals operating through the tota.

At first glance these crossings may appear as conflicts; but they are not. The difference between traverses is too profound to entertain a convergence or, for that matter, a divergence. Each traverse instead is autonomous, demanding the engagement of a particular language through which it represents, negotiates, intervenes and transforms the land that is perceived. In this sense, property lines, tanks, mapped entities, events, photographs, mantaps, gardens, and totas do not share a common ground in Bangalore; rather Bangalore shares in their many grounds.

This Bangalore, constituted by coexistent traverses, cannot be held to a boundary or a plan any more than Lambton could hold the ground that he chose for his baseline to be 'clear of tanks and cultivated grounds' even for the two months of his measurement. Neither can it be held to a past in a land that Colin Mackenzie in 1800 saw changing too fast for the 'Register'. 'In the process of time the original names are altered in common use; villages go to decay in one place, while new ones are built in others; Hamlets assume the place of Cusbas; and . . . as the original name is still preserved in the Register, a confusion is apt to occur and, from the difficulty of ascertaining doubtful places, concealments and frauds are practicable.' His orders were to 'fix' settlements 'by the nearest permanent landmarks, as Hills, Rocks, Rivers, and other villages and stations observed, so that no difficulty can well occur'.[1] It offered Governor General Wellesley, who ordered Mackenzie's survey, a firm basis for administration, producing, as he said, 'immediate and important benefits in establishing and conducting our government in the conquered provinces'.[2] The articulations of traversors in the hands of administrators thus assumed the status of 'truths' communicated through gazetteers but in due course also through textbooks and indeed, everyday vocabulary. Today they are defined 'subjects' of governance and disciplines instead of elements within open-ended traverses. Bangalore is among these subjects, largely accepted as a demarcated entity covering a definite area and having a distinct statistic. Like other subjects, it appears to hold out the possibility of study, containment and control.

Not surprisingly, however, Bangalore eludes this desire for clarity, and, as a result, studies and plans aimed at 'understanding' and 'controlling' it. Its elusiveness is amply displayed in the regular re-drawing of boundaries; land use violations and their 'regularisations'; squatter settlements; extensions of infrastructural dependencies; redefinitions of history and identity; and so on. The uncertainty and blurring injected by today's open economy merely underscores the point that Bangalore is not necessarily a demarcated entity to begin with.

It is time perhaps to return Bangalore to an open terrain, to the level surface that James Rennell in the early 1790s called a Tableland and described as 'the top of a vast flat mountain' on which the 'lofty eminences' are 'nothing more than inequalities'. Bangalore at the time was a point in maps before surveyors gave it a spatial dimension, and other enterprises, privileged by the East India Company, enforced its centrality and inequality. As a point on a map it was open to colonial power, but as a singular point it was open to the imagination and enterprise of traversors, to the beginnings of ventures that generated new subjects, sciences and, in the process, landscapes. We can choose to see Bangalore as such a point again today, one from which the Garden City emerged in an intersection of extraordinary enterprises and one from which new traverses can begin to cultivate new imaginations and fresh vocabularies for future interventions. This is surely the sense of the place that Kempegowda I envisioned when he designed the pettah of Bangalore in 1537: not as a spatial entity, but as an auspicious point that he initiated at a carefully chosen moment.

NOTES

Introduction

1 Francis Buchanan in his journey across the Indian peninsula made the observation in 1800 (Francis Buchanan, *A Journey from Madras through the countries of Mysore, Canara, and Malabar,* vol. I, Madras: Higginbotham and Co., 1870). Lord Valentia described it as such in 1804 (George Viscount Valentia, *Voyages and Travels to India, Ceylon, the Red Sea, Abyssinia and Egypt in the years 1802, 1803, 1804, 1805, and 1806,* vol. I, London: William Miller, 1809). In 1792 artist William Daniell wrote in his diary of a land 'barren, most probably in consequence of the war. From Bangalore, Severn Droog, Nundy Droog, Sheeva Gunga, Oolia Droog, with several other lesser hill forts, are distinctly seen'. For Major William Lambton, the 'neighbourhood of Bangalore' offered sightings that extended across tens of miles (William Lambton to George Buchan, Secretary of Government, British Library, IOR P/242/36 27 November 1801, 5140-41).

2 William Arthur, *A Mission to the Mysore,* (London: Partridge and Oakey, Paternoster Row, 1847).

3 Roderick Mackenzie, *A Sketch of the War with Tipoo Sultan,* (Calcutta, 1793), 49.

4 Winston Churchill, *My Early Life: A Roving Commission,* (New York: Charles Scribners Sons, 1958), 105.

5 Fazlul Hasan, *Bangalore through the Centuries,* (Bangalore: Historical Publications, 1970), 221.

6 Francis Henry Skrine, *Life of Sir William Wilson Hunter,* (London: Longmans, Green, and Co., 1901), 163.

7 United Nations Group of Experts on Geographical Names, Department of Economic and Social Affairs, Statistics Division, *Glossary of Terms for the Standardization of Geographical Names,* (New York: United Nations, 2002)

8 Francis Henry Skrine, *Life of Sir William Wilson Hunter,* (London: Longmans, Green, and Co., 1901), 302.

9 Immanuel Kant, 'What is Enlightenment?' in *Enlightenment: A Comprehensive Anthology,* ed., Peter Gay, (New York: Simon & Schuster, 1985).

10 Barbara Maria Stafford, *Voyage into Substance: Art Science, Nature, and the Illustrated Travel Account, 1760-1840,* (Cambridge: MIT Press, 1984), 2.

11 Colin Mackenzie, 'Biographical Sketch', *Journal of the Royal Asiatic Society,* vol. I, 1834, 337. Colonel de Bussy was the representative of the French East India Company at the court of the Nizam. Jean-Baptiste Tavernier and Jean de Thévenot were French travellers to India in the seventeenth century.

12 Thomas Daniell and William Daniell, *A Picturesque Voyage to India by Way of China,* (London, 1810).

The War

1 Walter Scott, *Chronicles of the Canongate*, edited by Claire Lamont, (Edinburgh: Edinburgh University Press, 2000), 269.

2 Marco Polo, *The Travels of Marco Polo*, (Penguin Books, 1958), 276, 279, 285, 294.

3 R.H. Phillimore, ed., *Historical Records of the Survey of India*, vol. I, (Dehradun: Survey of India, 1945), 238.

4 Robert Hyde Colebrooke, *Twelve Views of Places in the Kingdom of Mysore, the Country of Tippoo Sultan, from drawings taken on the spot*, (London, 1794).

5 Walter Hamilton, *The East-India Gazetteer*, (London: Parbury, Allen, and Co., 1828), vii.

6 Mark Wilks, *Historical Sketches of the South of India, in an attempt to trace the History of Mysoor; from the Origin of the Hindoo Government of that State, to the Extinction of the Mohammedan Dynasty in 1799*, vol. I, (London, 1810).

7 Robert Orme, *A History of the Military Transactions of the British Nation in Indostan, from the year 1745*, (London, 1763).

8 Colonel H.L. Thuillier and Lt. Colonel R. Smyth, *A Manual of Surveying for India detailing the Mode of Operations on the Trignometrical, Topographical and Revenue Surveys of India*, (Calcutta: Thacker, Spink and Co., 1875), 441.

9 Jean-Baptiste Bourgignon D'Anville, *A Geographical Illustration of the Map of India*. Translated by William Herbert, 1759, 56.

10 R.H. Phillimore, *Historical Records of the Survey of India*, vol. I, (Dehradun: Survey of India, 1945), 186.

11 James Rennell, *Memoir of a Map of the Peninsula of India*, (London: W. Bulmer and Co., 1793), 14, footnote.

12 An early admirer of Rennell's achievements was Capt. John Warren, responsible for a number of surveys of the Mysore Tableland in the early 1800s. 'We think very highly of the father of our Indian geography', he says, 'and yield to no one in admiration of his sagacity and skill in combining heterogeneous materials and extracting from conflicting statements results so nearly approaching to truth, as to leave little to his successors beyond the task of confirming his statements'. (R.H. Phillimore, *Historical Records of the Survey of India*, vol. I. Dehradun: Survey of India, 1945, 376).

13 Major Rennell, *The Marches of the British Armies in the Peninsula of India, during the Campaigns of 1790 and 1791*, (London: W. Bulmer and Co., 1792), 17.

14 Major Alexander Beatson, *Geographical observations on the Peninsula of India containing measured Routes, Bearings, Azimuths and Latitudes — with Views of the most remarkable Peaks and Hills throughout the British Possessions on the Coast of Coromandel from the River Kistnah to Cape Comorin; Extending also, to Seringapatam Bangalore, and other places in Mysore*, vol. I., (British Library, Mss. Eur. D 46).

15 Major Rennell, *The Marches of the British Armies in the Peninsula of India, during the Campaigns of 1790 and 1791*, (London: W. Bulmer and Co., 1792), 46.

16 Major H.M. Vibart, *The Military History of the Madras Engineers and Pioneers, From 1743 up to the Present Time*, vol. I, (London: W.H. Allen & Co., 1881), 221.

17 Major Rennell, *The Marches of the British Armies in the Peninsula of India, during the Campaigns of 1790 and 1791*, (London: W. Bulmer and Co., 1792), 50.

18 Roderick Mackenzie, *A Sketch of the War with Tipoo Sultan* (Calcutta, 1793), Appendix, 1.

19 Major Rennell, *The Marches of the British Armies in the Peninsula of India, during the Campaigns of 1790 and 1791*, (London: W. Bulmer and Co., 1792), 54.

20 Ibid, 54, 59.

21 R.H. Phillimore, ed., *Historical Records of the Survey of India*, vol. I, (Dehradun: Survey of India, 1945), 312.

22 Major Dirom, *A Narrative of the Campaign in India which terminated the war with Tipoo Sultan in 1792*, (London: W. Bulmer and Co., 1793), 242-3.

23 Robert Orme, *A History of the Military Transactions of the British Nation in Indostan, from the year 1745*, (London, 1763).

24 Robert Home, *Select Views in Mysore, The Country of Tipoo Sultan from Drawings taken on the spot with Historical Descriptions*, (London: Bowyer, 1794), 4.

25 Roderick Mackenzie, *A Sketch of the War with Tipoo Sultan*, (Calcutta, 1793), 23.

26 Robert Home, *Select Views in Mysore, The Country of Tipoo Sultan from Drawings taken on the spot with Historical Descriptions*, (London: Bowyer, 1794), 4.

27 Major Dirom, 'Bound Hedge', in Glossary, *A Narrative of the Campaign in India which terminated the war with Tipoo Sultan in 1792*, (London: W. Bulmer and Co., 1793).

28 Mark Wilks, *Historical Sketches of the South of India in an attempt to trace the History of Mysoor*, vol. II, (Madras: Higginbotham and Co., 1869, 2nd edition), 187.

29 Robert Hyde Colebrooke, *Twelve Views of Places in the Kingdom of Mysore, the Country of Tipoo Sultan, from drawings taken on the spot*, (London, 1794).

30 Roderick Mackenzie, *A Sketch of the War with Tipoo Sultan*, (Calcutta, 1793), 51.

31 John Blakiston, *Twelve Years' Military Adventure in Three Quarters of the Globe*, vol. I, (London: Henry Colburn, 1829), 56.

32 Major Dirom, *A Narrative of the Campaign in India which terminated the war with Tippoo Sultan in 1792*, (London: W. Bulmer and Co., 1793), 24.

33 Roderick Mackenzie, *A Sketch of the War with Tipoo Sultan*, (Calcutta, 1793), 31.

34 Ibid, 29, 31.

35 Robert Home, *Select Views in Mysore, The Country of Tipoo Sultan from Drawings taken on the spot with Historical Descriptions*, (London: Bowyer, 1794), 5.

36 Roderick Mackenzie, *A Sketch of the War with Tipoo Sultan*, (Calcutta, 1793), 31. According to Rennell 'Besides being in itself a fine town, 200 yards in length, by 750 broad, within the fortifications; it contained great magazines of grain, forage, and fuel; articles that were likely to be in great request, in the course of any siege: and the two latter began to be already wanted'. Major Rennell, *The Marches of the British Armies in the Peninsula of India, during the Campaigns of 1790 and 1791* (London: W. Bulmer and Co., 1792), 61.

37 Robert Hyde Colebrooke, *Twelve Views of Places in the Kingdom of Mysore, the Country of Tipoo Sultan, from drawings taken on the spot*, (London, 1794).

38 Fazlul Hasan, *Bangalore through the Centuries*, (Bangalore: Historical Publications, 1970), 14.

39 R.H. Phillimore, *Historical Records of the Survey of India*, vol. I, (Dehradun: Survey of India, 1945), 118.

40 Letter from Resident Arthur Cole to the Governor in Council, Robert Clive, dtd. 20 November 1799, (British Library IOR R/2/1/174 1799-1801).

41 Arthur Wellesley, 'Memorandum upon Seringapatam', in *Selections from the Dispatches and General Orders of Field Marshal the Duke of Wellington*, ed. Lieut. Colonel John Gurwood, (London: John Murray, 1851), 26-33.

42 The idea is invoked by Lord Valentia on his visit to Bangalore in 1804. Travelling the nascent British Empire in 1804, Valentia expresses surprise that Bangalore was not already the centre. Bangalore, he says, may not hold the advantage as regards large buildings when compared to Seringapatam; 'I doubt, however, whether this would not have been repaid by the additional salubrity of Bangalore'. George Viscount Valentia, *Voyages and Travels to India, Ceylon, the Red Sea, Abyssinia and Egypt in the years 1802, 1803, 1804, 1805, and 1806*, vol I, (London, William Miller, 1809), 431.

43 John Blakiston, *Twelve Years' Military Adventure in Three Quarters of the Globe*, vol. I, (London: Henry Colburn, 1829).

44 V. Balachandran, *Geomorphological, geological, geotechnical, hydrogeological features of the Bangalore Metropolitan Area and their bearing on City Development*, (Calcutta: Geological Survey of India, 1979).

45 Rev. William Arthur, *A Mission to the Mysore; with Scenes and Facts illustrative of India, its People, and its Religion* (London: Partridge and Oakey), 142, 143.

46 Major H. Bevan, *Thirty Years in India or A Soldier's Reminiscences of Native and European Life in the presidencies, from 1808 to 1838*, vol. I, (London: Pelham Richardson, Cornhill, 1839), 101.

47 Colonel James Welsh, *Military Reminiscences; Extracted from a Journal of nearly Forty Years' Active Service in the East Indies*, vol. I, (London: Smith, Elder and Co., 1830), 310.

48 John Blakiston, *Twelve Years' Military Adventure in Three Quarters of the Globe*, vol. I, (London: Henry Colburn, 1829), 316.

49 Major Dirom, *A Narrative of the Campaign in India which terminated the war with Tipoo Sultan in 1792*, (London: W. Bulmer and Co., 1793), 20.

50 Roderick Mackenzie, *A Sketch of the War with Tipoo Sultan*, (Calcutta, 1793), 162.

51 Lewis Rice, *Mysore: A Gazetteer compiled for Government*, vol. I, (Westminster: Archibald Constable and Company, 1897), 1897, 39.

52 B.P. Radhakrishna and R. Vaidyanadhan, *Geology of Karnataka*, (Bangalore: Geological Society of India, 1997), 163.

53 Francis Buchanan, *A Journey from Madras through the countries of Mysore, Canara, and Malabar*, vol. I, (Madras: Higginbotham and Co., 1870), 36.

54 Roderick Mackenzie, *A Sketch of the War with Tipoo Sultan*, (Calcutta, 1793), 90, 161.

55 Major Dirom, *A Narrative of the Campaign in India which terminated the war with Tipoo Sultan in 1792*, (London: W. Bulmer and Co., 1793), 69.

56 Ibid, 77-78.

57 Roderick Mackenzie, *A Sketch of the War with Tipoo Sultan*, (Calcutta, 1793), 181.

58 Anupama Chopra, *Sholay: The Making of A Classic*, (Delhi: Penguin Books, 2000), 8.

59 Major Dirom, *A Narrative of the Campaign in India which terminated the war with Tipoo Sultan in 1792*, (London: W. Bulmer and Co., 1793), 22.

The Survey

1 William Lambton, 'An Account of a Method for extending a Geographical Survey across the Peninsula of India', *Asiatic Researches*, vol. VII, 1803, 312.

2 William Lambton, 'An Account of the measurement of a Base Line on the Table land of the Mysoor Country in the year 1800', dtd. 18 October 1801, Public Diaries and Consultations, Fort St. George 27 November 1801, (British Library, IOR P/242/36, 5133-5176).

3 William Lambton, 'An Account of a Method for extending a Geographical Survey across the Peninsula of India', *Asiatic Researches*, vol. VII, 1803, 312.

4 William Lambton, 'A Plan of a Mathematical and Geographical Survey extending across the Peninsula of India proposed to be carried into execution by Brigade Major Lambton', Fort St. George, 10 February 1800, (British Library, P/254/52, 748).

5 W.A. Seymour, ed., *A History of the Ordnance Survey* (Folkstone: Dawson, 1980), 7.

6 William Roy, 'An Account of the Mode Proposed to be Followed in Determining the Relative Situation of the Royal Observatories of Greenwich and Paris', *Philosophical Transactions of the Royal Society* 77 (1787), 188-228, 224.

7 William Lambton, 'A Plan of a Mathematical and Geographical Survey extending across the Peninsula of India proposed to be carried into execution by Brigade Major Lambton', Fort St. George, 10 February 1800, (British Library, P/254/52, 756).

8 Ibid, 746-47.

9 'As the distinct nature of your undertaking', writes Webbe on behalf of the Governor of Madras, 'will probably make it necessary for you to traverse the peninsula from sea to sea more than once, His Lordship is aware that a scrupulous coincidence with Captain Mackenzie's plan will not always be practicable, but the same motives which have governed his Lordship's selection of you for this important undertaking induce him to rely with the most entire confidence that you will regulate your intercourse with captain Mackenzie in such a manner as shall best conduce to the promotion of science and of the great national objects to which your mutual labours are directed'. Josiah Webbe, Letter to Major of Brigade Lambton, 6 February 1800, (British Library, IOR P/254/52, 597).

10 Lord Mornington's minute, dtd. 4 September, 1799, (British Library, IOR P/254/41 6058-6062).

11 Colin Mackenzie, *Plan of the Mysore Survey and the manner on which it is proposed to be executed*, January 28 1800, (British Library, IOR P/254/52, 728-745).

12 R.H. Phillimore, ed., *Historical Records of the Survey of India*, vol. II, (Dehradun: Survey of India, 1950), 93.

13 Letter from the Court of Directors to the Government of Fort St. George dated 9 February 1810 in John Philippart, *The East India military calendar, containing the services of general and field officers of the Indian army*, by the editor of the Royal military calendar, vol. III, (London, 1826), 329.

14 Colin Mackenzie in Matthew H. Edney, *Mapping an Empire: The Geographical Construction of British India, 1765-1843*, (University of Chicago Press, 1997), 105.

15 R.H. Phillimore, ed., *Historical Records of the Survey of India*, vol. II, (Dehradun: Survey of India, 1950), 235.

16 William Lambton, 'Memoir, Containing an Account of the Measurement of a Base Line near St. Thomas's Mount in the Year 1802', (British Library, IOR F/4/152 2598, 22-64).

17 Clements Markham, *A Memoir of the Indian Surveys*, (2nd edition, Amsterdam: Meridian Publishing Co., 1968), 94.

18 John Philippart, *The East India military calendar, containing the services of general and field officers of the Indian army*, by the editor of the Royal military calendar, vol. III, (London, 1826), 102.

19 Matthew H. Edney, *Mapping an Empire: The Geographical Construction of British India, 1765-1843*, (Chicago: University of Chicago Press, 1997), 197.

20 R.H. Phillimore, ed., *Historical Records of the Survey of India*, vol. II, (Dehradun: Survey of India, 1950), 9.

21 John Keay, *The Great Arc: The Dramatic Tale of How India was Mapped and Everest was Named*, (Perennial, 2001), 51

22 William Lambton, 'A Plan of a Mathematical and Geographical Survey extending across the Peninsula of India proposed to be carried into execution by Brigade Major Lambton', Fort St. George, 10 February 1800, (British Library, P/254/52, 749).

23 William Lambton to George Buchan, Secretary of Government, (British Library, IOR P/242/36 27 November 1801, 5140-41).

24 S.G. Burrard, 'An Account of the operations of the Great trigonometrical Survey of India under Colonel Lambton', *Account of the Operations of the Great Trigonometrical Survey of India*, vol. XII, (Dehra Dun: Office of the Trigonometrical Branch, Survey of India, 1890), 8.

25 William Lambton, *A memoir containing an account of the principal operations of the Survey carried on in Mysoor in the year 1801 and explaining the General Principals on which it has been conducted,* Madras, Public Diaries & Consultations 26 Feb to 26 March, 26 Mar. to 30 Apr 1802, (British Library, IOR P/242/39-40).

26 William Lambton, 'An Account of the Trigonometrical Operations in crossing the Peninsula of India, and Connecting Fort St. George with Mangalore', *Asiatic Researches,* vol. X, 1811, 290-384.

27 George Everest, *An Account of a Measurement of Two Sections of the Meridional Arc,* vol. I, (London, 1847), 7.

28 Clements Markham, *A Memoir of the Indian Surveys,* 2nd edition, (Amsterdam: Meridian Publishing Co., 1968), 126.

29 William Lambton, 'An Account of a Method for extending a Geographical Survey across the Peninsula of India', *Asiatic Researches,* vol. 7, 1803, Table 1.

30 Francis Buchanan, *A Journey from Madras through the countries of Mysore, Canara, and Malabar,* vol. I, (Madras: Higginbotham and Co., 1870), 2.

31 Mrs. L. Bowring, 'Chit-chat with Friends at Home', in *Eastern Experiences,* L.B. Bowring, (London: Henry S. King and Co., 1872), 402.

32 Benjamin Heyne, *Report relative to the Mysore Survey, 1800-1802,* (National Archives, Foreign Department, Misc. 94).

33 *Webster's Dictionary.*

34 William Bryant Logan, *Dirt: The Ecstatic Skin of the Earth,* (New York: Riverhead Books, 1995), 125, 116.

35 B.P. Radhakrishna and R. Vaidyanadhan, *Geology of Karnataka,* (Bangalore: Geological Society of India, 1997), 277

36 Francis Buchanan, *A Journey from Madras through the countries of Mysore, Canara, and Malabar,* vol. II, (Madras: Higginbotham and Co., 1870), 116.

37 Lewis Rice, *Mysore: A Gazetteer compiled for the Government of India,* vol. II, (Westminster: Archibald Constable and Company, 1897), 148

38 Major R.H. Sankey, Letter to The Secretary to the Commissioner for the Government of the Territories of His Highness the Rajah of Mysore, Dated the 19 November 1866 (State Archives: Public Works Department, 13).

39 Lieut. John Warren, 'Observations on the Golden Ore found in the Eastern Provinces of Mysore, in the Year 1802', *Asiatic Annual Register, or View of the History of Hindustan, and of the Politics, Commerce, and Literature of Asia,* 1804, Miscellaneous Tracts, 1-7.

40 Ibid.

41 Robert H. Elliot, *Gold, Sport, and Coffee Planting in Mysore,* (Westminster: Archibald Constable and Co., 1894), 199.

The Picture

1 David Watkin, 'Introduction', in *Household Furniture and Interior Decoration,* Thomas Hope, (New York: Dover Publications), vi.

2 Martin Hardie and Muriel Clayton, 'Thomas and William Daniell: Their Life and Work', *Walker's Quarterly* Nos. 35-36 (1932). The Walker Galleries in London apparently acquired 'several hundred' of these works around the time of this publication.

3 Sidney Robinson, *Inquiry into the Picturesque,* (Chicago: The University of Chicago Press, 1991).

4 Giles Tillotson, *The Artificial Empire: The Indian Landscapes of William Hodges,* (Richmond: Curzon Press, 2000), 29.

5 Thomas and William Daniell, *Oriental Scenery*, (London, 1799), Plate XVII.

6 *Diary of William Daniell*, Private Collection, London.

7 Thomas and William Daniell, *Oriental Scenery*, (London, 1799), Plate XVIII

8 Lt. Colonel W.J. Wilson, *History of the Madras Army*, vol. II, (Madras: Government Press, 1882), 204-5. The day before the battle for the Bangalore pettah, Colonel Floyd, on a reconnoitering mission south of the fort area, sighted a detached section of 'Tippoo's infantry and guns, accompanied by large quantities of baggage on elephants and camels'. Not able to resist the temptation, he attacked. 'The charge was entirely successful at first, but was pursued too far, and detached parties of the enemy, taking advantage of the ground, which was rocky, and much intersected by steep ravines, began to rally'. Floyd, shot in the face, was forced to retreat, rescued by the timely intervention of Major Gowdie's infantry. 'The great disproportion in the loss was attributed to the low condition of the horses . . . unable to clear the ravines'.

9 William Gilpin, *Three Essays: on Picturesque Beauty; on Picturesque Travel; and on Sketching Landscape: To which is added a Poem on Landscape Painting*, (London, 1794), 14, 7, 8.

10 Ibid, 26-27

11 Sidney Robinson, *Inquiry into the Picturesque*, (Chicago: The University of Chicago Press, 1991), xii.

12 Giles Tillotson, *The Artificial Empire: The Indian Landscapes of William Hodges*, (Richmond: Curzon Press, 2000).

13 Ray Desmond, *The European Discovery of the Indian Flora*, (Oxford: Oxford University Press, 1992), 176; Partha Mitter, *Much Maligned Monsters: History of European Reaction to Indian Art*, (Oxford: Clarendon Press, 1977)

14 Pratapaditya Pal and Vidya Dehejia, *From Merchants to Emperors: British Artists and India 1757-1930*, (Ithaca: Cornell University Press, 1986), 97.

15 Edward Backhouse Eastwick, *A Handbook for India; Being the Account of the Three Presidencies. Part I – Madras*, (London: John Murray, 11859), i-ii.

16 Thomas Daniell and William Daniell, *A Picturesque Voyage to India by Way of China*, (London, 1810),

17 Martin Hardie and Muriel Clayton, 'Thomas and William Daniel: Their Life and Work', *Walker's Quarterly* Nos. 35-36 (1932).

18 Giles Tillotson, *The Artificial Empire: The Indian Landscapes of William Hodges*, (Richmond: Curzon Press, 2000), 43.

19 Mildred Archer, *Early Views of India: The Picturesque Voyages of Thomas and William Daniell 1786-1794*, (London: Thames and Hudson, 1980), 226-27.

20 Giles Tillotson, *The Artificial Empire: The Indian Landscapes of William Hodges*, (Richmond: Curzon Press, 2000), 42-3.

21 Mildred Archer, *Early Views of India: The Picturesque Voyages of Thomas and William Daniell 1786-1794*, (London: Thames and Hudson, 1980).

22 Mildred Archer and Ronald Lightbrown, *India Observed: India as viewed by British Artists 1760-1860*, (London: Victoria and Albert Museum, 1982), 12.

23 Mildred Archer, *Early Views of India: The Picturesque Voyages of Thomas and William Daniell 1786-1794*, (London: Thames and Hudson, 1980), 159.

24 Martin Hardie and Muriel Clayton, 'Thomas and William Daniel: Their Life and Work', *Walker's Quarterly* Nos. 35-36, (1932), 78

25 Francis Buchanan, *A Journey from Madras through the countries of Mysore, Canara, and Malabar*, vol. I, (Madras: Higginbotham and Co., 1870), 118.

26 Robert Home, *Select Views in Mysore, The Country of Tipoo Sultan from Drawings taken on the spot with Historical Descriptions*, (London: Bowyer, 1794), 9.

27 Captain Newbold, 'Summary of the Geology of Southern India', *Journal of the Royal Asiatic Society*, vol. 8, 1846, 144.

28 Benjamin Heyne, *Tracts, Historical and Statistical on India; with journals of several towns through various parts of the Peninsula*, (London, 1814), 31.

29 *Diary of William Daniell*, Private Collection, London.

30 Lewis Rice, *Mysore and Coorg: A Gazetteer compiled for the Government of India*, vol. II, (Bangalore: Mysore Government Press, 1877), 2.

31 R.D. Oldham quoted in *Geology of Karnataka*, B.P. Radhakrishna and R. Vaidyanadhan, (Bangalore: Geological Society of India, 1997), 331

32 J.H. Furneaux, ed., *Glimpses of India: A Grand Photographic History of the Land of Antiquity, the vast Empire of the East*, (Philadelphia: Historical Publishing Company, 1895), 419-20.

33 Lewin B. Bowring, *Eastern Experiences*, (London: Henry S. King & Co., 1872), 8-9.

34 Domingo Paes, 'Of the Things which I saw and contrived to learn concerning the Kingdom of Narsimga, etc.,' in *Vijayanagar*, ed., Vasundhara Filliozat, (Delhi: National Book Trust), 80.

35 Thomas Daniell and William Daniell, *Oriental Scenery* (London, 1799), Plate XVII.

36 Captain Newbold, 'Summary of the Geology of Southern India', *Journal of the Royal Asiatic Society*, vol. 8, 1846, 144.

37 B.P. Radhakrishna and R. Vaidyanadhan, *Geology of Karnataka*, (Bangalore: Geological Society of India, 1997), 75.

38 Ibid, John Rogers, 'The Dharwar Craton and the Assembly of Peninsular India', in *The Journal of Geology*, vol. 94, March 1986.

39 Geological Survey of India, *Inauguration of National Geological Monument, Peninsular Gneiss, Lalbagh, Bangalore, Karnataka*, (Calcutta: Geological Survey of India Press, 1975).

40 Lieut. Newbold, 'On the Processes prevailing among the Hindus, and formerly among the Egyptians, of quarrying and polishing Granite; its uses, etc.; with a few Remarks on the tendency of this Rock in India to separate in concentric exfoliation', *Journal of the Royal Asiatic Society*, vol. 7, 1843, 115.

41 Ibid, 113.

42 B. Mahanaleswar, M. Jayananda, J.J. Peucat, and N. Shadakshara Swamy, 'Archaean high-grade gneiss complex from Satnur-Halagur-Sivasamudram areas, Karnataka, southern India: Petrogenesis and crustal evolution', *Journal Geological Society of India*, vol. 45, Jan. 1995, 33-49. The name Charnockite comes from Job Charnock, known as the 'founder of modern Calcutta', whose gravestone there, taken from the Madras area, was made from this rock.

43 Lewis Rice, *Mysore: A Gazetteer compiled for the Government of India*, vol. II, (Westminster: Archibald Constable and Company, 1897), 309. Malingi is a town on the cut-bank across from Talakad.

44 Francis Buchanan, *A Journey from Madras through the countries of Mysore, Canara, and Malabar*, vol. I, (Madras: Higginbotham and Co., 1870), 407.

45 W.S. Caine, *Picturesque India: A Handbook for European Travellers*, (London: Routledge, 1898), 517-18.

46 Mark Wilks, *Historical Sketches of the South of India, in an attempt to trace the History of Mysoor; from the Origin of the Hindoo Government of that State, to the Extinction of the Mohammedan Dynasty in 1799. Founded chiefly on Indian Authorities collected by the Author while officiating for several years as Political Resident at the Court of Mysoor*, vol. II, (London, 1810), 452.

47 The words are those of Sri Thyagaraja, an exponent of the classical Carnatic music whom many regard as a saint.

48 Major R.H. Sankey, Letter to The Secretary to the Commissioner for the Government of the Territories of His Highness the Rajah of Mysore, Dated the 19 November 1866, (State Archives: Public Works Department)

49 Brief History and Principal Documents in Connection with the Cauvery Power Transmission Scheme, for the information of the Government of India, 1 March 1900. 'As a first step', continues the Dewan, 'it is proposed to convert a portion of the water power at the Falls into Electrical power and to transmit the same a distance of 90 miles to the Kolar Gold Fields, to be utilized in operating the machinery of the various mines in place of the Steam Power which is now used.' (British Library IOR R/2, 8/51[1-2]). This was apparently the first hydroelectric project in Asia and the engineers who designed it came from America after completing the plant at Niagara Falls.

50 Lewin B. Bowring, *Eastern Experiences*, (London: Henry S. King & Co., 1872), 7.

51 George Michell, ed., *Eternal Kaveri: Historical Sites along South India's Greatest River*, (Mumbai: Marg Publications, 1999), 16.

The Garden

1 N. Wallich, Superintendent of Botanical Garden to C.J. Metcalfe, Private Secretary to the Most Noble the Marquis of Hastings, dtd. 17 April 1819. Public Consultations, (British Library, IOR F/4/751 20526).

2 A. H. Cole, Resident at Mysoor to G. Strachey, Chief Secretary to Government, Fort St. George, dtd. 25 January 1819. Public Consultations, (British Library, IOR F/4/751 20526).

3 C.J. Metcalfe, Secretary to the Government, to G. Strachey, Chief Secretary to the Government of Fort St. George, dtd. 21 August 1819. Public Consultations, (British Library, IOR F/4/751 20526).

4 Ray Desmond, *The European Discovery of the Indian Flora* (Oxford: Oxford University Press, 1992), 107.

5 Richard Drayton, *Nature's Government: Science, Imperial Britain, and the 'Improvement' of the World*, (New Haven: Yale University Press, 2000), 89.

6 Stuart Gager, 'Botanic Gardens of the World', *Brooklyn Botanic Garden Record*, 27: 151-406, 262.

7 Richard Drayton, *Nature's Government: Science, Imperial Britain, and the 'Improvement' of the World*, (New Haven: Yale University Press, 2000), 270.

8 Ray Desmond, *Kew: The History of the Royal Botanic Gardens*, (London: The Harvill Press, 1995).

9 Richard Drayton, *Nature's Government: Science, Imperial Britain, and the 'Improvement' of the World*, (New Haven: Yale University Press, 2000), 108.

10 R.H. Phillimore, ed., *Historical Records of the Survey of India*, vol. II, (Dehradun: Survey of India, 1950), 113.

11 Ray Desmond, *The European Discovery of the Indian Flora*, (Oxford: Oxford University Press, 1992), 39.

12 Extract of Lord Clive's Minute, dtd. 18 March 1800, Boards Collection (British Library, IOR F/4/78 1750).

13 Roderick Mackenzie, *A Sketch of the War with Tipoo Sultan*, (Calcutta, 1793), 49.

14 Benjamin Heyne, Letter to Josiah Webbe dtd. 4 May 1800. Boards Collection, (British Library, IOR F/4/78.1750).

15 Public Consultations, 27 March 1802, (British Library IOR/F/4/123).

16 Francis Buchanan, *A Journey from Madras through the countries of Mysore, Canara, and Malabar*, vol. I, (Madras: Higginbotham and Co., 1870), 32.

17 Public Consultations, 27 March 1802, (British Library IOR/F/4/123).

18 George Viscount Valentia, *Voyages and Travels to India, Ceylon, the Red Sea, Abyssinia and Egypt in the years 1802, 1803, 1804, 1805, and 1806*, vol. I, (London, William Miller, 1809), 356

19 Benjamin Heyne, Report of the Company's Garden at Bangalore, dtd. 15 April 1806. Public Consultations, 29 April 1806, (British Library IOR F/4/275. 6129).

20 Benjamin Heyne, 'Sketch of a Plan for a Botanical Garden on the Madras Establishment' in a letter to the Right Hon'ble. Lord Clive, President and Governor in Council, Fort St. George, 2 May 1800. (British Library IOR/F/4/78). 53-72.

21 John Blakiston, *Twelve Years' Military Adventure in Three Quarters of the Globe: or Memoirs of an Officer who served in the Armies of his Majesty and of the East India Company, Between the Years 1802 and 1814*, vol. I, (London: Henry Colburn, 1829), 73-74.

22 W. Petrie to the Madras Government. Public Consultations, 3 June 1807, (British Library IOR F/4/275. 6129).

23 Lt. Col. Malcolm, Resident of Mysore, to G. Keeble, Secretary to Government, Fort St. George. Public Consultations, 4 June 1807, (British Library IOR F/4/275 6129).

24 Major Waugh to the Right Hon'ble The Governor in Council, Fort St. George dtd. 15 January 1819. Public Consultations, 25 January 1819, (British Library IOR F/4/751 20526).

25 Issac Burkill, *Chapters on the History of Botany in India*, (Nasik: Government of India Press, 1965), 107.

26 John Cameron, Letter dated July 20, *The Gardener's Chronicle and Agricultural Gazette*, Aug. 29, 1874, 266.

27 Lewin B. Bowring, *Eastern Experiences*, (London: Henry S. King & Co., 1872), 9.

28 Suryanath U. Kamath, 'The Early Long History of Lalbagh', in *Glass House: The Jewel of Lalbagh* (Bangalore: Mysore Horticultural Society, 1991), 7.

29 William Munro, 'Intelligence concerning the Progress of Agriculture and Horticulture on the table land of Southern India', *Transactions of the Agricultural and Horticultural Society of India*, vol. 6, 1838. William Munro was the Secretary of the Mysore Agri-horticultural Society.

30 Henry Spry, 'Report of the Agricultural and Horticultural Society of India for the Year 1839', *Transactions of the Agricultural and Horticultural Society of India*, vol. 7, 1839, 201.

31 Hugh Cleghorn, *The Forests and Gardens of South India* (London: W.H. Allen & Co., 1861), 334.

32 Ibid, 331.

33 Cleghorn's suggestion was made in response to the *Report on the Government Botanical and Horticultural Gardens at Ootacamund for 1853-55* by the garden's superintendent, William MacIvor. In answer to the increasing demand for vegetables for European soldiers, MacIvor had proposed 'a much more efficient and extended system of producing seeds than that now on hand'. He recommended the establishment of at least one other branch garden. Cleghorn saw it as an opportunity to recommend Bangalore.

34 Dr Cleghorn, Professor of Botany, to J. Pycroft, Chief Secretary to Government, Fort St. George, dtd. 28 March 1856, (British Library, IOR F/4/2681. 183465).

35 Hugh Cleghorn, *The Forests and Gardens of South India*, (London: W.H. Allen & Co., 1861), 334.

36 Ray Murphy, ed., *Edward Lear's Indian Journal: Watercolours and extracts from the diary of Edward Lear (1873-75)*, (Jarrolds Publishers, 1953), 176.

37 G.H. Krumbiegal, 'A Note on the Development of Horticulture in Mysore and the Organization of the Department of Horticulture and Botany', (1920), 19.

38 John Dixon Hunt, *The Dictionary of Art*, vol. XII (1996).

39 Francis Buchanan, *A Journey from Madras through the countries of Mysore, Canara, and Malabar*, vol. I, (Madras: Higginbotham and Co., 1870), 28, 76-79. Buchanan's categories are repeated by Lewis Rice a century later in *Mysore: A Gazetteer compiled for the Government of India*, vol. I, (Westminster: Archibald Constable and Company, 1897), 101.

40 Ibid, 154.

41 Satpal Sangwan 'Natural History in Colonial Context: Profit or Pursuit? British Botanical Enterprise in India 1778-1820,' in *Science and Empires: Historical Studies about Scientific Development and European Expansion*, eds., Patrick Petitjean, Catherine Jami, and Anne Marie Moulin, (Boston: Kluwer Academic Publishers, 1992).

42 Mysore Horticultural Society, 'Dr. M.H. Marigowda', in *Glass House: The Jewel of Lalbagh*, (Bangalore: Mysore Horticultural Society, 1991).

43 Francis Buchanan, *A Journey from Madras through the countries of Mysore, Canara, and Malabar*, vol. I, (Madras: Higginbotham and Co., 1870), 76.

44 Lewin B. Bowring, *Eastern Experiences*, (London: Henry S. King & Co., 1872), 9.

45 Prince Albert, 'At the Banquet Given by The Right Hon. The Mayor, Thomas Farncombe, To Her Majesty's Ministers, Foreign Ambassadors, Royal Commissioners of the Exhibition of 1851, and the Mayors of the Hundred and Eighty Towns, at the Mansion House, (March 21st, 1850), *The Principal Speeches and Addresses of His Royal Highness The Prince Consort*, (London: John Murray, 1862), 111, 112

46 John Tallis, *Tallis's history and description of the Crystal Palace, and the exhibition of the world's industry in 1851 / illustrated by beautiful steel engravings, from original drawings and daguerreotypes by Beard, Mayall, etc.*, (London: John Tallis and Co.)

47 Ibid, iii.

48 Lothar Bucher and Richard Lucae in *Crystal Palace*, John McKean, (London: Phaidon Press, 1994), 32.

49 Gottfried Semper in *Crystal Palace*, John McKean, (London: Phaidon Press, 1994), 36.

50 L. Hanumiah, 'The Glory of Lalbagh and Glass House', in *Glass House: The Jewel of Lalbagh*, (Bangalore: Mysore Horticultural Society, 1991), 21.

51 M.H. Marigowda, 'Man and Plants — An Inseparable Bondage', in *Glass House: The Jewel of Lalbagh*, (Bangalore: Mysore Horticultural Society, 1991), 100.

52 Robert H. Colebrooke, 'North West View of Nandydroog', *Twelve Views of Places in the Kingdom of Mysore*, (London, 1794).

53 Lewin B. Bowring, *Eastern Experiences* (London: Henry S. King & Co., 1872).

54 Roderick Mackenzie, *A Sketch of the War with Tipoo Sultan*, (Calcutta, 1793), 149.

55 Ibid, 151.

56 M.H. Krishna, *A Guide to Nandi*, (Bangalore: Government Press). The term 'spot' is used often in the *Visitor's Book* on Nandi Hill to characterise the place.

57 Colonel James Welsh, *Military Reminiscences; Extracted from a Journal of nearly Forty Years' Active Service in the East Indies*, vol. I, (London: Smith, Elder and Co., 1830), 311-12.

58 John Cameron, 'Letter from the Superintendent, Government Gardens, Bangalore, to L. Ricketts Esq., Inspector General of Forests and Plantations, No. 106 dated the 23 August 1890', (Lalbagh Library).

59 C.V. Raman, *Visitor's Book*, Nandi, 20 December, 1986.

60 John Cameron, 'Letter from the Superintendent, Government Gardens, Bangalore, to L. Ricketts Esq., Inspector General of Forests and Plantations, No. 106 dated the 23 August 1890', (Lalbagh Library).

61 Colin Mackenzie, 'Source of the Pennar River', in *Oriental Repertory*, vol. II, ed., Alexander Dalrymple, (London: George Bigg, 1796).

Epilogue

1 R.H. Phillimore, ed., *Historical Records of the Survey of India* Vol. II, (Dehradun: Survey of India, 1950), 213.

2 Lord Mornington's minute, dtd. 4 September, 1799 (British Library, IOR P/254/41 6058-6062)

INDEX

Historical Maps and Images